REFLECTIONS ON PROBATION

A Companion Resource for
Developing Practitioners

Edited by
Jennifer Grant, Laura Haggar and
Michelle McDermott

First published in Great Britain in 2025 by

Policy Press, an imprint of
Bristol University Press
University of Bristol
1–9 Old Park Hill
Bristol
BS2 8BB
UK
t: +44 (0)117 374 6645
e: bup-info@bristol.ac.uk

Details of international sales and distribution partners are available at
policy.bristoluniversitypress.co.uk

© Bristol University Press 2025

British Library Cataloguing in Publication Data
A catalogue record for this book is available from the British Library

ISBN 978-1-4473-7264-6 paperback
ISBN 978-1-4473-7265-3 ePub
ISBN 978-1-4473-7266-0 ePdf

The right of Jennifer Grant, Laura Haggar and Michelle McDermott to be identified as editors of this work has been asserted by them in accordance with the Copyright, Designs and Patents Act 1988.

All rights reserved: no part of this publication may be reproduced, stored in a retrieval system, or transmitted in any form or by any means, electronic, mechanical, photocopying, recording, or otherwise without the prior permission of Bristol University Press.

Every reasonable effort has been made to obtain permission to reproduce copyrighted material. If, however, anyone knows of an oversight, please contact the publisher.

The statements and opinions contained within this publication are solely those of the editors and contributors and not of the University of Bristol or Bristol University Press. The University of Bristol and Bristol University Press disclaim responsibility for any injury to persons or property resulting from any material published in this publication.

Bristol University Press and Policy Press work to counter discrimination on grounds of gender, race, disability, age and sexuality.

Cover design: Liam Roberts Design
Front cover image: Unsplash/Pawel Czerwinski

Contents

List of figures and tables	vi
List of abbreviations	vii
Notes on contributors	viii
Acknowledgements	xiv

Introduction   1
Jennifer Grant, Laura Haggar and Michelle McDermott

PART I   Contextualising reflection within probation practice

1. Psychological perspectives on reflective processes in criminal justice contexts   11
Adrian Needs
2. Reflective practice in probation work: sustaining reflexivity in times of turbulence   29
Anne Burrell
3. Probation staff reflective practice: can it impact on outcomes for clients with personality difficulties?   44
Dominic Pearson and Daniele Molino
4. Enhancing professional growth through self-understanding   63
Laura Sibret

PART II   The organisational space for reflection

5. Fostering reflective practice as part of leadership   81
Jennifer Grant
6. Thinking about safeguarding   99
Mike Nash

7	A relational role in the prison environment *Lauren Stevens*	116
8	Creating space for reflection and connection: learning from the creative arts and the third sector *Jennifer Walmsley and Laura Haggar*	134

PART III Reflections on contemporary issues of diversity in probation practice

9	Reflections of racially minoritised staff in the COVID-19 pandemic *Ashlea Swinford*	157
10	Reflections on probation: co-creating the probation experience with Black male service users *Nicole Nyamwiza*	174
11	Reflections of female probation practitioners: navigating the challenges of working with male offenders *Michelle McDermott, Laura Haggar and Jennifer Grant*	192
12	Unspoken journeys: reflections of lesbian probation practitioners *Kath Wilson, Daniella Nudd, Hollie Neal and Victoria Jones*	210

PART IV Teaching, learning and professional development

13	'SCOPE' for reflection: a framework of transformative outcomes for probation officer training *Ben Keysell*	229
14	De-mystifying the mirror: a framework for the assessment of reflective practice *Julie Eden-Barnard*	248
15	Critical reflection: key principles for Professional Qualification in Probation students and assessors providing feedback *Ceri Halfpenny*	266

| 16 | Navigating trauma in higher education: reflections on applying trauma-informed approaches to teaching criminology and Professional Qualification in Probation (PQiP) students
Megan Thomas | 282 |
| 17 | Extended Reality: a new dimension for reflective learning
Laura Haggar, Michelle McDermott and Amy Meenaghan | 301 |

Conclusion 319
Laura Haggar, Michelle McDermott and Jennifer Grant

Index 322

List of figures and tables

Figures

8.1	'I need' poem developed by staff members	144
8.2	'What I want to see' poem developed by staff members	147
16.1	The five core values of a trauma-informed approach	285
16.2	The five components required to apply a trauma-informed approach and achieve positive outcomes in teaching and learning	294

Tables

13.1	Transformative outcomes (SCOPE)	243
14.1	Aligning levels of reflection, thinking skills and higher education levels	254
14.2	What are the attributes of a 'good' reflective practitioner?	255

List of abbreviations

BFT	BearFace Theatre
CJS	criminal justice system
DPR	Declarative-Procedural-Reflective (model)
EDM	Exceptional Delivery Model
HE	higher education
HMIP	HM Inspectorate of Probation
HMPPS	HM Prison and Probation Service
MAPPA	Multi-Agency Public Protection Arrangements
MoJ	Ministry of Justice
NCJAA	National Criminal Justice Arts Alliance
OPD	Offender Personality Disorder
PBL	Problem-Based Learning
PD	personality difficulty
PP	Personal Practices
PQiP	Professional Qualification in Probation
PTA	practice tutor assessor
RNR	Risk-Need-Responsivity (model for offender rehabilitation)
RP	reflective practice
RPSS	Reflective Practice Supervision Standards
SEEDS	Skills for Effective Engagement Development and Supervision
SFO	serious further offfences
SPO	senior probation officer
STICS	Strategic Training in Community Supervision
TR	Transforming Rehabilitation
VR	Virtual Reality
XR	Extended Reality

Notes on contributors

Anne Burrell is currently employed on a fractional contract as a practice teacher assessor in the Probation Service, primarily working with learners on the Professional Qualification in Probation programme, and with Probation Services officer grade staff on their Vocational Qualification 3 award, alongside delivering training and mentoring. Anne holds a Certificate of Qualification in Social Work and has a long-standing career in probation work, including as a main grade practitioner, a senior probation officer and as a practice development assessor, prior to becoming a practice teacher assessor. She is currently undertaking a PhD with supervisors at De Montfort University, exploring professionalism in probation practice, and the implications of professional identity for probation practitioners.

Julie Eden-Barnard is Senior Lecturer at De Montfort University. She predominately teaches the Professional Qualification in Probation and the Masters in Community and Criminal Justice Leadership programmes. Prior to being in academia, Julie was a probation practitioner. During her time in probation, she developed expertise in working with women and also had experience of being a practice tutor assessor. Her research interests include the experiences of criminal justice involved women, reflective practice, and creative and participatory research methods.

Jennifer Grant is Senior Teaching Fellow at the University of Portsmouth, involved in the teaching and course leadership of the BA Hons in Community Justice. She has ongoing research in the area of male violence committed against women and girls, with a focus on non-contact sexual offending. Prior to this she worked in the probation service as a probation officer and senior probation officer.

Notes on contributors

Laura Haggar is Senior Lecturer at the University of Portsmouth, teaching across both campus and distance learning undergraduate and postgraduate programmes. Laura's current research focuses upon women in the justice system, the use of technology as a tool for probation practitioners, and probation attrition. Laura joined the university in 2019 to teach on the Professional Qualification in Probation and prior to this had a career as a probation officer.

Ceri Halfpenny joined the Probation Service in 2006. As a probation officer she managed individuals under Integrated Offender Management (IOM) and Multi-Agency Public Protection Arrangements (MAPPA), worked in court and was a programmes facilitator. She was a senior probation officer for five years. This role included chairing MAPPAs, managing the IOM team, women's lead and being an internal assessor for HM Inspectorate of Probation. She joined the University of Portsmouth in 2019. She is passionate about delivering an excellent learning experience for Professional Qualification in Probation students and helping to equip and inspire the next generation of probation officers. Her research interests include probation practice, reflective practice, desistance, rehabilitation, care-experience and penology.

Victoria Jones has held various roles in prison and probation since the 2000s, including operational management of Approved Premises. She later conducted safeguarding and fatal incident investigations for the Ombudsman. Currently, she lectures at De Montfort University, teaching the Professional Qualification in Probation and the Masters in Criminal Justice Leadership.

Ben Keysell is Senior Teaching Fellow at the University of Portsmouth. He has taught for five years on the BA Community Justice degree for trainee probation officers. He has also completed research on Transformative Learning Outcomes for learners on the Professional Qualification in Probation. Prior to his academic career, he worked for 18 years in the Probation Service, working across both the public and private sectors, including eight years as a practitioner before moving into Training/Learning and Development. Previous posts include Head of Professional Skills

Training for the National Offender Management Service and Learning & Development Business Partner for Interserve Justice.

Michelle McDermott is Principal Lecturer in Community Justice responsible for the academic component of the Professional Qualification in Probation delivered at the University of Portsmouth. Her current research focuses on decision-making of probation practitioners, and the retention of front-line staff in the Probation Service. Prior to joining academia in 2019 Michelle had a career in the Probation Service spanning 18 years as a front-line practitioner and with leadership positions across HM Prison and Probation Service in Learning and Development.

Amy Meenaghan is Principal Lecturer in Psychology and Offending Behaviour and the Subject Area Lead for Psychology in the School of Criminology and Criminal Justice at the University of Portsmouth. Her research interests include decision-making and offender behaviour, and the use of immersive technologies in education, training and research.

Daniele Molino gained their professional doctorate at the University of Portsmouth, where they are also Teaching Fellow in Forensic Psychology. He is the module coordinator for the Theory into Practice module on the MSc Forensic Psychology. He is British Pyschological Soceity chartered and a Health and Care Professions Council registered practitioner psychologist. Outside of his role in academia, Daniele has worked in a variety of forensic settings, from forensic units, to prison, mental health services, courts and probation, where he currently practices as a senior forensic psychologist on the London Offender Personality Disorder Pathway.

Mike Nash was involved in the early development of multi-agency working for the management of potentially dangerous offenders. He later worked in a lifer prison (unique at the time) as a probation officer, and in a maximum security prison as a senior probation officer. Joining the University of Portsmouth in 1991, he has held a variety of roles including head of department and director of community justice. Mike's research and publications have predominantly focused on the roles of criminal justice practitioners in working with, assessing and supervising high risk and dangerous offenders. He has also worked as a trainer with various police and probation services, organisations such as the Parole Board and spoken at gatherings in countries such as South Korea and Hong Kong.

Adrian Needs, PhD, worked in the prison service for 13 years, undertaking high security with violent and sexual offenders, then moving to develop staff training. Additional work included hostage and firearms incident negotiation and in-service counselling. A major impetus for going into academia was a leading role with the British Psychological Society in developing national standards for training and qualification in forensic psychology. He also contributed to working parties on homicide, suicide, disasters and psychological trauma and conducted research with, for example, veterans and horses. Now 'retired', Adrian has two British Psychological Society Lifetime Achievement Awards – and involvement in reconciliation after conflict.

Hollie Neal is Senior Lecturer at De Montfort University delivering the Professional Qualification in Probation. Prior to this role, she worked in West Midlands Probation as a probation practitioner, practice tutor assessor and senior probation officer. She lives with her wife and daughter, Emmy, who she would like to dedicate her chapter to.

Daniella Nudd is Senior Lecturer at De Montfort University delivering the Professional Qualification in Probation. Previous to this, she worked across Nottinghamshire and Derbyshire for 20 years as a probation officer and then senior probation officer.

Nicole Nyamwiza is Senior Lecturer in Criminology at the University of Law in Bloomsbury, London. Nicole's research focuses on the relationship between deviance and Blackness, and how this shapes Black people's experiences of the criminal justice system in England and Wales. Nicole has held academic posts at the University of Portsmouth and Kingston University, London. Her experience in academia has focused on offending behaviour, criminal justice and social policy. Nicole is also a qualified probation officer, with a specialism in managing people who engage in serious group offending. Her professional and academic background has provided her with an excellent practical understanding and insight into criminal behaviour and all aspects of community and custodial supervision

Dominic Pearson, PhD, is Associate Professor in Clinical Research and Practice in Forensic Psychology at the University of Portsmouth. He is the MSc Forensic Psychology Programme Lead, and module coordinator for the Assessment and Interventions module. He is a practitioner psychologist, British Pyschological Society chartered and Health and Care Professions Council registered, with over 20 years' experience working for or with the prison and probation services; studying community-oriented approaches to rehabilitation and risk management.

Laura Sibret obtained her BA(Hons) in Criminology and Criminal Justice from Griffith University in 2018 and her MPhil in Criminological Research from the University of Cambridge in 2020. Her academic research centres around preventative measures of sexual offences outside of current practices; in particular, it has involved exploring prevention mechanisms of child sexual abuse and the examination of interpersonal dynamics among sexual offenders. Her doctoral focus is on non-offending minor-attracted individuals, with a specific emphasis on formulating mental health preventative measures. She currently teaches at the University of Portsmouth across undergraduate and master's level courses. She also taught on the Professional Qualification in Probation, which generated an interest in self-reflection.

Lauren Stevens is Lecturer in Rehabilitation and Desistance at the University of Portsmouth. She has been teaching the Professional Qualification of Probation and Criminology over the last four years, and has also spent five years working at a category B prison in England working with families and prisoners during visitation prior to her teaching career. She is a PhD candidate within Criminology and Criminal Justice, and is very passionate about research in the areas of prison, probation, rehabilitation, desistance, crime prevention and offender management.

Ashlea Swinford qualified as a probation officer in 2020. They managed complex, high risk cases and undertook specialist responsibilities including court duty, diversity champion and mental health lead. In 2021, Ashlea began a professional doctorate researching the effectiveness of diversity and inclusion policies on the experiences of Black and minority ethnic staff. She currently teaches on the probation training programme, including lessons in rehabilitation, change theories and reflective practice.

Megan Thomas is Senior Teaching Fellow in the School of Criminology and Criminal Justice at the University of Portsmouth. With extensive teaching experience at various academic levels, she is committed to fostering student learning both in traditional and distance learning environments. As a course leader for the Professional Qualification in Probation, she contributes to developing future professionals in the field. Her research interests centre on professional cultures in probation and trauma-informed approaches, reflecting a dedication to enhancing practices within the criminal justice system.

Jennifer Walmsley is Executive Director for BearFace Theatre community interest company, which she co-founded in 2012 and has been developing and delivering arts based programmes across Hampshire and surrounding counties, predominantly working with men and women in prison and probation. With an MA in Applied Theatre, she has over 20 years' experience as a group worker and is passionate about people, connection and the power the arts have in strengthening community ties. Jennifer strongly believes in creative action for social change.

Kath Wilson is Associate Professor at De Montfort University, primarily involved in delivering the Professional Qualification in Probation. She has written around LGBTQIA+ issues and the criminal justice system for a number of years, highlighting some of the many inequities that remain in the system. Previous to this she worked for the Probation Service in various roles across the West Midlands over a 16-year period.

Acknowledgements

This work is a collaborative endeavour, born from a shared belief in the importance of creating time and space for reflection within and around probation practice. We hope these contributions offer insight, encouragement and a deeper understanding of how reflective practice can transform our work and the lives we touch. No matter your role within probation or your interest in the field, may this book aid in fostering a reflective approach that strengthens your impact.

This compendium is dedicated to our families who have supported us in our probation journeys and beyond. Thank you for your love and patience in making this book possible.

Introduction

Jennifer Grant, Laura Haggar and Michelle McDermott

Synopsis and aims

This edited collection delivers authentic reflective insights into probation practice. Its initial chapters will contextualise reflection, before considering the organisational space for reflective practice, diversity, and the implications for teaching and learning. It purposefully highlights contemporary issues of diversity in probation practice, given the diverse workforce of the Probation Service and the caseload of people on probation. Aimed at trainee probation officers, probation practitioners and those supporting their learning and development, this compendium provides the reader with real-world discussion about reflection in the probation context. In addition to probation specialists, its contributors include those from prison, third-sector organisations and mental health perspectives, to consider probation practice in different settings. Each chapter will provide prompts for reflective development, so its ideas can be immediately applied in practice. Its content will therefore enable the reader to develop their reflective practice skills, regardless of their level of experience.

Reflective practice is fundamental to probation practice and staff well-being. It is an integral element of effective training and continuous professional development (Coley, 2016) and encourages ethical probation practice, which is essential when working with the diverse population of people on probation (Burrell, 2022). Reflective practice also supports staff with the emotional toll of their work (Webster et al, 2020), enhancing their resilience and reducing the risk of burnout. Yet remarkably little has been written about reflective practice within probation, with much of the knowledge in this area based upon the adoption of practices within other sectors, such as nursing and social work. Jasper (2013) views reflective practice as a concept for learning, from which professionals can learn from their experiences to better understand and develop practice. Reflective practice can therefore be a way for the practitioner to take some time to consider their experiences and analyse them, to further their decision-making and professional development (Butani et al, 2017).

With reflective practice utilised across a wide range of settings we can draw on academic writing and research from other professions such as teaching, nursing and social work, to inform our understanding. In the similar profession of social work, where professional judgement decisions are also made in challenging situations, reflective practice offers practitioners the ability to reflect on the rationale for decision-making and consider future development (Gould and Baldwin, 2004). This also allows clearer decision-making in the moment via reflection-in-action (Schon, 1991), using their knowledge of theory and practice (Lyons et al, 2019). Given that experiencing an event is insufficient for deeper learning (Smart, 2017), reflecting on the experience enables the individual to both learn and develop professionally (Leigh, 2016). This process therefore should entail critical reflection, wherein the practitioner can also consider the influence of their assumptions and biases on their practice (Thompson and Thompson, 2018). Critical reflection provides practitioners with an outlet to problem-solve situations in a structured way (Malthouse et al, 2015), avoiding the pitfalls of rumination and bias (Smart, 2017). In probation, this means that reflection enhances both learning from an experience and the resulting quality of probation practice (Ainslie, 2020).

It is, therefore, unsurprising that reflective practice is strongly incorporated into the trainee probation officer programme. A key aspect of the training links to the student's ability to reflect on theory and practice to demonstrate critical reflection (Coley, 2016). There is also an emphasis on continuous professional development, and thus the use of theory in practice throughout their career. While the foundations of reflective practice form a key part of probation training, there is a need to provide practitioners with ongoing tools to enable this. Several chapters of this book acknowledge the barriers to reflection within the current Probation Service (Ainslie et al, 2022). Yet, reflective practice is a solution to some of the current concerns regarding staffing, well-being and retention in the organisation (Tidmarsh, 2024). Moreover, reflection provides a tool for practitioners to navigate practice ethically while addressing some of the current concerns about the impact of gender, race, sexuality and other protected characteristics on probation work and its staff (Petrillo, 2007; Woods, 2015; HMIP, 2021). Reflective practice is also integral to the professionalism of officers (Coley, 2016), which is pertinent given the current creation of professional registration for practitioners (HMPPS, 2024). This compendium will therefore offer a diverse range of insights which are relevant to all levels of experience in probation practice.

We begin this compendium by contextualising reflection within probation practice. Adrian Needs opens this discussion by addressing the holistic nature of reflection and provides the foundation for considering reflective practice in criminal justice contexts. Anne Burrell sets the scene, as she evaluates the importance of reflective practice in the current probation context, providing an opportunity for practitioners to reflect on how they can build reflexivity into their daily work. Dominic Pearson and Daniele Molino consider reflective practice within the context of the Offender Personality Disorder pathway programme, paying attention to the benefits and barriers to group-based reflective practice. Laura Sibret ends this section by providing an opportunity to review how personal self-reflection can enhance professional reflection. Through these chapters, the reader is invited to consider their own use of reflection within professional practice and reflect upon the ways that this can be developed holistically.

A spotlight is shone on the organisational context in Part II of this compendium, given its significance in providing opportunity and support for reflective practice. Jennifer Grant begins this section by discussing the significance of the senior probation officer role in embedding a culture of reflective practice within the organisation. The further chapters in this section discuss differing inter-agency perspectives, with Mike Nash reflecting on the evolving role of the Probation Service in regards to safeguarding and multi-agency working. Lauren Stevens then considers multi-agency working in the prison context, pertaining to civil staff, with space for probation practitioners to reflect on their practice in this context also. Jennifer Walmsley and Laura Haggar close this section by introducing the concept of creative reflective practice, utilising applied theatre and trauma-informed practice to support practitioners.

Key reflections on contemporary issues of diversity in probation practice are provided by contributors in Part III. Ashlea Swinford explores her experiences of working in the COVID-19 pandemic to prompt debate and reflection on safe working practices for minority ethnic practitioners, and Nicole Nyamwiza reflects on working with Black and minority groups in probation, providing consideration to a co-created approach. In considering approaches to working as a female practitioner, Michelle McDermott, Laura Haggar and Jennifer Grant reflect on the barriers and opportunities that gender can bring to the supervisory relationship. Current issues in relation to lesbian women as both probation practitioners and people on probation are then discussed by Kath Wilson, Daniella Nudd, Hollie Neal and Victoria Jones. This diverse range of contributors highlights the impact of intersectionality, not only on the probation caseload but also on the experiences of those working within the service.

The final section focuses on teaching, learning and professional development. This discusses the trainee probation officer programme from both the student and assessor perspectives, as well as the use of technology in probation training more widely. Ben Keysell proposes a 'transformative framework' of learning outcomes to enhance the integration of theory and practice through all aspects of teaching and learning, with concluding thoughts on continuous professional development. Perspectives on assessment of reflection are offered by Julie Eden-Barnard, who presents a Reflective Practice Assessment Framework, which provides key principles to consider when designing reflective practice assessments. The resulting feedback from assessment is then considered by Ceri Halfpenny, who shares best practice for both students and assessors for reflective assignments. Megan Thomas moves to teaching and discusses the practical application and benefits of trauma-informed teaching and learning in higher education. Widening the context to probation training more generally, Laura Haggar, Michelle McDermott and Amy Meenaghan draw on their research to explore the potential of technology to enhance reflective practice. The compendium will then provide a short conclusion, wherein it will provide the reader an opportunity to further reflect on key themes featured in this book.

This edited collection has been designed with practitioners at every stage of their career in mind, given reflection has ongoing benefits for well-being and continuous professional development. This book is designed as a collection rather than a continuous text with a beginning and an end, so readers may notice common themes if read as an entire volume. Despite the many barriers to reflection in daily practice, this compendium seeks to highlight the opportunities for reflection so invites the reader to pause for thought using reflective prompts at the end of each chapter. This book is an invitation, albeit a call, to take the time to reflect. We really hope that there is something for everyone in this collection and that, most of all, you enjoy reading it.

References

Ainslie, S. (2020) A time to reflect?, *Probation Quarterly*, 17: 9–12.

Ainslie, S., Fowler, A., Phillips, J. and Westaby, C. (2022) 'A nice idea but …': Implementing a reflective supervision model in the National Probation Service in England and Wales, *Reflective Practice*, 23(5): 525–538. doi: https://doi.org/10.1080/14623943.2022.2066075

Burrell, A. (2022) The reflective practitioner in transition: Probation work during reintegration of Probation Services in England and Wales, *Probation Journal*, 69(4): 434–451. doi: https://doi.org/10.1177/02645505221117537

Butani, L., Bannister, S., Rubin, A. and Forbes, K. (2017) How educators conceptualize and teach reflective practice: A study of North American pediatric medical educators, *Academic Pediatrics*, 17(3): 303–309. doi: https://www.sciencedirect.com/science/article/abs/pii/S187628591630540X

Coley, D. (2016) Reflective practice: The cornerstone of all we do, Probation Institute. Available from: https://static1.squaresp ace.com/static/5ec3ce97a1716758c54691b7/t/5ed7a65e8756c 4572d39731d/1592837014154/Reflective+Practice

Gould, N. and Baldwin, M. (eds) (2004) *Social Work, Critical Reflection and the Learning Organization*, Ashgate.

HMIP (HM Inspectorate of Probation) (2021) Race equality in probation: The experiences of black, Asian and minority ethnic probation service users and staff. Available from: https://www.justiceinspectorates.gov.uk/hmiprobation/inspections/race-equality-in-probation/

HMPPS (HM Prison and Probation Service) (2024) Probation professional register policy framework. Available from: https://assets.publishing.service.gov.uk/media/66fa78c0a31f45a9c765e e6e/2024_09_30_Prof_Reg-Probation_Professional_Register_ policy_framework.pdf

Jasper, M. (2013) *Beginning Reflective Practice*, Cengage Learning.

Leigh, J. (2016) An embodied perspective on judgements of written reflective practice for professional development in higher education, *Reflective Practice*, 17(1): 72–85. doi: http://dx.doi.org/10.1080/14623943.2015.1123688

Lyons, A., Mason, B., Nutt, K. and Keville, S. (2019) Inside it was orange squash concentrate: Trainees' experiences of reflective practice groups within clinical psychology training, *Reflective Practice*, 20(1): 70–84. doi: https://psycnet.apa.org/doi/10.1080/ 14623943.2018.1559804

Malthouse, R., Watts, M. and Roffrey-Barentsen, J. (2015) Reflective questions, self-questioning and managing professionally situated practice, *Research in Education*, 94(1): 71–87. doi: https:// doi.org/10.7227/RIE.0024

Petrillo, M. (2007) Power struggle: Gender issues for female probation officers in the supervision of high risk offenders, *Probation Journal*, 54(4): 394–406. doi: https://doi.org/10.1177/ 0264550507083538

Schon, D. (1991) *The Reflective Practitioner: How Professionals Think in Action*, Ashgate.

Smart, F. (2017) Poetic transcription with a twist: An approach to reflective practice through connection, collaboration and community, *Innovations in Education and Teaching International*, 54(2): 152–161. doi: https://doi.org/10.1080/14703297.2016.1258323

Thompson, S. and Thompson, N. (eds) (2018) *The Critically Reflective Practitioner* (2nd edn), Palgrave.

Tidmarsh, M (2024) Legacies of change: Probation staff experiences of the unification of services in England and Wales, *British Journal of Criminology*, 64(2): 468–486. doi: https://doi.org/10.1093/bjc/azad042

Webster, N., Doggett, L. and Gardner, S. (2020) If you want to change the world you have to start with yourself: The impact of staff reflective practice within the Offender Personality Disorder pathway, *Probation Journal*, 67(3): 283–296. doi: https://doi.org/10.1177/0264550520939180

Woods, J.B. (2015) The birth of modern criminology and gendered constructions of homosexual criminal identity, *Journal of Homosexuality*, 62(2): 131–166. doi: https://doi.org/10.1080/00918369.2014.969053

PART I

Contextualising reflection within probation practice

1

Psychological perspectives on reflective processes in criminal justice contexts

Adrian Needs

Many supervisors of individuals taking their first steps in reflective writing and practice will be familiar with patterns that suggest that a student or trainee doesn't quite 'get it'. Common patterns include presenting a narrative that is almost entirely descriptive, or a focus on justifying decisions rather than questioning them. The essence of a genuinely reflective process is self-questioning, making it an inherently dialogical activity (Brown and Sawyer, 2016). Having an idea of what kinds of questions to ask can be very helpful in getting started. Otherwise the injunction to engage in reflection could be compared to Karl Popper asking his students to 'observe'; the predictable response, which made Popper's point, was 'observe what?' (Fransella, 1975). Yet experience with that other form of questioning, known as interviewing, tells us that the 'same old questions' tend to elicit the 'same old answers'. There are helpful guides available, although some students' introduction to reflective writing may have been via a generic university protocol with the appearance and inspirational capacity of a box-ticking requirement.

Once in practice, challenges can escalate. Academic knowledge may seem difficult to apply to situations that do not come 'clearly defined and readily packaged' and practitioners need to explore, engage and create 'from an array of complex and potentially competing demands and priorities' (Lane and Corrie, 2006: 23–24). For several years, worrying numbers of submissions by trainee forensic psychologists on the British Psychological Society's post-MSc route to qualified status were being returned by assessors as showing insufficient evidence of reflection. They exhibited procedural competence but failed to capture the self-awareness, critical and original thinking, contextual sensitivity and problem-solving which characterise a resilient, environmentally aware and ethically attuned professional capable of autonomous, effective judgement and action in complex and unfamiliar situations (see Chapter 14 regarding key principles for reflective writing assessments). Exercise of routine, prescribed practice on its own corresponds to a lower place in the skills hierarchy (Sookermany, 2012). Lane and Corrie (2006) also commented that in psychology, at least, the scientist-practitioner ideal has proved elusive, not helped by the products of academic paradigms sometimes seeming of questionable relevance and realism.

Reflective practice itself has been criticised for a cognitive, detached, 'in the head' bias. Embodied awareness, including feeling and doing, has been given relatively little attention (Jordi, 2011). The irony is that, outside of the prevailing orthodoxy, in the last couple of decades ideas about the nature of cognition have been reformulated to encompass such aspects. This heterogeneous movement has been accompanied by growing concerns over the dominance of what might be seen as unhelpfully simplistic forms of knowledge creation and utilisation. The present chapter raises the possibility that the effectiveness of reflective practice might be enhanced by increasing familiarity with critiques of taken-for-granted forms of knowledge and with developments in understanding processes that might (or arguably should) be involved in reflection.

Critiques of prevalent forms of knowledge

Variables as abstractions

At its best, the language of 'variables' that permeates fields such as intervention programmes and risk assessment can furnish useful short-hand terms for thinking and communicating about the world. However, it is easy to forget that the map is not the territory, the menu not the meal (Bateson, 1972). Favoured terms such as 'impulsivity' are abstractions, standing in for often complex and context-dependent processes (Polaschek, 2012). Interpreting research usually involves navigating definitions and measurements, frequently with statistical techniques initially devised with a eugenicist's eye for objectification and categories (Kennedy-Shaffer, 2024). Controversy has persisted over whether direct extrapolation from group data to specific individuals is justified, unlikely to be the case with data from markedly different contexts and populations and where contradictory individual patterns are obscured (Diener et al, 2022). Experimental paradigms have been criticised for tending to sacrifice realism and relevance for internal controls: rigour within a suspension of disbelief. Beyond laboratories, quantitative research has sometimes been seen as based upon restricted measurements, such as crude ratings with insufficient attention to the situations and circumstances of people's lives (Case and Haines, 2014).

Disregard of such contextual aspects makes extrapolation to new settings 'notoriously unreliable', with many phenomena sensitive to the smallest of differences (Diener et al, 2022). In real-world criminal justice settings, lack of attention to characteristics of settings such as quality of interpersonal relationships with staff more generally, along with associated factors such as staff training and morale, can lead to the 'evaporation' of effectiveness of offending behaviour programmes during rollout and insufficient information to understand why (Hough, 2010). Ironically, trends in what we take as knowledge are not themselves immune to contextual influences, such as the increasingly competitive, business-oriented ethos of universities or managerialism and under-funding of agencies within the criminal justice system. Practitioners within the latter often have their own orthodoxies. As in most settings, using expected terminology can signify a professional identity and membership of a group, while demonstrating an approved narrative of concepts and reasoning influences access to resources and opportunities.

The web of relations

A preoccupation with reified variables (where fluid and provisional processes become like chemical elements) and neglect of context are two sides of the same coin: what early systems theorists termed 'building blocks' are isolated from the kind of 'web of relations' in which they occur in nature. The latter is the reality faced by practitioners, even though they may succumb to shortcut heuristics and biases which involve giving undue weight to a single issue or piece of information. The Western penchant for taking things apart should be at least balanced by an attempt to see what they are part *of* (Clarke and Crossland, 1985). Without this, in trying to understand what is essentially a system by reducing it to its component parts, there is a danger that 'the analytical method destroys what it seeks to understand' (Kernick, 2006: 3). The complex behaviour of human beings cannot be reduced to single factors such as brain malfunction or other putative deficits. Venturing more deeply into this perspective makes us more aware of 'multi-factor problems that require tracking many complex interactions, feedback loops, highly correlated processes and outcomes simultaneously'; in real-world dynamics, causal effects change over time and outcomes are rarely proportional to inputs or precipitating events (Diener et al, 2022: 26). This contrasts with the clockwork-like universe suggested by classical Newtonian science or the dualisms (such as mind–body, rationality–emotion, inner–outer, subject–object) of Cartesian philosophy.

People as systems

A dynamical systems perspective is far from restricted to what is 'external' to individual living beings. Not that the distinction between organism and environment is entirely straightforward, even though it may seem as self-evident as the demarcation of space and time before Einstein; but how should we categorise food just eaten, a tool in use or a functioning artificial limb (Palmer, 2004)? Several authors, from Merleau-Ponty onwards, have used the example of the white stick through which a blind person knows the world. Rather than just being regarded as separate entities, mind, stick and environment can be seen from a functional perspective as coming together to constitute a system of information transmission. From this standpoint, mind is not a disembodied processor detached from engagement with the world (Barrett et al, 2010). Yet to act autonomously, living beings must maintain integration and viability as they interact with their environment (which, of course, includes living beings similar to themselves). Since the pioneering work of biologists Maturana and Varela self-creating and self-maintaining living systems have been referred to as 'autopoietic'.

Ideally, at least, we need to hold ourselves together and keep going in life while (or rather through) maintaining a sense of continuity of our own being, making adaptive sense of the world we are part of in accordance with our purposes, be able to make choices and keep ourselves on track, while throughout engaging with others facilitated by a sense of connectedness and participation. These elements can be seen as broadly corresponding to the interdependent needs or motives identified as 'identity, meaning, control and belonging' postulated in Ashforth's (2001) framework for understanding organisational role transitions. A core idea is that these are activated and in need of realignment, renegotiation or reconciliation when an individual's circumstances alter. For example, former members of the armed forces sometimes struggle with the loss of military identity, outlook, confidence and camaraderie. This adaptation of Ashforth's framework can also be applied to transitions such as major life events, therapeutic/rehabilitative change and the abruptly disruptive episodes of potential trauma (Needs and Adair-Stantiall, 2018). More generally, in the words of Robert C. Gallagher: 'Change in life is inevitable – except from a vending machine.'

Getting stuck

Existing resolutions of the processes involved in identity, meaning, control and belonging tend to be resistant to change. They provide a foundation of familiarity and predictability. A preference for stability and consistency leads individuals to attempt to be selective in the people, situations and activities they engage with, to influence situations through behaviour in characteristic ways and even to ignore or neutralise discrepant information, perhaps by denigrating the source (see Needs and Adair-Stantiall, 2018). Another option is to bring about a state of affairs that appears to confirm an otherwise tenuous anticipation or interpretation;

George Kelly (1955, as cited in Needs and Jones, 2017) famously illustrated this by suggesting that, if you really want to prove the neighbours' animosity towards you, go and throw stones at their windows! Systems can also be constrained by 'path dependence', the narrowing effect of previous development on outlooks, circumstances and opportunities. This is evident in many individuals sanctioned by the criminal justice system who live with the consequences of stigma and mistrust.

Well-used patterns can become 'attractor states' to which the system tends inexorably to return (Hayes and Yasinski, 2015). With people identified as personality disordered, this has been seen in terms of repeatedly bringing to bear certain themes in interpreting interpersonal events. This tends to be accompanied by intolerance of ambiguity, closed-mindedness with regard to alternative possibilities and perspectives, along with domination by internal experiences and concerns (Salvi et al, 2023). Consequences of rigid, inflexible patterns of thinking and action in professional roles range from limiting to catastrophic (Needs, 2010) and often accompany poor mental health and suboptimal functioning more generally. Closed-mindedness facilitates relating to people as objects rather than subjects, becoming mired in repeated patterns and difficulty in engaging in personal change. Conversely, openness to others, to experiencing and to alternative possibilities is a prerequisite of non-defensive mutuality, flexible adaptation and renewal (Cooper et al, 2012; Kyselo, 2016).

Getting together

Openness is also a precondition of 'intersubjectivity', a fundamental (some would say *the* fundamental) process in human development from the earliest days onwards; in this 'we make sense of each other and of the world together' (De Jaegher, 2015: 113). Intersubjectivity has a profound effect on our ways of experiencing the world (De Jaegher, 2015), but is not a single process. Stevanovic and Koski (2018) identified and traced the developmental origins of several processes that can be present, synthesised and fluctuating in any interaction episode. These include the exercise of anticipation and attention towards a co-interactant's intentions, current focus and likely behaviour to oneself. From origins soon after birth, such a stance is refined and comes to extend to groups, including their roles, norms and sanctions. Emotional satisfaction (and avoidance of upset) is a key driver and Stevanovic and Koski (2018) further highlight issues of power and knowledge. The whole is permeated by mutuality, reciprocity and responsiveness to the extent that each 'incorporates' the other in the experience of engagement (Fuchs and De Jaegher, 2009). Interactions create an 'emergent' dynamical system that transforms behaviour and social understanding over time, in a way that is not reducible to the coupled parts in isolation (Fuchs and De Jaegher, 2009), analogous to how the creation of water molecules requires the interaction of hydrogen and oxygen atoms and 'wetness' resides in neither. As Hanne De Jaegher and colleagues have pointed out, participating in each other's sense-making transforms making sense *of* the other into making sense *with* the other. The emergence of new insights, experiences and plans through intersubjectivity is a crucial process in constructive conversations, including psychotherapy (Needs and Adair-Stantiall, 2018).

There is, however, considerable scope during an individual's development for these processes to be limited or distorted, contributing to the problems in attachment, personal validation or childhood trauma encountered in many clients in the criminal justice system. Fluctuations between 'attunement and alienation', mutuality and tension, along with conflict, differences, perceived rejection and failures of understanding are all part of social interaction (Fuchs and De Jaegher, 2009). In many instances the misunderstandings and irritations that arise can function 'like questions that lead to answers in the subsequent course of the interaction' (Fuchs and De Jaegher, 2009: 471), although many individuals in (but far from confined to) criminal justice settings have problems in negotiating either answers or questions. Negotiation (Murakami, 2003) and repairs of ruptures are ubiquitous in professional contexts, especially helping and change-oriented professions including probation, and working through them can have emergent benefits. Additionally, however, qualitative research suggests that activities such as risk assessment are not immune to extraneous influences (including maintaining credibility in the eyes of colleagues or supervisors [Shingler et al, 2020]).

Inhabiting a position

Interactions between people also imply potential 'positions' and themes (Murakami, 2003). A position invokes a set of concepts, images, tropes, metaphors, ways of speaking and self-narratives (Murakami, 2003) and can evoke or explicitly invoke congruent, sometimes complementary, culturally embedded routines. This is a core process in impression management (for example, meeting expectations of professional conduct in order to instil confidence and trust). Cumulative interpersonal experience and participation in a culture contribute to a common foundation, while adopting particular motivational and perceptual perspectives has been seen as a basis for agency and self-regulation (Cooper et al, 2012). In addition, comparison of perspectives can generate new perspectives (Brown and Sawyer, 2016). Positions are permeated not only by culture, groups and narrative constructions of the world but by personal aspects such as memories. They can also, when entered into in reflection or daily life, be endowed with a voice.

The idea of activities such as reflection, self-regulation and problem-solving involving 'inner speech' has a long history and has been seen as involving dialogical exchanges (such as questions and answers, arguments and counter-arguments) between perspectives (for more on practising self-reflection, see Chapter 4). Such positions or voices can correspond to the perspectives of particular other people, including fictional ones, or those of a group, culture or society, and be in various forms of dialogical relationship reflecting aspects such as dominance, integration and accessibility (Stewart, 2018). Like relations between people, those between self-positions may be adversely affected by lack of openness (Cooper et al, 2012). Together, they constitute in Bakhtin's term a 'polyphony', are contextualised (although some contexts are repetitive) and have an important role in identity change.

There is growing recognition of, for example, the role of identity changes in desistance from offending and research on how assumptions about the sort of person one might become (and perceived consequences) can impede potential trajectories (see Needs and Adair-Stantiall, 2018). Reflection upon one's own personal and professional development also provide a valuable source of insights into change processes which might operate in clients. Methods for facilitating these – and elaborating new positions – with both clients and self are available (Needs and Jones, 2017). Such work should take place from a stance of 'dispositional reciprocity' and participation in the alternative standpoint, with mutual acknowledgement of agency and perspective even when the meaning of the interaction is initially uncertain (Radley, 1977; Crone and Huemer, 2018). This is essentially a 'second person' stance, where the other person is regarded as a 'you'. It stands in contrast to the 'third person' standpoint of detached observers familiar from academic research, where the other person is a 'they', 'he/she' or an example of a category.

A new understanding of 'cognition'

It was noted previously that reflective practice has been criticised as being excessively cognitive. In some quarters, criticised views of cognition have been developing and jostling with each other over the last few decades. There has been a move to more holistic and integrated perspectives than where the focus is on living beings in relation to their natural environments. These perspectives are centred upon '4e' cognition, in which cognitive activity is seen as 'enactive', 'embodied', 'embedded' and (more controversially) 'extended'. Some authors have recommended that we remove 'extended' and go down to '3e'. Others have recommended that we add 'ecological', to foreground sensitivity to contextual changes. At the risk of a proliferation of terms which takes us away from the fundamental nexus of individual and environment, we might also explore the addition of 'ethical' cognition. This could involve examining whether we might be falling into the rationalisations and excuses of moral disengagement, a self-righteous identity and self-serving narrative, or neglect of second-person engagement and tolerance of ambiguity (Needs, submitted).

Enactive

The mind is not best seen as a passive, detached receiver of inputs from the environment, which are then reconstituted into centralised representations and finally translated into behaviour

(Hutchins, 2010). An alternative view is that what we do and experience arises from (and for) our engagements with our environments. Although there is a natural world that exists independently of ourselves, this can be distinguished from the effective environments or 'worlds' of individuals; those worlds are 'enacted' or 'brought forth' through actions. Our worlds are experienced primarily through multiple 'affordances', or possibilities for action. In the words of Laroche et al (2014: 7): 'I bring forth an experience of the other that emerges from the consequences of my activity towards him.' Or, in those of Rietveld et al (2018: 42): 'Someone who does not have the ability to read English cannot be responsive to the possibility this sentence offers of being read.' Cognition is thus in all senses an inherently relational process (Thompson and Stapleton, 2009). We know the world according to how we relate to it (Radley, 1977).

The world that we bring forth is created from a perspective of concerns and interests, of what is significant to an individual's autonomous existence (Laroche et al, 2014; Maiese, 2018). Clearly, a starving person is likely to be preoccupied with getting food and a tired person may look for somewhere to sit. Perhaps less immediately obvious are the concerns from Ashforth's (2001) framework that we interpreted as necessary properties of the functioning autopoietic system: identity, meaning, control and belonging. Since these refer to processes that are essential to the system's continued viability, they might be expected to be rarely too far in the background of an individual's landscape of affordances. How often they are in the foreground is likely to depend on the individual's state of autopoietic equilibrium. Disequilibrium instigates compensatory self-organisational activity, including selective openness and responsiveness to relevant affordances (Ramstead et al, 2016). When called into question by events an individual might redouble attempts to affirm or restore a valued identity, narrative, source of self-efficacy or affiliation, or perhaps ignore or denigrate the source. Affective consequences are more than likely.

There are other ramifications. For example, places or trajectories of action can offer multiple and sometimes well-established affordances. In interaction with a state of disequilibrium, these can come to 'solicit' action rather than just present possibilities. This results in 'a bodily readiness for what you can do next' (Ramstead et al, 2016: 58). (Such processes are worth exploring in relation to serial offending, accounts of which often tend to fall back on stereotypes, circular reasoning or obsolete typological approaches [Needs, 2022].) In addition, the coordinated activities of many individuals over time tend to give rise to an emergent 'niche', a context of multiple affordances such as a subculture (Ramstead et al, 2016). In the course of 'intentional and narrative engagement' with their environments, individuals have an active role in structuring their milieux (Thompson and Stapleton, 2009: 28). The 'dog eat dog', 'look after Number One' outlook associated with the extreme end of the criminal spectrum can, if unchecked, be perpetuated by a prison subculture which reflects this (Needs and Adair-Stantiall, 2018).

Embodied

A bodily aspect is, unsurprisingly, at the core of 'embodied' cognition. As living beings, we have bodies that enable us to be immersed in yet differentiate ourselves from our environments, to participate in the world with agency, self-regulation and the co-regulation of relational dynamics and to experience emotions and other feelings (Hutchins, 2010; Laroche et al, 2014; Kyselo, 2016). Cognition in real-life contexts has been referred to as 'embodied action' (Thompson and Stapleton, 2009), with interaction between people characterised as taking place between embodied perspectives (Laroche et al, 2014). We may be familiar with the feeling that there are more possibilities than we can currently grasp and articulate; a bodily 'felt sense' can be outside of conscious experience, implicit rather than explicit and struggling for expression, with a failure to do so leaving a sense of incompleteness (Jordi, 2011). However, situations such as childhood play, sports, yoga, creative activity and intimacy demonstrate that it is possible to attend in a non-conceptual sense *through* the body to activity and environment in the present moment (Buttingsrud, 2018).

Embedded and extended

Complementary to embodied cognition, 'embedded' cognition highlights how cognition is 'afforded and constrained by ongoing interactions between body and environment, emphasizing an intimate relationship between external artifacts and cognitive processes'; this differs from embodied cognition in that the latter 'amounts to the claim that knowledge is grounded in sensorimotor routines and experiencing' (Pouw et al, 2014: 53). Using external resources, such as a notebook, promotes flexible cognitive activity in a continuous coupling that reduces cognitive load. 'Extended' cognition would suggest, more radically, that the notebook in effect becomes an intrinsic part of the cognitive activity. To some, such as Maiese (2018), this is a step too far, with the idea of cognition reaching beyond an organism concerned with its own boundaries seen as contradicting the enactive approach and adding nothing of value to the embedded perspective.

Others have disagreed explicitly or implicitly with this. Vold (2018) cited research and theorising which suggest that the loss of familiar relationships with objects and locations has profound effects not predicted by the embedded view. It is tempting to speculate, in line with the earlier discussion based on Ashforth's framework, that some of the objects we use, surround ourselves with or put on display support our sense of who we are, our outlook, what gives us confidence and a sense of belonging; this might also be applied to the affordances of place. Kyselo (2016) argued that life and development are characterised by a continuous interplay between separateness and integration with the environment ('distinction' and 'participation'). From a functional perspective, the coupling of mind and environment forming a unitary system (Barrett et al, 2010) parallels the idea of intersubjective systems emerging between people. It is consistent with a form of science oriented towards the connectedness as well as separateness of being.

Conclusion

Fifty years ago, I read Gregory Bateson's *Steps to an Ecology of Mind*. Its demonstration of how major insights can be gained from unfamiliar ways of seeing the world stayed with me. R.D. Laing's *The Divided Self* highlighted the importance of people's experiences and viewpoints. At university, studying psychology, much seemed contrived and rarefied. Then I stumbled upon personal construct theory. It focuses upon how people's behaviour and feelings are inextricably linked to and best understood through their sense-making, rather than the externally imposed categories of 'objective' frameworks. In my subsequent doctorate, despite initial resistance from those who objected to studying subjectivity, it proved possible to do a reasonable approximation of studying subjectivity, objectively.

In HM Prison Service I found this approach invaluable in interviewing and attempting to facilitate personal change with hundreds of prisoners in high security. Engaging with individuals' perspectives proved essential in hostage-taking episodes and firearms incidents with the police. These further sharpened awareness of multiple interacting factors and possibilities that had been encouraged by recognition of contextual factors, including preceding life events and situations of homicides and the effects of prison environments. Involvement in formulating national standards for qualification of forensic psychologists left questions about conceptualising professional competence.

An academic role was intended to enable elaboration of these interests, but proved a culture shock. Much was remote from the world of professional practice, in which for the most part there was little interest and less knowledge, despite pretentions which sometimes accompanied extraordinarily manipulative behaviour. This intensified a sense of duty to prepare students for the realities of the field of practice to which many aspired. It was clear that there was a need to emphasise the role of questioning in reflection, particularly identifying alternatives, anticipating possible obstacles and counter-arguments while fostering resilience.

In addition, the discourse of 'variables' assumes a life of its own and must be treated critically to avoid becoming too divorced from reality. It is necessary to appreciate contextual factors and processes, including properties generated through interaction. Intersubjectivity in interactions between people is central to their development, although sustaining aspects such as identity can also constrain and interactions can be problematic. Rigidity is particularly detrimental to what Schön (1984) termed reflection in action. We do not have to be held in the grip of a single perspective or 'position' but we can be, just as we can be limited by what we apprehend or the patterns that we help bring about, without necessarily being aware that we are limited or limiting. We may fail to realise how we are affected by and affect other people, situations and outcomes. Ideally, we should have ways of opening our awareness that take us beyond the narrowing consequences of primarily conceptual reflection (Buttingsrud, 2018). This is what the students mentioned at the start also needed to discover: reflective practice can be liberating.

Reflective prompts

These examples can be used within frameworks such as those of Kolb, Gibbs, the Sunflower Health protocol, contextualised for reflection 'in' or 'on' action (Schön, 1984):

- How/why am I using these labels (for example, impulsive, angry)? What processes are actually going on? What is affecting these?
- How are elements of this situation connected? How does the other person/other people seem to be experiencing the situation we are in (including me/my actions)? How are we affecting each other and what are we generating?
- Is the other person/myself dominated by particular perceptions or issues? Including: how they see/want to see themselves, position(s)/role(s) they seem to be enacting; understanding of own life story, on life/world in general; 'comfort zone' and willingness/ability to make and act consistently with choices; affiliations, allegiances, what believe others would think.
- How is the other person/myself reacting to anything questioning, undermining or not fitting with the above? Openness to alternative ways of seeing/doing?
- How do I 'know' all of the above? What information am I using and how confident can I be? Are there alternative possibilities or explanations?

References

Ashforth, B.E. (2001) *Role Transitions in Organizational Life: An Identity-based Perspective*, Lawrence Erlbaum Associates.

Barrett, L.F., Mesquita, B. and Smith, E.R. (2010) The context principle, in B. Mesquita, L.F. Barrett and E. Smith (eds) *The Mind in Context*, Guilford Press, pp 1–24.

Bateson, G. (1972) *Steps to an Ecology of Mind: Collected Essays in Anthropology, Psychiatry, Evolution, and Epistemology*, University of Chicago Press.

Brown, H. and Sawyer, R.D. (2016) Dialogic reflection: An exploration of its embodied, imaginative, and reflexive dynamic, in H. Brown, R.D. Sawyer and J. Norris (eds) *Forms of Practitioner Reflexivity: Critical, Conversational, and Arts-based Approaches*, Palgrave Macmillan, pp 1–12.

Buttingsrud, C. (2018) Embodied reflection, presented at the Embodied Cognition and the Arts Conference CTSA UCI 8-10, December 2016.

Case, S. and Haines, K. (2014) Youth justice: From linear risk paradigm to complexity, in A. Pycroft and C. Bartollas (eds) *Applying Complexity Theory: Whole Systems Approaches to Criminal Justice and Social Work*, Policy Press, pp 113–139.

Clarke, D.D. and Crossland, J. (1985) *Action Systems: An Introduction to the Analysis of Complex Behaviour*, Methuen.

Cooper, M., Chak, A., Cornish, F. and Gillespie, A. (2012) Dialogue: Bridging personal, community, and social transformation, *Journal of Humanistic Psychology*, 53(1): 70–93. https://psycnet.apa.org/doi/10.1177/0022167812447298

Crone, K. and Huemer, W. (2018) Self-consciousness and intersubjectivity: Dimensions of the social self, *Phenomenology and the Cognitive Sciences*, 17(2): 225–229. https://doi.org/10.1007/s11097-017-9547-6

De Jaegher, H. (2015) How we affect each other: Michel Henry's 'pathos-with' and the enactive approach to intersubjectivity, *Journal of Consciousness Studies*, 22(1–2): 112–132.

Diener, E., Northcott, R., Zyphur, M.J. and West, S.G. (2022) Beyond experiments, *Perspectives on Psychological Science*, 17(4): 1101–1119. https://doi.org/10.1177/17456916211037670

Fransella, F. (1975) *Need to Change?* Methuen.

Fuchs, T. and De Jaegher, H. (2009) Enactive intersubjectivity: Participatory sense-making and mutual incorporation, *Phenomenology and the Cognitive Sciences*, 8: 465–486. https://psycnet.apa.org/doi/10.1007/s11097-009-9136-4

Hayes, A.M. and Yasinski, C. (2015) Pattern destabilization and emotional processing in cognitive therapy for personality disorders, *Frontiers in Psychology*, 6(107): 1–13. http://dx.doi.org/10.3389/fpsyg.2015.00107

Hough, M. (2010) Gold standard or fool's gold? The pursuit of certainty in experimental criminology, *Criminology and Criminal Justice*, 10(1): 11–22. https://doi.org/10.1177/1748895809352597

Hutchins, E. (2010) Cognitive ecology, *Topics in Cognitive Science*, 2(4): 705–715. https://psycnet.apa.org/doi/10.1111/j.1756-8765.2010.01089.x

Jordi, R. (2011) Reframing the concept of reflection: Consciousness, experiential learning, and reflective learning practices, *Adult Education Quarterly*, 61(2): 181–197. https://psycnet.apa.org/doi/10.1177/0741713610380439

Kennedy-Shaffer, L. (2024) Teaching the difficult past of statistics to improve the future, *Journal of Statistics and Data Science Education*, 32(1): 108–119. https://doi.org/10.1080/26939169.2023.2224407

Kernick, D. (2006) Wanted – new methodologies for health service research. Is complexity theory the answer?, *Family Practice*, 23(3): 385–390. https://doi.org/10.1093/fampra/cml011

Kyselo, M. (2016) The enactive approach and disorders of the self: The case of schizophrenia, *Phenomenology and the Cognitive Sciences*, 15: 591–616. https://doi.org/10.1007/s11097-015-9441-z

Lane, D.A. and Corrie, S. (2006) *The Modern Scientist-practitioner: A Guide to Practice in Psychology*, Routledge.

Laroche, J., Berardi, A.M. and Brangier, E. (2014) Embodiment of intersubjective time: Relational dynamics as attractors in the temporal coordination of interpersonal behaviors and experiences, *Frontiers in Psychology*, 5: Article 1180. https://doi.org/10.3389/fpsyg.2014.01180

Maiese, M. (2018) Can the mind be embodied, enactive, affective, and extended?, *Phenomenology and the Cognitive Sciences*, 17(2): 343–361. https://link.springer.com/article/10.1007/s11097-017-9510-6

Murakami, K. (2003) Orientation to the setting: Discursively accomplished intersubjectivity, *Culture and Psychology*, 9(3): 233–248. https://doi.org/10.1177/1354067X030093005

Needs, A. (2010) Systemic failure and human error, in C. Ireland and M. Fisher (eds) *Consultancy and Advising in Forensic Practice: Empirical and Practical Guidelines*, Wiley-Blackwell, pp 203–219.

Needs, A. (2022) Serial and mass murder, in L.R. Kurtz (ed) *Encyclopedia of Violence, Peace and Conflict*, vol 2 (3rd edn), Elsevier, pp 72–82.

Needs, A. (submitted) Reconciliation as transition: A view from dynamical systems and forensic psychology, *Journal of Reconciliation Studies*.

Needs, A. and Jones, L. (2017) Personal construct psychotherapy, in J. Davies and C. Miles (eds) *Individual Psychotherapy with Clients in Forensic Settings*, Wiley, pp 121–141.

Needs, A. and Adair-Stantiall, A. (2018) The social context of transition and rehabilitation, in G. Akerman, A. Needs and C. Bainbridge (eds) *Transforming Environments and Rehabilitation: A Guide for Practitioners in Forensic Settings and Criminal Justice*, Routledge, pp 31–62.

Palmer, D.K. (2004) On the organism-environment distinction in psychology, *Behavior and Philosophy*, 32: 317–347. https://www.jstor.org/stable/pdf/27759490.pdf

Polaschek, D.L. (2012) An appraisal of the risk-need-responsivity (RNR) model of offender rehabilitation and its application in correctional treatment, *Legal and Criminological Psychology*, 17: 1–17. http://dx.doi.org/10.1111/j.2044-8333.2011.02038.x

Pouw, W.T.J.L., van Gog, T. and Paas, F. (2014) An embedded and embodied cognition review of instructional manipulatives, *Educational Psychology Review*, 26(1): 51–72. https://doi.org/10.1007/s10648-014-9255-5

Radley, A. (1977) Living on the horizon, in D. Bannister (ed) *New Perspectives in Personal Construct Psychology*, Academic Press, pp 221–244.

Ramstead, M.J., Veissière, S.P. and Kirmayer, L.J. (2016) Cultural affordances: Scaffolding local worlds through shared intentionality and regimes of attention, *Frontiers in Psychology*, 7: Article 1090. https://doi.org/10.3389/fpsyg.2016.01090

Rietveld, E., Denys, D. and van Westen, M. (2018) Ecological-enactive cognition as engaging with a field of relevant affordances: The skilled intentionality framework (SIF), in A. Newen, L. de Bruin and S. Gallagher (eds) *Oxford Handbook of 4E Cognition*, Oxford University Press, pp 41–70.

Salvi, C., Iannello, P., Cancer, A., Cooper, S.E., McClay, M., Dunsmoor, J.E., et al (2023) Does social rigidity predict cognitive rigidity? Profiles of socio-cognitive polarization, *Psychological Research*, 87: 2533–2547. http://dx.doi.org/10.21203/rs.3.rs-1781915/v1

Schön, D.A. (1984) *The Reflective Practitioner: How Professionals Think in Action*, Basic Books.

Shingler, J., Sonnenberg, S.J. and Needs, A. (2020) 'Their life in your hands': The experiences of prison-based psychologists conducting risk assessments with indeterminate sentenced prisoners in the United Kingdom, *Psychology, Crime and Law*, 26(4): 311–326. https://doi.org/10.1080/1068316X.2019.1652750

Sookermany, A.M. (2012) What is a skillful soldier? An epistemological foundation for understanding military skill acquisition in (post) modernized armed forces, *Armed Forces and Society*, 38(4): 582–603. http://dx.doi.org/10.1177/0095327X11418320

Stevanovic, M. and Koski, S.E. (2018) Intersubjectivity and the domains of social interaction: Proposal of a cross-sectional approach, *Psychology of Language and Communication*, 22(1): 39–70. https://psycnet.apa.org/doi/10.2478/plc-2018-0003

Stewart, T.T. (2018) Dialogue, inquiry, changing roles, and the dialogical self, in F. Meijers and H. Hermans (eds) *The Dialogical Self in Education: Cultural Psychology of Education*, Springer, pp 35–47.

Thompson, E. and Stapleton, M. (2009) Making sense of sense-making: Reflections on enactive and extended mind theories, *Topoi*, 28: 23–30. http://dx.doi.org/10.1007/s11245-008-9043-2

Vold, K. (2018) Overcoming deadlock: Scientific and ethical reasons to embrace the extended mind thesis, *Philosophy and Society*, 29(4): 489–504. https://doi.org/10.1007/s11245-008-9043-2

2

Reflective practice in probation work: sustaining reflexivity in times of turbulence

Anne Burrell

The current context for probation work is challenging. The final annual report by the outgoing Inspector for Probation Justin Russell noted that 'the Probation Service is struggling' (HMIP, 2023c: 17), highlighting ongoing issues of sufficient staffing. His Majesty's Inspectorate of Probation (HMIP) also expressed concern that the location of probation work in HM Prison and Probation Service has resulted in a detrimental diminution of flexibility and freedom in probation practice. Russell proposed a further reorganisation, to place probation services within local control, which he sees as essential to effective probation work – while also recognising the challenges of further structural change (HMIP, 2023f).

Additionally, the nature of how probation work is currently conducted continues to be shaped by the remote working measures introduced during the lockdown as a result of the COVID-19 pandemic (the Exceptional Delivery Model arrangements were in response to the pandemic; see HMIP [2020]). Some aspects of the shifts in practice now appear embedded into practitioner routines, and it therefore seems important to seek to evaluate the implications for the recruitment and training of front-line probation workers, at both probation service officer and probation officer grades – and, for the purposes of this chapter, the specific challenge of becoming a reflective practitioner.

In this context, it is constructive to note that practitioners moving into probation work since 2021 will have little or no familiarity with practice during the Transforming Rehabilitation (TR) era of split services; and that recruits to probation training between 2020 and 2023 will have experienced the delivery of their training, and much of their practice with their supervisees, being conducted remotely. While this may mean being unencumbered by memories of how things used to be, or indeed perceptions of how things should be, it seems timely and constructive to consider specific elements of probation practice which may be lost in the processes of change. One aspect of the work which seems vulnerable in this context is that of reflexivity, and opportunities to practise reflectively in a busy and challenging working environment.

The nature of probation work is, inevitably, demanding on many levels, as well as potentially hugely rewarding. The chapter examines the evolution of reflective practice in probation, and the reasons why it is both valued, and difficult to achieve and to sustain – notably at a time of continuing change in organisational culture and approaches. The chapter asserts that reflective practice is a key tool available for practitioners to navigate their way through the challenges. It aims to develop a narrative which enables developing practitioners to continue to recognise the value of reflective practice, as well as to effectively carve out opportunities in which they can operate as reflective practitioners themselves.

What reflective practice is, and why it is important

The notion of the reflective practitioner originated in the work of Schön in his consideration of what he described as the 'artistry' of professional practice (1991: 18). Schön (1991) argued that reflective practice was a response to the increasing complexity of the work of professionals, notably in health, education and criminal justice services, where the 'technical rationality' which had previously underpinned practice, and which was key to effective problem-solving, had become compelled to adapt to a world of increasing complexity, and so uncertainty.

Famously, Schön (1983: 42) differentiated between the 'high ground' of professional practice, where technical and rational decision-making remained a possibility, and what he called the 'swampy lowland, where situations are confusing "messes" incapable of a technical solution'. It is worth noting that Schön regarded the swampy lowland as the location for the most significant and challenging decision-making for professional practitioners. It also seems likely that any probation practitioner will identify with Schön's terminology as a vivid exposition of their working lives.

Schön (1983) noted that the 'swampy lowland' is characterised by complexity and instability, often occurring on several levels (for example, personal, economic, legal and moral). For probation practitioners, key factors related to their supervisees in these scenarios will be the effects of previous and current trauma. Much of the focus of interventions in probation work revolves around the mechanisms frequently utilised by people on probation to manage such trauma, notably drugs and alcohol; issues in forming and sustaining healthy relationships; and attitudes and beliefs which can be challenging (for instance, using aggression to resolve problems; discriminatory attitudes; beliefs which support criminal behaviour).

For Schön (1983), reflective practice involves framing a unique problem situation in order to seek to change it, and so to resolve it. He suggested that each scenario demands new learning, as the practitioner navigates their way through each individual's personal context and issues. Additionally, the practitioner needs the skills and personal qualities to demonstrate resilience and persistence when there are unexpected problems and outcomes. This pattern, of improvement, lapse and relapse, will be readily identified by any practitioner as characteristic of probation practice.

It is possible to see that probation work demands resources of knowledge and skills, aligned with a capacity for adaptation, and an engaging and constructive approach. These qualities and factors are discussed in a series of papers produced by HMIP in 2023, investigating the links between probation supervision and positive outcomes (HMIP, 2023d; 2023e). The final report in the series notes that, for positive progress on probation, 'practitioner skills are key, and, when utilised in combination with all the available information, appropriate professional judgements can be exercised' (HMIP, 2023e: 24). So, an OASys Initial Sentence Plan could be seen as a way to ensure that the probation practitioner is enabled to obtain all the relevant information required, and on which they can then base an informed judgement as to what is needed in the sentence plan, in order to address the risks and needs of the person subject to supervision. The review process will formally recognise the modifications to the original plan, as further information is gleaned, and the supervisory relationship develops over time, with the practitioner navigating the challenges of the cycle of change alongside the supervisee.

Within this context, it is the knowledge base, and the practice skills, of the trained professional which enable the process of reframing to occur. It is helpful to note that Argyris and Schön describe professional practice as being influenced by 'theories of action' which inform and shape what people actually do, and which they describe as 'theories created by people to make events come about' (1978: 5). Further, they note that 'all human beings – not just professional practitioners, need to become competent in taking action *and* simultaneously reflecting on this action to learn from it' (Argyris and Schön, 1978: 10, emphasis mine).

In this context, it is vital to note that Schön (1991) asserts that reflective practice is essentially active – not a meditative nor a solitary process, but an engagement with people, in real time, with their specific issues; and that possible strategies for problem-solving in themselves can generate controversy, both in defining the problem, and in reframing it. Schön argues that, inevitably, the processes of reflection, and of reframing, will involve criticism and potential conflict, as the practitioner seeks to challenge the existing problem-solving strategies of the person on probation – which, self-evidently, have proved unhelpful and possibly dangerous to the supervisee and to others.

Schön (1991) suggests that this process is inherently experimental, both in the practitioner's evaluation of the problem situation, and their reframing of it, alongside how they can engage the person on probation with that reframing effectively. He considers that 'the therapist (practitioner) must become adept at converting his [sic] relationship with the patient (person on probation) into a world of inquiry in which thoughts and feelings can be seen as sources of discovery rather than as triggers to action' (Schön, 1991: 161). He further discusses the key qualities of self-awareness of the practitioner's own experiences, alongside empathy for the supervisee, as key to creating the 'worthwhile special relationship' (Schön, 1991: 161).

This model of practice is embedded into the training model for qualified probation officers, in which reflective accounts are a key assessment method for the practice component of the award. Goldhill (2010: 68), in a paper considering the content and approaches of probation officer training, suggests that 'without reflective practice, the essence of probation work is lost'. Further, that reflexivity enables a distinction 'between the *professional* and the *technical* practitioner' (Goldhill, 2010: 58, emphasis mine).

While Goldhill's study explores the challenges of enabling the development of reflexivity in the probation officer training programme, she reinforces that reflective practice is vital in the day-to-day work of probation practitioners. This reflects the context for probation work, which is the arena for multiple decisions of varying gravity – for example, whether to make a statutory contact a home visit, reporting to the office, or a telephone contact; whether to disclose sensitive information, and, if so, to whom, and for what purposes. Enforcement is likely to be the context for much of the most challenging reflection required of practitioners – whether to take enforcement action at all; and, if so, to what level – with recall to custody being the most draconian measure available, and thus a decision not to be taken lightly.

It is apparent, therefore, that reflective practice is a highly challenging and demanding process. In his study of practitioners' perspectives regarding reflective practice, undertaken in a National Probation Service (NPS) region in 2015/2016, shortly after the Transforming Rehabilitation reorganisation of probation work, Coley (2016) recounts that, for practitioners, reflective practice involves a process of thought and consideration following each meeting with a person on probation. This can include identifying the supervisee's responses, alongside thinking about what the practitioner could have done better, and evaluating the feelings, as well as the thoughts, generated by the encounter. Participants referred to reflective practice as an ongoing process with colleagues, in what Coley describes as a process which is 'ad hoc and unstructured, as probation officer colleagues turn to each other throughout their working day to discuss, share and vent their feelings' (2016: 43). Other respondents considered the collaborative nature of reflective practice, notably with supervisors, such as senior probation officers; and which is likely to be a more formal and structured process. Inevitably, such practices were identified as demanding time and space – time which was seen as elusive to carve out of a hectic and demanding work schedule, in which 'firefighting' was seen as the inevitable consequence of high caseloads and staff shortages.

In this context, it is also worth noting that, in the final chapter of *The Reflective Practitioner*, Schön (1991) ruminates on the perspective that the bureaucratisation of professional organisations – such as the Probation Service – would inevitably result in the prioritisation of technical expertise over reflection. He argues that bureaucracies seek predictability and stability in order to operate smoothly; and that 'surprise, which is essential to learning', is inimical to smooth organisational functioning (Schön, 1991: 327). Schön (1991: 329) suggests that the uncertainties of reflective practice sit uncomfortably within a bureaucratic organisation; and, moreover, that 'bureaucracies tend to resist a professional's attempt to move from technical expertise to reflective practice'. In the contemporary context of probation work, epitomised by the well-rehearsed issues of excessive workloads, and associated retention of staff, it is worth considering strategies which could, nonetheless, foster reflective practice in challenging circumstances.

Enabling reflective practice

Given these considerations regarding the meanings and purposes of reflective practice, set within the context of current probation work, what are the implications for practitioners, and particularly early career probation workers, for developing and safeguarding their own reflective practice? It would now be helpful to look at recent work which might contribute to our understanding, with a view to enabling effective reflective practice.

Key tensions, highly relevant to reflective practice, are the definition of the practitioner role and the purposes of the probation task. While any practitioner would recognise the distance travelled from the Victorian era of advising, assisting and befriending, to the current Probation Service aims of assessment, protection and change, it remains apparent that the motivations to undertake probation work have consistently been characterised as altruistic and enabling (see, for instance, Mair and Burke, 2011; Mawby and Worrall, 2013). Annison et al suggest that 'accounts of English probation's self-identity over its history feature origin stories that are essentially egalitarian in character', identifying core values of a commitment to 'participation, communitarianism, and collectivism' (2023: 15). While the supervisory relationship remains at the core of probation work, it is also the case that probation work requires relational skills at many levels, with a range of organisations, with differing aims and approaches, but with whom liaison and collaboration are essential for effective practice. In this context, Ainslie et al (2022: 526) suggest that the current probation landscape 'is characterised by emotionally complex and challenging interactions'.

In addition, the Probation Service at the time of writing (spring/summer 2024) is seeking to navigate its way into a unified public service, located within the UK Civil Service, and on a trajectory to merging with the Prison Service into One HM Prison and Probation Service. The introduction to this chapter outlines some of the tensions generated by these processes; similarly, Coley, drawing on the work of Gardner, identifies that 'organisational cultures provide a pivotal influence upon reflective practice within any agency, creating *either* constructive, challenging *or* disabling environments' (2016: 16, emphasis mine). In this context, he identifies a range of factors which can enhance, or diminish, opportunities for reflective practice, noting that organisational change, which is inherently unsettling, can be problematic in generating practice which is truly reflective.

Ainslie et al (2022) suggest that staff supervision is one key tool in supporting and enabling reflective practice, although they recognise that supervision itself has potentially conflicting purposes – that of maintaining accountability and oversight of risk management; and being attentive to practitioner well-being (for more on this, see Chapter 2). It is of note that, in Coley's (2016) study of reflective practice in the National Probation Service, undertaken in 2016 (that is, post-TR, and prior to reunification), some participants reflected fondly on the period of probation, shortly before to the roll out of TR, when the SEEDS (Skills for Effective Engagement, Development and Supervision) model was rolled out. Among other features, this model incorporated structured reflective supervision between senior probation officers and practitioners, alongside collaborative team approaches to the day-to-day work. Chapter 5 further explores the complexities of delivering staff supervision within the current probation landscape.

Equally, and while it is certainly the case that organisations can aid the capacity for reflective practice in its staff, Coley (2016: 47–48) concluded that 'probation officer understandings of what it means to be a reflective practitioner encompass interpersonal skills application and an attitude of self-awareness'. He further identified that practitioners themselves were creating agency, in order to safeguard their opportunities to reflect, notwithstanding the pressures of workloads, and the specific demands of the then NPS caseloads. Notably, a specific opportunity for shared learning was identified around the findings of Serious Further Offence reviews – a pertinent and relevant suggestion, at a time when the reputation of the Probation Service has been severely tarnished by a succession of Serious Further Offence inquiries (HMIP, 2023a). In a recent study of the impact of inspection on probation practitioners, Phillips concluded that 'staff experience case interviews for reflection and validation' (2023: 124). It is possible to feel a shred of anguish for probation practitioners, who appear grateful for the opportunity to reflect on their casework within the highly robust context of an inspection – suggesting that practitioners otherwise have few opportunities to do so; and that there is a thirst to utilise their skills of reflection even in this most testing of settings.

In the context of navigating organisational change and its impact, a more recent study, conducted in 2021 in a West Midlands Probation Delivery Unit, examined practitioner responses to the reunification of probation services. Kyle Hart, a probation practitioner himself, explored practitioner self-evaluation of their confidence, competence and commitment to the Probation Service following reunification. The findings of the study (Hart, 2023) contrasted the differing levels of confidence, and of job satisfaction, within discrete groups of practitioners, categorised in terms of longevity of career, and their locations for practice prior to the reintegration of probation services in 2021. Hart (2023) identified that significant deficits for practitioners revolved around training, and continuous professional development, mostly arising from limited opportunities to shadow experienced practitioners, and the paucity of face-to-face training.

The issue of methods of delivery of training has arisen across a number of studies. Relatedly, Goldhill (2010) discusses the significance of reflexivity in informing ethical decision-making, alongside questioning of the practitioner's own professional identity. Her study of attitudes to reflective practice among trainee probation officers identified that distance learning presented an additional barrier and inhibitor to the effective outcome of becoming a reflective practitioner. This perspective is reinforced in the Annual Report of the Probation Inspectorate for 2022–23, which identified that the recruitment of waves of new trainee probation officers and probation service officers had created

> an influx of inexperienced new staff … to be trained and mentored, [which] has created its own problems. Working remotely and receiving all their training online during the pandemic, new staff found it difficult to access the practical support and advice that comes with sharing an office with more experienced colleagues. (HMIP, 2023c: 7)

While the Probation Service has recently been returning to more hybrid working methods, it nonetheless remains the case that most staff will be working remotely for varying periods of their working week, with the consequent impact for opportunities for collaboration and support from colleagues, and so of empowerment. In this context, and writing in 2020, during the period of lockdowns as a result of the COVID-19 pandemic, and at the height of largely remote working, Ainslie (2020) identified the value of reflective practice as 'self-care', as a strategy to navigate the tensions of undertaking the challenges of probation work largely in isolation, and of taking place within the personal space of the practitioner. Ainslie (2020) asserts that reflective practice is highly dependent on feedback from others; and that it is therefore imperative to provide a theoretical framework, and robust opportunities for self-reflection, throughout the practitioner's career.

And so, Schön's (1983) swampy lowlands cannot solely apply to the circumstances of people who are subject to probation supervision but must encompass the experiences of practitioners too. What is apparent is that Coley's (2016) assertion, that a significant feature of reflective practice is the element of criticality – that is, the capacity to be both self-aware *and* self-critical – remains imperative for effective probation work, and particularly at a time of further organisational change.

This inquiring approach has parallels with notions of professional curiosity, discussed at length in a succession of Inspectorate reports as a key skill for probation work. The HMIP report produced in January 2023, subsequent to the Serious Further Offence review into the case of Damien Bendall, refers to 'professional curiosity' no fewer than five times. Professional curiosity, in essence, describes a mindset of healthy scepticism, in which the perspective of the person or situation under scrutiny is not accepted at face value, but is explored for gaps in the narrative, and for contradictions in the explanations (HMIP, 2023a). So, the skills of reflexivity, and of professional curiosity, mutually reinforce and enhance effective professional practice.

And a final point – Ainslie (2020) asserts that, additionally, reflective practice is vital in enabling anti-discriminatory approaches in probation work – an acutely relevant observation, at a time when the Probation Service has been identified as retreating from such effective practice – notably by the Probation Inspectorate, which, in a report produced in 2021, made reference to a lack of training in this area, and consequent limitations in practice (HMIP, 2021). Worryingly, in a follow-up report written in 2023, the Inspectorate found little evidence of progress and identified dissatisfaction among both staff, and people subject to probation supervision. The report concluded with several recommendations to address these issues, including 'learning programmes that enable probation staff to … *reflect* on their anti-discriminatory practice' (HMIP, 2023b: 12, emphasis mine).

To summarise – a review of relevant literature appears to concur with Schön's perspective, that reflective practice is not just desirable, but essential, for professional practitioners. The current turbulent environment of probation work can present challenges to reflexivity; and yet, relatedly, emphasises the intrinsic value of a reflective approach for practitioner confidence, development and well-being. Moreover, Schön (1983) suggests that the nature of the professional relationship, the therapeutic alliance, is predicated on mutual respect, and on transparency and accountability on the part of the practitioner – approaches and characteristics which are highly reliant on a reflexive and self-aware approach.

Author reflections

The chapter has focused on the principles of reflective practice; evaluated its place and purpose in contemporary probation work; and considered some of the challenges to sustaining reflective practice in turbulent times, while emphasising the imperative to seek to do so. The author's personal reflections also incorporate a further critical aspect of reflection, in enabling and enhancing anti-discriminatory practice.

Schön (1991) argues that reflection is a means to frame and to analyse our experience, with a view to informing action, and this perspective appears highly relevant to a personal scenario in which reflection became a drive to explore the processes and impact of TR, and the current landscape of the reintegrated Probation Service. For the author, this resulted in the decision to undertake a PhD research project – itself the outcome of a lengthy period of reflection, much of it painful to encounter. For a time, post-TR, I was an employee of both a Community Rehabilitation Company and the NPS, in differing job roles – a disconcerting and disturbing time. The decision to undertake the project reflects my sense of loss of professional identity at that time, linked to what I perceived to be the dilution and diminution of professionalism in probation work. In the work for the project undertaken so far, it is notable that participants have welcomed the opportunity to reflect on their role, to consider their commitment and loyalty to their practice, and to remind themselves of their 'why?' for doing probation work. These responses suggest that the drive to be a reflective practitioner remains strong, with probation workers seeking out, and locating, relevant opportunities for reflection – an encouraging feature of current probation practice, which appears both commendable in thought, and nurturing in action.

Conclusion

In the context thus outlined, it is worth considering a recent paper which presents early findings from a large-scale, longitudinal study being undertaken by researchers at Liverpool John Moores University and elsewhere (Millings et al, 2023). The paper provides an account which suggests that, while respondents at all levels in the newly reunited Probation Service continue to express feelings of trauma and loss as a consequence of the TR restructure and its aftermath, it is also of note that many respondents nonetheless feel optimistic regarding the longer-term future of probation work; and, perhaps more pertinently, to retain a strong sense of loyalty to their role.

These findings resonate with the early themes which have been possible to identify in my own current research project, in which participants have expressed a similar commitment, alongside holding a strong sense of professional identity as probation practitioners, which they perceive to be reflective of their personal and professional values. In both studies, such attitudes and approaches have been expressed by practitioners of both probation officer and probation service officer grade, with varying levels of experience of probation work. Again, in this context, it is important to be continually reminded that the service is increasingly staffed by practitioners recruited to the reunited Probation Service, who hold no memory of the preceding decade of organisational change; and that practitioner optimism appears to be tempered with a resolution to take action to improve the delivery of probation work, to the benefit of practitioners, and to those subject to probation supervision – for whom there continues to be a widely expressed sense of duty.

While the landscape and narrative of probation work remains turbulent, and in what appears to be a protracted state of flux, it is also worth reminding ourselves of the inherent commitment of probation practitioners, and their motivation to continue to effect positive change in the lives of the people whom they supervise. Participants in the author's research project have reiterated that the most satisfying aspect of the role for them is to work alongside people, over a period of time, to effect personal change, and so to enable their supervisees' reintegration into their social world – at its simplest, to advise, assist and befriend. These values have been at the core of probation work since its inception and seem to encapsulate a sense of true vocation. Navigating these personal motivations, alongside the contemporary challenges of public protection and risk management, appears to reinforce the essential nature of reflexivity – to do the job, and to do it well. The duality of the probation role is a key characteristic of the work, in recognising the status of many of the people with whom we work as both perpetrators and victims of crime; and in navigating the challenges of the therapeutic elements of the supervisory relationship, alongside the imperative to be alert to issues of risk. Such complexities of practice and of decision-making demand critical reflection, in order to enable positive outcomes.

Reflective prompts

- How can you build reflexivity into your day-to-day practice?
- How will reflexive practice elevate the work you currently do?
- With whom, and where, can reflective practice occur?
- What are your barriers to daily reflexive practice, and how can you overcome these?
- What resources are available to support you in developing reflective practice?

References

Ainslie, S. (2020) A time to reflect?, *Probation Quarterly*, 17: 9–12.

Ainslie, S., Fowler, A., Phillips, J. and Westaby, C. (2022) 'A nice idea but ...': Implementing a reflective supervision model in the National Probation Service in England and Wales, *Reflective Practice*, 23(5): 525–538. https://doi.org/10.1080/14623943.2022.2066075

Annison, H., Burke, L., Carr, N., Millings, M., Robinson, G. and Surridge, E. (2023) Making good? A study of how senior penal policy makers narrate policy reversal, *The British Journal of Criminology*, 64(3): 726–743. https://doi.org/10.1093/bjc/azad054

Argyris, C. and Schön, D. (1978) *Organizational Learning: A Theory of Action Perspective*, Addison-Wesley.

Coley, D. (2016) Reflective practice: The cornerstone of all we do, Probation Institute. Available from: https://static1.square space.com/static/5ec3ce97a1716758c54691b7/t/5ed7a65e8 756c4572d39731d/1592837014154/Reflective+Practice

Goldhill, R. (2010) Reflective practice and distance learning: Problems and potentials for probation training, *Reflective Practice*, 11(1): 57–70. https://doi.org/10.1080/14623940903500085

Hart, K. (2023) Exploring probation practitioners' transition to the new unified service, Probation Institute. Available from: https://static1.squarespace.com/static/5ec3ce97a1716758c54691b7/t/65085d6f022e0e08e79d82f4/1695047027236/Exploring+probation+practitioners%E2%80%99+transition+to+the+new+unified+service.pdf

HMIP (His Majesty's Inspectorate of Probation) (2020) A thematic review of the Exceptional Delivery Model arrangements in response to the COVID-19 pandemic, HMIP. Available from: https://www.justiceinspectorates.gov.uk/hmiprobation/wp-content/uploads/sites/5/2020/11/A-thematic-review-of-the-EDM-arrangements-in-probation-services-in-response-to-the-COVID-19-pandemic.pdf

HMIP (2021) Race equality in probation: the experiences of black, Asian and minority ethnic probation service users and staff, HMIP. Available from: https://www.justiceinspectorates.gov.uk/hmiprobation/inspections/race-equality-in-probation/

HMIP (2023a) Independent Serious Further Offence review of Damien Bendall, HMIP. Available from: https://wwwjusticein spectorates.gov.uk/hmiprobation/wp-content/uploads/sites/5/2023/01/Independent-serious-further-offence-review-of-Damien-Bendall-1.pdf

HMIP (2023b) Race equality in probation follow up: A work in progress, HMIP. Available from: chrome-extension://efaidnbmn nnibpcajpcglclefindmkaj/https://www.justiceinspectorates.gov.uk/hmiprobation/wp-content/uploads/sites/5/2023/09/Race-equality-in-probation-follow-up-thematic-inspection-v1.0.pdf

HMIP (2023c) HMIP annual report, 2022–2023, HMIP. Available from: https://www.justiceinspectorates.gov.uk/hmiprobation/wp-content/uploads/sites/5/2023/09/2022-2023-HMIP-Probation-Annual-Report-v1.0.pdf

HMIP (2023d) Examining the links between probation supervision and positive outcomes – completion and proven reoffending, *HMIP Probation Research and Analysis Bulletin*, 2023/03, HMIP. Available from: https://www.justiceinspectorates.gov.uk/hmiprobation/wp-content/uploads/sites/5/2023/08/Examining-the-links-between-probation-supervision-and-positive-outcomes-completion-and-proven-reoffending.pdf

HMIP (2023e) The role of engagement for positive outcomes in probation, *HMIP Research and Analysis Bulletin*, 2023/05, HMIP. Available from: https://www.justiceinspectorates.gov.uk/hmiprobation/wp-content/uploads/sites/5/2023/08/The-role-of-engagement-for-positive-outcomes.pdf

HMIP (2023f) Chief Inspector calls for an independent review of the Probation Service, publishing his final annual report, HMIP. Available from: https://www.justiceinspectorates.gov.uk/hmiprobation/media/press-releases/2023/09/annual-report-2022-2023/

Mair, G. and Burke, L. (2011) *Redemption, Rehabilitation and Risk Management: A History of Probation*, Routledge.

Mawby, R. and Worrall, A. (2013) *Doing Probation Work: Identity in a Criminal Justice Organisation*, Routledge.

Millings, M., Burke, L., Annison, H., Carr, N., Robinson, G. and Surridge, E. (2023) A necessary but painful journey: experiences of unification in a probation service region, *Probation Journal*, 70(4): 331–349. https://doi.org/10.1177/02645505231182822

Phillips, J. (2023) An analysis of inspection in probation and its impact on practitioners, practice and providers, *Probation Journal*, 70(2): 124–142. https://doi.org/10.1177/02645505211041577

Schön, D. (1983) *The Reflective Practitioner: How Professionals Think in Action*, Basic Books.

Schön, D. (1991) *The Reflective Practitioner: How Professionals Think in Action*, Ashgate.

3

Probation staff reflective practice: can it impact on outcomes for clients with personality difficulties?

Dominic Pearson and Daniele Molino

The government's Offender Personality Difficulties (OPD) pathway strategy (NOMS/NHS, 2015) began in 2012 with key aims to reduce reoffending and risk of harm to others, develop a competent workforce, and improve psychological well-being and access to services. To achieve these high-level outcomes, a number of more concrete proximal outcomes were specified, notably to: reduce the number and severity of incidents of misconduct; reduce the number and severity of incidents of self-destructive behaviour; improve clients' access to and progression through services; and improve the quality of the relational environment. A psychologically informed management approach was adopted because personality difficulties (PDs) are strongly associated with treatment noncompletion (for example, Shaw and Edelmann, 2019). To maintain this psychologically informed approach, 'reflective practice spaces' – the focus of the present chapter – have been provided for practitioners.

What is currently uncertain is the extent to which the positive impact of such reflective practice (RP) spaces in criminal justice settings is likely to extend, beyond practitioner well-being and confidence, to concrete client outcomes. This is of particular relevance following the independent review of the case of Joseph McCann (HM Inspectorate of Probation, 2020) where failures in case management were attributed to a confirmatory bias among staff and a lack of any real analysis of his behaviour. Therefore, ten years since the implementation of RP in the OPD pathway, the present chapter examines the literature regarding the impact of staff RP practices on outcomes for probation clients; to determine future directions for research and on-the-ground support for this aspect of the initiative.

To support reflection on the contribution of RP spaces, we refer to the fidelity framework (Borrelli et al, 2005); a methodological strategy to enhance the reliability and validity of interventions. According to Borrelli et al (2005), the overall goal of the framework is to enhance confidence that changes in the outcome variable (for example, further offending) are due to the explanatory variable (the RP spaces). Milne (2014) provides six key fidelity steps, or questions, for inclusion in any systematic evaluation: (1) what is the right way to supervise; (2) has training in the right supervision been done; (3) has supervision been done right; (4) did supervision result in the right initial impacts with the supervisee; (5) did supervision result in the right therapy with clients; (6) did supervision result in the right clinical outcomes. The latter queries the effect of supervision on the client's daily life, otherwise known as the 'acid' test of good supervision (Ellis and Ladany, 1997: 485). Some time ago, Day (2012) highlighted a gap in research in forensic settings regarding whether clinical supervision provides better outcomes for clients. The aforementioned fidelity steps guide Part I, and in Part II we will discuss learning from research relating to the clinical supervision and training of staff, before integrating the two parts in our summary and recommendations.

Part I: Staff reflective practice

The what and why of staff reflective practice (fidelity step 1)

In RP spaces on the OPD pathway, staff meet voluntarily to 'discuss team or individual issues; consider their emotional reactions, thoughts and ways in which they could adapt; and develop their clinical practice' (Webster et al, 2020: 286). These spaces entail group discussions in which both trainee and qualified probation officers reflect, under the facilitation of a psychological therapist and a PD-specialist probation practitioner, on complex pathway-eligible cases. Although RP sessions were facilitated by different disciplinary staff, reflection followed a consistent model; namely Gibbs' (1988) reflective cycle.

The OPD pathway strategy emphasised a whole systems approach involving a range of providers working in partnership to deliver a pathway of services in a range of settings from high security to the community. RP as a conceptual model is regarded as crucial for staff working with PD offenders (Scaillet and Taylor, 2018). Group RP provides an opportunity, alongside clinical supervision, to focus on potentially destructive team dynamics and systemic processes which may arise. Reflection in groups can assist in recognising how these patterns may be manifesting between team members. Scaillet and Taylor (2018) highlight the benefit of group RP in analysing why a situation went wrong including recognising the impact of working with the client group, individuals with PD who have offended. Therefore, the rationale for RP on the OPD pathway initiative is predominantly to assist practitioners in managing the practitioner–client working alliance and resolving impasses, to thereby enhance clinical outcomes for clients. Group RP sessions can be attended by any staff member; providing a space to discuss issues, whether team or individual, and reflect on emotional reactions.

As a national organisation, the Probation Service recently introduced a new model for supervising staff (including those on the OPD pathway), named Reflective Practice Supervision Standards (RPSS). Within RPSS, senior probation officers were trained in a more structured, reflective and developmental approach relative to previous approaches to probation staff supervision. RPSS is part of an expansion of the Skills for Effective Engagement Development and Supervision (SEEDS; Rex and Hosking, 2014) programme which had a specific focus on developing practitioners' client engagement skills; see Chapters 2 and 5 for further exploration of this. RPSS's squarer focus on staff supervision and support aimed to enhance practitioner autonomy and resilience.

Implementation (fidelity steps 2–3)

Staff 'buy-in' to a programme's theoretical basis has been implicated in previous evaluations of the implementation of offender supervision programmes, as discussed in Part II. In relation to the OPD pathway and PD clients, attachment theory was specified as the core model (Campbell and Craissati, 2018). Ansbro (2019) interviewed six qualified probation practitioners ($N=6$) monthly for six months regarding the utility of attachment theory concepts, in relation to three cases each. She found that while some concepts from attachment theory were useful, that is, the practitioner as a secure base and the relevance of early attachment experience for understanding current functioning, other concepts were less useful. Specifically, the use of mentalisation received mixed reviews with practitioners finding this a nebulous concept or simply common sense. Some disagreed that clients lacked reflective function, preferring available alternative explanations (for example, learning difficulty). The identification of an 'attachment style' per client was found to be a poor fit to actual experience and have no applied value whatsoever. Ansbro's (2019) findings offer a basis to believe that the OPD pathway's core model may not have been implemented with fidelity.

Experience of training in the probation model for supervising staff, RPSS, was explored in an interview study of 33 probation practitioners and 28 supervisors (Ainslie et al, 2022). Findings indicated that the RP model under RPSS was a 'nice idea but…' and failed to reach its full potential. One obstacle was that supervision was both contested and congested: delivery of reflective supervision was juxtaposed with the pressure to oversee practice in the context of public protection and the risk of serious further offences. A key impediment to adoption was the operational reality of constrained time. Practitioners struggled to identify the impact of the RPSS – partly owing to the difficulty of attributing change to the training itself due to changes in manager or existing managers already using a particular approach. According to the practitioners, the quality of supervision was contingent on the supervisor–supervisee dynamic and the approach of the supervisor, RP training notwithstanding. Undoubtedly this variation in capacity was affected by the noted absence of senior leader support either in modelling the reflective approach, or regarding implementation of RPSS following the training. These qualitative findings supported and expanded on results from a large scale ($N=1,509$) quantitative survey by the same researchers (Westaby et al, 2021). This research, which included staff on the OPD pathway, suggests problems in the implementation of staff RP and we return to this later when reflecting on our experience in this setting.

Impact/outcomes (fidelity steps 4–6)

A perceived beneficial impact for practitioners was identified in research soon after the first implementation of the OPD pathway; although this focused on consultation training and formulation (for example, Shaw et al, 2017; Radcliffe et al, 2020). Shaw et al (2017) investigated the impact on the professional relationship between practitioners and their clients of probation practitioners completing collaborative case formulations. They concluded that completing case formulations collaboratively with clients may have a small beneficial impact on the practitioner–client relationship quality. Contrary to expectations, however, there was no association between completing formulations and practitioners' perceptions of client engagement, compliance or motivation to desist. Then, in a small study of selected probation practitioners ($N=5$) who had benefited from professional psychology consultation, Radcliffe et al (2020) identified the process through which they felt relationship quality improved. Reflection was said to lead to developing a connection to their client's experience, new self-awareness and a fresh sense of clarity about the whole picture of the person they were working with. Impact of this reflection included perception of a positive change in client presentation, for example, being less suspicious and more emotionally open, but did not include changes to 'concrete' client outcomes.

Staff's experience of the impact specifically of RP on the OPD pathway has only been considered in one study (Webster et al, 2020). Webster and colleagues' most prevalent theme, based on interviews and focus groups with 32 members of probation and health service staff, was that RP was useful. Specifically, it was deemed beneficial to have a dedicated space to offload, talk about how others feel and receive support. Again, the impact of this was seen as being mainly on practitioner well-being, rather than noticeably on direct delivery with clients. Specifically, having a space away from constant demands assisted some staff with managing workload pressures. However, as this was soon after the first implementation of the OPD pathway, it was unknown if the sessions did indeed reduce burnout. Given the limited adoption of RP, summarised earlier, one may have doubts. Furthermore, there was an absence of testimony by those who *did not* find the service useful. There is a need for research to explore specifically whether, and how, RP sessions impact on direct experience with clients.

Part II: Learning from literature on clinical supervision of staff

Clinical supervision is generally held as beneficial to professionals (Mor Barak et al, 2009; Galletti et al, 2021). Mor Barak et al's (2009) meta-analysis of 25 studies with social and mental health workers found moderately positive associations for desired outcomes including well-being, job satisfaction and one's sense of competence and achievement. Clinical supervision was also found to protect against negative outcomes for staff such as depression, burnout and wishing to quit the job. The strongest association with desired outcomes was for task assistance, that is, supporting supervisees in their learning and development. Consistent with social exchange theory (Cook, 1977), practitioners who experience good supervision through task assistance, in a context of effective relationships with supervisors, reciprocate with positive feelings and work-related behaviours. Changes to confidence could however be seen as changes to the practitioner, that have no bearing on the client. There is limited research focusing on the clinical, or client-level, outcomes of supervision.

A systematic review of 11 controlled studies with human service professionals was provided by Milne et al (2011). Only two studies assessed impact on the supervisee's clients. Rating the impact of supervision from -3 to +3, the authors found an impact on supervisors of 2.0 and on supervisors' clients of 2.5 – cautioning that the latter was only from two studies. One of these was by Bambling et al (2006), investigating the impact on therapists treating people with depression. The main interest was in the impact of supervision on two features: (1) the working alliance; and (2) client outcomes, that is, drop-out, symptom reduction and client evaluation of treatment. Alongside a group receiving no supervision, the authors provided two different forms of 'alliance focused supervision': alliance skill (therapist skill); and alliance process (therapist awareness). The outcomes for the no supervision group were similar to previous studies of the treatment approach, however those in both forms of supervision had better alliance and client outcomes, that is, lower drop-out, lower end of treatment symptom rates, and a more positive view of treatment. In all groups the adherence to the specific treatment model was no different. The authors identify some important limitations to their review, however they conclude that 'supervision can play a role in developing the working alliance and enhancing treatment outcome' (Bambling et al, 2006: 327).

A specific focus on the impact of clinical supervision regarding client outcome, specifically patient safety, was provided in a systematic review by Snowdon and colleagues (2016). Although allied health, nursing and medical disciplines were eligible, the overwhelming majority of the 32 studies retrieved were medical ($N=29/32$). Of the 32, $n=28$ investigated the impact on patient safety of direct supervision, that is, where a more experienced supervisor was present to oversee a procedure. The remaining four studies examined the effect of reflective supervision. While direct supervision was effective in reducing patient mortality, reflective supervision had no effect in the one study focusing on this. Regarding patient complications, the impact of reflective supervision was negative, that is, associated with a higher risk of occurrence, but again this result was from a single study. While the authors concluded that direct supervision is associated with a reduced risk of negative outcomes in patient safety among medical professionals, due to limited research they were unable to comment on the effectiveness of reflective supervision nor on the effectiveness of clinical supervision with non-medical health professionals in general.

The few studies found by Milne et al (2011) and by Snowdon et al (2016), despite the thorough systematic review methodology, indicate an under-emphasis in the literature on the impact of supervision on client outcomes. Findings are however supportive of clinical supervision impacting on client outcomes where the support is experienced as direct task assistance, echoing a conclusion from studies of occupational outcomes (Mor Barak et al, 2009).

Training in effective probation supervision

A considerable amount of knowledge has developed about how to reduce further offending via structured rehabilitation programmes. Interventions are effective when delivered at an intensity proportionate to the client's assessed risk of reoffending, focusing on criminogenic needs and using cognitive-behavioural techniques (see Lipsey and Cullen, 2007). These are the empirically supported risk-needs-responsivity principles (RNR; Bonta and Andrews, 2007). Although this research has focused on isolated intervention programmes, it explores the core skills for routine probation practice and, of relevance to clinical supervision, has led to the implementation of training aimed at developing effective practices.

A set of core practices for probation practitioners was identified after a meta-analysis by Dowden and Andrews (2004). They found the following core practices, when delivered within RNR-based intervention, to be positively related to reduced reoffending: relationship-building factors; structuring skills of problem-solving; prosocial modelling and reinforcement; effective use of authority; cognitive restructuring; and advocacy/brokerage. These practices were infrequently found, however (≤16 per cent of studies), and it was unclear whether the component studies in the meta-analysis extended beyond specialist intervention programmes to routine probation supervision.

The core practices of relationship-building, structuring and problem-solving, prosocial modelling and brokering access to community resources underpinned the Citizenship supervision programme which I (DP) was closely involved in developing. Citizenship is a structured supervision programme based on the RNR principles, that aims to engage the client in the process of change; co-producing a formulation or 'theory of change', before connecting the client with community resources that match the proposed pathway to desistance (Bruce and Hollin, 2009). To implement Citizenship across front-line staff, a practitioner-led steering group was assembled comprising different grades of probation and psychology practitioners, and chaired at Assistant Chief Officer level. These personnel were central in staging a series of rolling Citizenship training events covering the procedures and practices. Notably, Citizenship was adopted as core business and steps were taken to ensure the programme fitted with existing policies – such as national standards for the management of offenders, and procedures – such as ensuring the local case records system integrated Citizenship activity codes and worksheets. Thus, systems for monitoring and evaluation were built-in from the outset so that these were not an additional burden on practitioners whose priority was delivery. Over the following years, routine monitoring of electronic records was supplemented by regular targeted case file inspections, led by the steering group with supportive management follow-up action to enhance delivery. Inspection findings catalysed team-level reflection on how to embed the core practices. This 'whole organisation' continuous development approach was successful with widescale (78 per cent) implementation of Citizenship across probation practitioners.

Evaluation of Citizenship proceeded, following a pilot study, by comparing all clients supervised in the two years after implementation ($n=3,819$) with all clients supervised in the one year prior to implementation ($n=2,110$). For the clients subject to Citizenship, time to reconviction over two years was significantly increased (Pearson et al, 2011). Citizenship reduced the hazard of reconviction by 31 per cent, with nearly one-third fewer clients under Citizenship being reconvicted compared to under usual practice. Support for the effectiveness of Citizenship was also obtained with a defined group of medium-high risk clients in a neighbouring probation area using a randomised trial design (Pearson et al, 2016). Here Citizenship supervision produced a non-significant 20 per cent reduction in the hazard of reconviction, although a statistically significant reduction was seen among the highest risk cases. Although the weaker overall result may be an artefact of the research design, instead it was thought to relate to the limited (38 per cent) acceptance and implementation of the programme among the staff at all levels in this neighbouring 'adopting' organisation.

The Citizenship experience resonates with accounts of the RNR-based staff training programme, which also developed the core staff practices, named Strategic Training in Community Supervision (STICS: Bourgon et al, 2010). STICS involved a three-day training workshop, followed by monthly peer support meetings, and monthly individual clinical supervision with one of the trainers focusing on developing and applying skills based on submitted samples of audiotaped sessions. Approximately one year after the initial workshop, the trainers facilitated a one-day group refresher course involving interactive exercises and exploring difficulties with applying STICS to ongoing cases. Although all skill/technique quality comparisons between STICS supervised clients and the control group favoured STICS, Bourgon et al (2010) reported that the use of some skills deteriorated over time – for example, relationship skills and cognitive-behavioural techniques. Individualised feedback was beneficial in mitigating skills fade by encouraging the officer to practise the specific skill. Clearly, as with Citizenship, there was a need to provide direct clinical support to practitioners in continually applying the training following the initial training. This conclusion finds support from a recent meta-analysis of the effect of training criminal justice staff on the core staff practices (Labrecque et al, 2023). Although clients of trained practitioners, across the 25 studies, were less likely to be arrested or convicted than clients of untrained practitioners, these reductions in reoffending doubled when fidelity to the core practices was rated as high compared to low.

Given that it may be the more reflective and competent staff that actually access ongoing clinical supervision, one might question whether it is staff selection, initial training or their clinical supervision which has more influence on probationer outcomes, as investigated by Makarios et al (2016). Staff characteristics and staff training were associated with substantively important reductions in reoffending, while the domain of staff supervision showed weaker effects. Makarios and colleagues recognised that the latter variable did not index the quality of supervision, but contend that the aptitude of the staff and how well they are trained on the model used by the programme may be of most importance.

Reflection and implications

This review found support for a positive impact of clinical supervision on staff well-being and sense of competence, but limited evidence for the impact of reflective individual or group supervision on client-level outcomes. As discussed in Radcliffe et al (2020), RP fosters the connection to the client's experience (or highlights the need for it), emphasises new self-awareness, and provides a new perspective on case and risk management issues; however, it has limited impact on client outcomes. The same limited impact has been found for collaborative case formulations (Shaw et al, 2017). Following Mor Barak et al's (2009) meta-analytic evidence, to exert an impact on probationer outcomes RP sessions should be task-oriented, for example, focus on practitioner skills in developing working alliance, rather than generic reflective spaces. In my (DM's) experience practicing on the OPD pathway in London since 2020, group 'consultations' have been deliberately task-focused, oftentimes at the expense of other significant professional issues, such as personal well-being and resilience. Probation practitioners and trainees attend these spaces to obtain a new understanding of the case and offload (Webster et al, 2020). Most importantly however, they seek guidance, direction and, crucially, to understand if something in their practice has been missed or should be addressed. Although RP sessions are task-oriented, reflection is reliant on recollection and self-insight: sessions do not involve direct monitoring/supervision (for example, basing reflection on shadowing or monitoring of sessions with clients; although this can often be achieved if the practitioner is open to joint working the case). As such, in what follows we reflect on what, currently, may be preventing the level of support required for RP spaces to have a significant influence on client outcomes. It is important to highlight that what follows draws heavily upon, and is subjective to, my (DM's) pathway experience. As such, this may not reflect the reality of working in OPD services outside of the capital.

Reflection on the impact of workloads on engagement with reflective practice spaces

While clinical supervision is certainly important in identifying problems and helping to guide professional development, it may need to be more closely aligned with theory and research on learning and performance in the workplace, and to consistently include observational learning, try-outs and constructive feedback (Milne et al, 2011). Central to this is adherence to the model of reflection (Gibbs, 1988). Reflecting on my own practice and that of my colleagues, not one of these conditions is currently being satisfied. Probation practitioners' attendance at RP sessions is directly influenced by heavy caseloads, and as such they may not regularly attend the one-hour monthly supervision meeting that is offered to them (Scaillet and Taylor, 2018). While attendance is monitored and 'strongly encouraged', this does not come with a reduction in practitioners' existing responsibilities, translating into being 'pushed from above and pushed from below' (see Westaby et al, 2023: 49).

This workload conflict is consistent with the findings of Ainslie et al (2022) showing that RP models did not reach their full potential. A range of pressures – societal, emotional and professional – to obtain management oversight in the context of public protection and the risk of serious further offences, may have impacted on probation practitioners' confidence in RP and, consequently, any opportunity for learning to significantly impact on client outcomes. Through supporting probation practitioners, I have found similar shared concerns. These concerns reflect the pressure of the work practitioners are allocated, compounded by a lack of dedicated clinical support, impacting on their professional optimism. The notion that the benefit of professional support is magnified by practitioner resilience, with such support acting to reduce the effect of cynicism on self-evaluated performance, does have empirical backing (Wang et al, 2023).

Reflection on the impact of wider organisational support on the delivery of reflective practice spaces

In Part I we discussed research indicating that the OPD pathway's core model may not have been implemented with fidelity (for example, Ansbro, 2019). Indeed, if we follow Milne's (2014) steps from the fidelity framework (Borrelli et al, 2005) with reference to current delivery in London, we can identify this to be the case. In particular, professionals from a variety of disciplinary backgrounds have been required to hold supervision spaces without adequate training or guidance in a model to follow (step two). Supervision being done right (step three) also appears to be lost in service provision, when probation practitioners are unclear over the goals they are trying to achieve, and experience pressures that do not allow them adequately to use that minimal one-hour monthly space they are granted. The crystallisation and implementation of learning from the supervision (steps four and five) therefore become hard to deliver. These are fundamental foundations that need to be addressed prior to even beginning to consider the most important question of whether supervision has resulted in the right clinical outcomes (step six). It is indeed not surprising that research has been lacking in this regard as, we would argue, the delivery of RP has been too fragmented to allow for this process to be followed and its efficacy to be evaluated.

Conclusion

As such, we turn focus to how we can move forward, what can we learn from this, and most importantly how can we ensure that clinical supervision provided to probation practitioners is not only effective in supporting their emotional and professional well-being, but also equips them to influence client outcomes directly. The present review, particularly the successful 'whole organisation' approach of Citizenship supervision, has highlighted some of the ways forward that may be considered. These include the need to:

- adopt, and most importantly maintain, a core, consistent model of supervision across different sites, providing facilitator training in following specific reflection models and principles;
- link reflection processes to the implementation and development of the evidence-based core staff practices (for example, cognitive restructuring), in order to increase the likelihood of impacting on client outcomes;
- ensure the model is frontline practitioner-led, and actively supported at senior management level, not just at initial workshop training but also through regular and sustained monitoring of implementation;
- build-in monitoring and evaluation from the outset, in order for practitioners to focus on their delivery, without being impacted by additional pressures and responsibilities.

The application of a standardised and monitored model of reflection in the whole organisation could support probation practitioners' professional movement, identifying similar support processes no matter where they move within probation.

We also wish to highlight that it is important for clinical supervision of probation practitioners to be more than a simple 'tick box' exercise. As both practitioners and researchers, more is needed. More effort and planning is required to deliver a model of reflective practice that is clear and consistent in its message and delivery, so that it is more than a 'nice idea' (Ainslie et al, 2022). Rigorous monitoring and evaluation of these sessions is required; not merely in terms of practitioners' attendance, but crucially regarding the use of the space. As probation, or psychologically informed, practitioners we should be reflecting upon a number of issues:

- whether group consultation sessions are attended and focused as appropriate including by following models of reflection. This includes maintaining an emphasis on developmental and qualitative functions (skills development and task performance) as well as attending to practitioner resources/resilience.
- Whether the reflective space allows for an examination of the true nature of the dynamics, discussions and reflections that are taking place there, such as recognising whether probation practitioners are effectively using the space instead of passively being present.
- Whether facilitators are directly supported in the delivery of group reflective practice, by ensuring training on facilitation of groups is delivered, and participant attendance is regularly monitored and actively monitored by local senior probation officers. Such organisational support would allow probation practitioners to perceive the group as 'not just another meeting' but an effective resource to support their well-being and work with probationers.

Once these practices are achieved, we can move on to a stage where the effects of reflective practice and supervision on probationer outcomes can truly be explored by research, both quantitatively and qualitatively. Ultimately, we need to strive for a professional context where reflective practice is no longer an afterthought, but is an integral mechanism supporting the assessment and risk management process of our work within probation.

Reflective prompts

- What interventions have I made, and where is this leading the client/me?
- How can I use this space to acknowledge and think constructively about the reasons for what went well or not so well?
- How might the context in which the work is happening be affecting its impact?
- What one thing would I like to have done differently? What else?
- What guidelines or evidence-based practices are relevant here?

References

Ainslie, S., Fowler, A., Phillips, J. and Westaby, C. (2022) 'A nice idea but …': Implementing a reflective supervision model in the National Probation Service in England and Wales, *Reflective Practice*, 23(5): 525–538. https://doi.org/10.1080/14623943.2022.2066075

Ansbro, M. (2019) A qualitative examination of attachment-based concepts in probation supervision, *Probation Journal*, 66(2): 181–200. https://doi.org/10.1177/0264550519833458

Bambling, M., King, R., Raue, P., Schweitzer, R. and Lambert, W. (2006) Clinical supervision: Its influence on client-rated working alliance and client symptom reduction in the brief treatment of major depression, *Psychotherapy Research*, 16(3): 317–31. https://doi.org/10.1080/10503300500268524

Bonta, J. and Andrews, D.A. (2007) Risk-need-responsivity model for offender assessment and rehabilitation, User Report 2007-06, Public Safety Canada. Available from: https://www.publicsafety.gc.ca/cnt/rsrcs/pblctns/rsk-nd-rspnsvty/index-en.aspx

Borrelli, B., Sepinwall, D., Ernst, D., Bellg, A.J., Czajkowski, S., Greger, R., et al (2005) A new tool to assess treatment fidelity and evaluation of treatment fidelity across 10 years of health behaviour research, *Journal of Consulting and Clinical Psychology*, 73: 852–860. https://doi.org/10.1037/0022-006x.73.5.852

Bourgon, G., Bonta, J., Rugge, T. and Gutierrez, L. (2010) Technology transfer: The importance of on-going clinical supervision in translating what works to everyday community supervision, in F. McNeill, P. Raynor and C. Trotter (eds) *Offender Supervision: New Directions in Theory, Research, and Practice*, Willan, pp 91–112.

Bruce, R. and Hollin, C.R. (2009) Developing citizenship, *EuroVista: Probation and Community Justice*, 1(1): 24–31. Available from: https://www.cep-probation.org/wp-content/uploads/2019/01/VOl-1.1-Developing-Citizenship.pdf

Campbell, C. and Craissati, J. (2018) Introduction, in C. Campbell and J. Craissati (eds) *Managing Personality Disordered Offenders: A Pathways Approach*, Oxford University Press, pp 1–25.

Cook, K.S. (1977) Exchange and power in networks of interorganizational relations, *Sociological Quarterly*, 18(1): 62–82. https://doi.org/10.1111/j.1533-8525.1977.tb02162.x

Day, A. (2012) The nature of supervision in forensic psychology: Some observations and recommendations, *The British Journal of Forensic Practice*, 14(2): 116–123. https://psycnet.apa.org/doi/10.1108/14636641211223675

Dowden, C. and Andrews, D.A. (2004) The importance of staff practice in delivering effective correctional treatment: A meta-analytic review of core correctional practice, *International Journal of Offender Therapy and Comparative Criminology*, 48(2): 203–214. https://doi.org/10.1177/0306624X03257765

Ellis, M. and Ladany, N. (1997) Inferences concerning supervisees and clients in clinical supervision: An integrative review, in C.E. Watkins (ed), *The Handbook of Psychotherapy Supervision*, Wiley, pp 447–507.

Galletti, M., Moscara, M., Mattei, G., Balducci, J., Sacchetti, A., Venturi, G., et al (2021) Group clinical supervision in adult mental health settings, *Minerva Psichiatrica*, 62(2): 94–102. http://dx.doi.org/10.23736/S2724-6612.21.02113-0

Gibbs, G. (1988) *Learning by Doing: A Guide to Teaching and Learning Methods*, Further Education Unit, Oxford Polytechnic.

HM Inspectorate of Probation (2020) Independent review of the case of Joseph McCann. Available from: https://www.justiceinspectorates.gov.uk/hmiprobation/wp-content/uploads/sites/5/2020/06/Independent-review-of-the-case-of-Joseph-McCann.pdf

Labrecque, R.M., Viglione, J. and Caudy, M. (2023) The impact of community supervision officer training programs on officer and client outcomes: A systematic review and meta-analysis, *Justice Quarterly*, 40(4): 587–611. https://doi.org/10.1080/07418825.2022.2120062

Lipsey, M.W. and Cullen, F.T. (2007) The effectiveness of correctional rehabilitation: A review of systematic reviews, *Annual Review of Law and Social Science*, 3: 297–320. https://doi.org/10.1146/annurev.lawsocsci.3.081806.112833

Makarios, M., Lovins, L., Latessa, E. and Smith, P. (2016) Staff quality and treatment effectiveness: An examination of the relationship between staff factors and the effectiveness of correctional programs, *Justice Quarterly*, 33(2): 348–367. https://doi.org/10.1080/07418825.2014.924546

Milne, D. (2014) Beyond the 'acid test': A conceptual review and reformulation of outcome evaluation in clinical supervision, *American Journal of Psychotherapy*, 68(2): 213–230. https://doi.org/10.1176/appi.psychotherapy.2014.68.2.213

Milne, D., Sheikh, A.I., Pattison, S. and Wilkinson, A. (2011) Evidence-based training for clinical supervisors: A systematic review of 11 controlled studies, *The Clinical Supervisor*, 30(1): 53–71. https://doi.org/10.1080/07325223.2011.564955

Mor Barak, M.E., Travis, D.J., Pyun, H. and Xie, B. (2009) The impact of supervision on worker outcomes: A meta-analysis, *Social Service Review*, 83(1): 3–32. https://doi.org/10.1086/599028

NOMS/NHS (National Offender Management Service/National Health Service) (2015) The offender personality disorder pathway strategy, Gateway reference 04272. Available from: https://www.england.nhs.uk/commissioning/wp-content/uploads/sites/12/2016/02/opd-strategy-nov-15.pdf

Pearson, D.A., McDougall, C., Kanaan, M., Bowles, R.A. and Torgerson, D.J. (2011) Reducing criminal recidivism: Evaluation of citizenship, an evidence-based probation supervision process, *Journal of Experimental Criminology*, 7: 73–102. https://doi.org/10.1007/s11292-010-9115-3

Pearson, D.A., McDougall, C., Kanaan, M., Torgerson, D.J. and Bowles, R.A. (2016) Evaluation of the citizenship evidence-based probation supervision program using a stepped wedge cluster randomized controlled trial, *Crime & Delinquency*, 62(7): 899–924. https://doi.org/10.1177/0011128714530824

Radcliffe, K., Carrington, B. and Ward, M. (2020) Exploring offender managers' experiences of psychologically informed consultation on relationships with service users within the offender personality disorder pathway, *Mental Health Review Journal*, 25(4): 317–328. https://psycnet.apa.org/doi/10.1108/MHRJ-11-2019-0042

Rex, S. and Hosking, N. (2014) Supporting practitioners to engage offenders, in I. Durnescu and F. McNeill (eds), *Understanding Penal Practice*, Routledge, pp 271–280.

Scailllet, C. and Taylor, C. (2018) Staff selection and training, in C. Campbell and J. Craissati (eds) *Managing Personality Disordered Offenders: A Pathways Approach*, Oxford University Press, pp 26–53.

Shaw, J. and Edelmann, R. (2019) Predictors of engagement, understanding and dropout from a community based cognitive skills programme, *The Journal of Forensic Psychiatry & Psychology*, 30(6): 993–1005. https://doi.org/10.1080/14789949.2019.1660908

Shaw, J., Higgins, C. and Quartey, C. (2017) The impact of collaborative case formulation with high risk offenders with personality disorder, *The Journal of Forensic Psychiatry & Psychology*, 28(6): 777–789. https://doi.org/10.1080/14789949.2017.1324579

Snowdon, D.A., Hau, R., Leggat, S.G. and Taylor, N.F. (2016) Does clinical supervision of health professionals improve patient safety? A systematic review and meta-analysis, *International Journal for Quality in Health Care*, 28(4): 447–455. https://doi.org/10.1093/intqhc/mzw059

Wang, Y., Xu, S. and Zhang, X. (2023) Pull and push: The effect of social support and professional resilience on the relationship between correctional officers' cynicism and service impact, *International Journal of Offender Therapy and Comparative Criminology*, 67(16): 1659–1680. https://doi.org/10.1177/0306624X221139067

Webster, N., Doggett, L. and Gardner, S. (2020) If you want to change the world you have to start with yourself: The impact of staff reflective practice within the Offender Personality Disorder pathway, *Probation Journal*, 67(3): 283–296. https://doi.org/10.1177/0264550520939180

Westaby, C., Fowler, A., Phillips, J. and Ainslie, S. (2021) An evaluation of the implementation of reflective practice supervision standards in the national probation service, Sheffield Hallam University. Available from: https://shura.shu.ac.uk/28842/1/SEEDS2%20RPSS%20Report%20Final.pdf

Westaby, C., Phillips, J., Ainslie, S. and Fowler, A. (2023) 'Pushed from above and pushed from below': Emotional labour and dual identities amongst senior probation officers in England and Wales, *European Journal of Probation*, 15(1): 40–59. https://doi.org/10.1177/20662203221144119

4

Enhancing professional growth through self-understanding

Laura Sibret

Self-reflection has been adopted as professional practice within a variety of professional contexts such as policing (Wood, 2020); social work (Ferguson, 2018); therapy (Bennett-Levy et al, 2009); and probation (Goldhill, 2010). Schön (1991), who advanced the concept of the reflective practitioner, highlights the ever-changing and sometimes chaotic situations within which these practitioners operate. The nature of their work involves addressing serious problems but when asked about their approaches they speak of intuition, experience and trial-and-error (Schön, 1991). Given this, it becomes crucial for practitioners to develop specific skills and attributes which support fair and non-judgemental probation practice, in order to maintain good quality therapeutic alliances (Burrell, 2022). Schön (1991) argues that through reflection-in-action, defined as the ability to reflect on an event as it is developing, practitioners cultivate their flexibility and adaptability to deal with complex and unpredictable circumstances. Therefore, the reflective practitioner becomes central to being an effective probation practitioner, as is emphasised throughout the Professional Qualification in Probation (PQiP) (Ainslie, 2020). However, Ainslie et al (2022) highlight the current challenges in practising self-reflection, including managerialism, quality assurance and high workloads. The study emphasises the value probation practitioners place on reflective supervision, indicating conflicts between the demands of the role and available space for reflective practice. This chapter will consider self-reflection as a means of achieving higher levels of reflection outside of the workplace.

The development of self-reflection more generally is hindered by several aspects including the different definitions, explanations and applications that can be found. This chapter will draw upon psychological tools including self-awareness, emotional literacy and personal practices, with the aim of defining self-reflection and thus encouraging probation practitioners to practice self-reflection within their personal lives. The desired outcome is to have a better understanding of the self-reflection process, which can then be applied to professional practice. Additionally, discovering more about oneself should lead individuals to a more nuanced understanding of their decision-making processes, including the impact of their emotional state on this. The rationale for the application of self-reflection within personal lives stems from the adaptation of the Declarative-Procedural-Reflective (DPR) model used for therapy skill development, herein co-opted for probation practice. This model highlights the connection between personal and professional identities, making it relevant for probation practice.

Declarative-Procedural-Reflective model

The DPR model (Bennett-Levy, 2006; Bennett-Levy and Thwaites, 2007; Bennett-Levy et al, 2009) serves as a framework for therapist skills development and is cited regularly in contemporary work (for example, Burgess et al, 2013; Davis et al, 2015; Haarhoff and Thwaites, 2016). This model illustrates the intricate process through which therapy skills are acquired and refined, highlighting the interplay between declarative, procedural and reflective systems (see figure 1 in Chaddock et al, 2014). Although it was originally conceptualised for therapy learning, it is highly applicable to how probation practitioners learn their skills. The DPR is outlined as follows:

- *Declarative system:* encompasses the theoretical understanding of probation practice including skills and approaches, providing

practitioners with the foundational knowledge necessary for effective interventions. Simply put, it is the repository of information and knowledge about practice gained through reading materials, professional development and training (Bennett-Levy, 2006).
- *Procedural system:* involves the practical use of skills, honed through repeated practice and feedback. It is the application of declarative knowledge (that is, skills-in-action).
- *Reflective system:* involves the critical examination and integration of personal experiences, client interactions and supervisory feedback, fostering self-awareness and professional growth. Through reflection, practitioners can understand how the implications of knowledge influence actions and how those actions can then adapt existing knowledge or consolidate it (Bennett-Levy et al, 2009).

While initially conceptualised for therapy learning, the DPR model transcends disciplinary boundaries and finds relevance in diverse professional contexts, including the training and development of probation practitioners. Much like therapists, probation practitioners acquire and refine their skills through a dynamic interplay of declarative, procedural and reflective processes. As they navigate complex interpersonal dynamics and legal frameworks, probation practitioners draw upon their theoretical knowledge, practical skills and reflective insights to effectively engage with clients, assess risks and facilitate rehabilitation (Goldhill, 2010; Burrell, 2022). Thus, the DPR model offers a versatile framework for understanding and enhancing skills development across a spectrum of helping professions, including therapy and probation practice.

This model distinguishes between the 'personal self' and the 'therapist self' (Chaddock et al, 2014), here adapted to the 'practitioner self'. This distinction suggests that as practitioners develop particular skills, they are actively developing a 'practitioner self'. These skills in turn continue to be influenced by the pre-existing 'personal self'. For instance, interpersonal skills such as communication skills and attitudes, determined by the 'personal self', will dictate how they present in the 'practitioner self'. This indicates the need for self-awareness of the practitioner's own biases, influences, perspectives and so on to ensure they are not expressed in the 'practitioner self' and, consequently, reflected in their interaction with their person on probation (Burrell, 2022).

Self-awareness and reflective practice

The processes of reaching self-awareness and engaging in reflective practice are inextricably linked within the literature. Distinguishing between each concept is crucial to understanding their importance and interconnectedness: 'Self-awareness is the continuous process of understanding and knowing of one's own identity, beliefs, thoughts, traits, motivations, feelings and behaviour and to recognise how they affect others in different ways' (Rasheed, 2015: 212). Eckroth-Bucher (2010) highlights that it is a process of introspection through the exploration of the previously mentioned characteristics. However, introspection has been shown to be a more nuanced process to engage in than previously thought. Research by Eurich (2018) demonstrated that individuals report lower well-being as a result of introspection. This finding was a particular result of individuals engaging in the process incorrectly by asking questions such as 'why' rather than 'what'. The former encourages more negative thinking while the latter encourages self-reflection and beneficial change. Rasheed et al (2019) highlight the dynamic nature of attaining self-awareness by identifying it as an ongoing developmental process. Since it has been shown to be possible to train self-awareness (Ashley and Reiter-Palmon, 2012; Rasheed et al, 2019) this means that introspection is also likely to improve if engaged through productive self-insight. Self-reflection then becomes the process through which to achieve self-awareness (Sutton et al, 2015). Ultimately, developing self-awareness will lead to the development of self-knowledge which will aid personal development (Carden et al, 2022).

Defining self-reflection is difficult given the multitude of approaches and motivators for engaging in the process. Elliot (1991, as cited in Chant et al, 2004: 25) defines it as a process requiring 'critical thought, self-direction, and problem-solving coupled with personal knowledge and self-awareness'. Self-reflection can encourage practitioners to understand and address any mismatch between adopted theories (for example, their beliefs and values) and their current theories-in-action (Osterman and Kottkamp, 2004). Mismatches between the two can be borne through habit, external pressure and/or unacknowledged biases, thus are important to uncover to support effective probation practice.

Reflection and probation

Research has shown that engaging in reflection can actively help relieve the pressures and emotional demands of probation work (Coley, 2020; Webster et al, 2020). As highlighted in a number of chapters in this compendium, probation practitioners' daily encounters with their person on probation can be unpredictable and involve a significant amount of emotional work (Fowler et al, 2018). Given the responsibility to rehabilitate people on probation, and having significant power to change these individuals' lives, it is essential for practitioners to have the ability to understand their emotional states and those of their person on probation (Ainslie et al, 2022). This connects with Knight's (2014) findings regarding the importance of emotional literacy for practitioners working within the criminal justice system. Knight (2014) defines emotional literacy as:

> knowledge of our own emotions and the ability to recognise and respond empathically to the emotions of others. It includes an awareness of the causes, triggers and expression of emotions in ourselves and in others, and requires an underpinning value base of respect, positive regard and a non-judgmental approach towards offenders. (Knight, 2014: 194)

By cultivating emotional literacy, practitioners can forge meaningful connections with those under their supervision, fostering an environment conducive to positive change. Moreover, emotional literacy equips practitioners with the ability to comprehend the underlying motivations behind an individual's behaviour, aiding in the formulation of effective intervention strategies (Knight, 2014). This not only enhances the quality of support provided but also enables practitioners to manage their own emotional responses, thereby forging resilience in the face of challenging circumstances. Both sensitivity and self-awareness are inherently important to achieve emotional literacy, and therefore maintain therapeutic alliances in challenging circumstances, and with high-risk offenders (Knight and Modi, 2014). These circumstances highlight the emotional impact of the work probation practitioners undertake (Westaby et al, 2020).

The expansion of the DPR model acknowledges the emotional toll of working with clients, so is relevant to include in supporting practitioners to engage in self-reflection. Bennett-Levy and Finlay-Jones (2018) have introduced the model of Personal Practices (PPs), which refer to activities or programmes that therapists engage in for their own self-care, professional development and personal growth (for example, counselling). The model identifies four kinds of motivations that usually underpin engagement in PPs: personal problems; personal growth; self-care; and therapist skill development. The model is framed within the context of the two selves: the 'personal self' and the 'therapist self'. Bennett-Levy and Finlay-Jones (2018) propose that the process of reflection, involving flexible transitioning between personal self-reflections and therapist self-reflection, is central to the enhancement of therapist skilfulness. The model suggests that PPs may lead to five core outcomes: personal development/well-being; enhanced self-awareness; interpersonal beliefs/attitudes/skills; reflective skills; and conceptual/technical skills. This integration of PPs aligns seamlessly with the DPR model, as it not only enhances the reflective system but also ensures that the continuous interplay between personal growth and professional skill development is deeply embedded in the practitioner's approach, thereby strengthening both the personal and practitioner self. This is supported in the probation context by Coley (2020), who argues that there needs to be a more clinical approach to supervision where self-reflection is a core part of the professional development of practitioners (see Chapter 5 for further discussion on this relating to leadership practices). For probation practitioners, integrating self-reflection into their personal practices becomes instrumental for professional development and personal growth. Similarly to therapists, probation practitioners can engage in activities or programmes aimed at enhancing self-awareness, interpersonal skills and overall well-being. These practices may include personal reflection sessions and mindfulness exercises, which can also help in coping with the demands of emotional labour (Phillips et al, 2020).

Emotional labour is the term used to describe the manner in which individuals regulate and display emotions to accomplish a goal of their work (Hochschild, 1983). This is a crucial aspect of probation work and requires the ability to regulate one's genuine emotions regarding a situation, which can relate to individual casework and have the potential to impact professional relationships. Indeed, emotional labour involves engaging with positive emotions while potentially suppressing negative ones. Practitioners have described experiences that range from positive demonstrations, such as showing happiness for a client's success, to suppression of negative feelings, such as disgust for their offences, for the purposes of strengthening the rapport with their person on probation (Westaby et al, 2020). The study also highlights the laborious aspects of emotional labour, as the act of suppressing emotions has been linked to burnout due to the high levels of surface acting. Surface acting involves the display of emotions which are not actually felt by the individual (Hochschild, 1983). Researchers have indicated a need for mindfulness practices to increase resilience given the potential links between emotional labour, burnout and probation practice (Phillips et al, 2020). That mindfulness can be classed as a PP is a reminder as to how engaging in self-care and self-reflection can aid well-being inside and outside of the workplace. Probation practitioners have indicated that their work is relentless (Phillips et al, 2016) and spills over into their personal lives, affecting their daily routines, parenting techniques and relationships with others (Westaby et al, 2016). Therefore, the integration of PPs becomes relevant to provide a space for practitioners to explore this aspect of the 'practitioner self' and the interplay with the 'personal self'. Consequently, PPs would strengthen the 'personal self' and provide support to the 'practitioner self'.

Integration of self-reflection

PPs as formal interventions and techniques can be engaged with over an extended period of time, which can span years. They should always have a reflective focus which can focus both on personal and professional development (Bennett-Levy, 2019). Examples of PPs, according to the literature, are 'personal therapy, meditation programs (mindfulness, compassion, loving-kindness), self-practice/self-reflection programs (therapists practising therapy techniques on themselves and reflecting on the experience), and experiential/personal development groups' (Bennett-Levy, 2019: 133).

Given the application of this model to probation work there are certain changes which need to be made in their application. While probation practitioners may not be able to practice therapy techniques on themselves (unless having had training/experience with therapy), the use of self-reflection is precisely the purpose of this chapter. The following suggestion for self-reflection is an adaption of Bennett-Levy's (2019) self-practice/self-reflection programmes:

- Practitioners should focus on a mild to moderate professional or personal problem, for example, a rupture that has occurred in a personal relationship.
- Self-reflective questions can be about the 'personal self' such as: 'What was your experience of noting how your actions were driven by your thoughts?', 'To what extent does this experience resonate with others from your past?'. The other type of questions are 'bridging questions' which form the bridge from the 'personal self' to the 'practitioner self' such as 'How does this experience relate to your understanding of theory (in this example, relating to the therapeutic alliance)?' and 'How can I use PPs to address the impact of this situation?'. The bridging questions are the core of this PP as they allow for the 'personal self' to act as a vehicle for the development of the 'practitioner self'.
- The concluding 'reflective bridge' explicitly connects learning from the 'personal self' to the 'practitioner self' and vice versa. This can include the use of questions such as 'What is the impact of my PP experience for my work with my person on probation?', 'What does my PP experience mean for my understanding of my professional practice?' (adapted from Bennett-Levy, 2019: 137). In the context of probation

practice, these questions can be further tweaked to consider the implications of working with a diverse range of people on probation.

According to Haarhoff and Thwaites (2016) consistent engagement with self-reflective practice will then lead to the development of the following:

- *Reflective practice:* The process of introspection can take place under various contexts, such as supervision, self-monitoring and the maintenance of reflective journals.
- *Reflective skill:* Ability to reconstruct past occurrences, including an examination of one's own emotional reactions and behavioural patterns.
- *Reflection as a process:* Focused attention on a specific issue, reconstructing the sequence of events, and conceptualising and synthesising dilemmas through self-analysis and problem-solving.
- *Reflective system:* The fundamental mechanism driving the practitioner's knowledge and expertise, facilitating the adaptation of strategies to address the unique needs of individual clients.

Haarhoff and Thwaites' (2016) outcomes can be further explored by using the DPR model while incorporating PPs:

- *Reflective practice as a personal and professional PP:* Through the integration of reflective practice as a PP, probation practitioners can explore the skill in both personal and professional contexts. The exploration of the interaction which occurs between the personal and professional self would provide insight into both domains and allow the probation practitioner to become increasingly familiar with reflective practice. Self-reflection will need to be consistently applied within the personal sphere given that, within the professional setting, it should be part of supervision meetings. The DPR model provides the structure to do so, which will lead to gaining insight into decision-making processes across domains and should help improve well-being and resilience. The methodology used to conduct the self-reflection, such as journaling, for example, is dependent upon each individual's preference.

- *Reflective skills in context:* The use of reflective journals provides a valuable for the exploration of past occurrences. The ability to go back and see one's progression can be valuable in identifying how the reflective skill has progressed. Journaling would also offer the ability to draw connections across personal and professional domains as events can be explored chronologically. This provides space to understand the connection between personal events and professional ones. Journaling about personal life events allows officers to explore how the 'personal self' influences the 'practitioner self'. Conversely, reflecting on professional experiences can reveal how their work impacts their personal life. This dual approach enables officers to maintain a healthy balance and adapt their practices to better address the needs of their person on probation.
- *Reflection as a process in personal and professional growth:* Reflection should be conducted methodically by focusing attention on specific events and understanding which actions need to be made moving forward. The DPR model provides a blueprint through which to do this.
- *Reflective system across different domains:* A reflective system, when developed across both personal and professional domains, will allow practitioners to continually develop their declarative knowledge, procedural skills, and reflective abilities. Through the incorporation of regular PPs such as mindfulness, self-monitoring and peer discussions, the process can ensure a mutually beneficial exercise which will benefit both domains.

Example of self-reflection

To demonstrate the DPR model of reflection here is an example of an experience in the early stages of my career:

- *Declarative:* As an education professional, I am committed to creating engaging and informative content for my university modules. Drawing upon my declarative knowledge of the subject matter and pedagogical principles, I developed content for a class with high expectations for its reception.
- *Procedural:* When the content was presented to the students, it became apparent that there were challenges. Feedback indicated

that some students were struggling with the material, leading to frustration and disengagement. Initially, I felt confident that the content was appropriate and believed that the existing supplementary resources would be sufficient. As a result, I directed students to these resources, anticipating they would find them helpful.

- *Reflective:* Upon further reflection, I realised that my initial response was not addressing student' needs as their engagement with the additional resources was not improving their understanding. I took a step back and tried to understand my response regarding their concerns. I acknowledged that my perception of the material is influenced by my declarative knowledge. In this case, I had made assumptions about their ability to engage with the content for which I had prior knowledge in the subject matter, and they did not. I recognised that I had been reluctant to admit I had made an error – doing well in my career is important to my 'personal self', and any form of failure felt contradictory to this. However, as I stepped back and critically evaluated the situation, I acknowledged the validity of the students' feedback and that taking action meant this was not an error, but a shared learning experience. In response to the students' feedback, I took proactive steps to reassess and improve the content to better align with the students' learning needs and abilities. I immediately developed additional guidance materials to supplement the existing resources, providing students with clearer instructions and explanations to facilitate their understanding. I utilised the PP of journaling to provide an outlet for self-reflection. This meant I also collaborated with colleagues to address these issues for the following year, incorporating feedback from both students and faculty to create a more inclusive and accessible learning experience.

The model highlights how my 'personal self' was impacting my 'professional self'. Self-reflection upon my professional situation added valuable insight into my 'personal self' about wanting to do well in the early stages of my career. Using PPs and self-reflection has provided me with understanding and confidence in how to engage in similar situations in the future.

Engaging in self-reflective practice has become a crucial skill that I return to, so I can consistently understand how my personal and professional selves interact and which steps I can take to either leverage or impede said interaction (Bennett-Levy, 2019). Through this experience, I learned the importance of adaptability in the face of failure. By embracing feedback, acknowledging shortcomings and taking proactive steps to address them, I was able to transform a challenging situation into an opportunity for growth and improvement.

Conclusion

Self-reflection is recognised as a vital component of effective probation practice, allowing practitioners to navigate complex and dynamic work environments while fostering personal and professional growth. Drawing from literature across various fields, this analysis explored some practical challenges and potential benefits of self-reflection in probation settings. The discussion emphasises the importance of integrating self-reflection into practitioner's personal lives and PPs to enhance practitioner self-awareness, emotional literacy, emotional well-being and resilience. By leveraging frameworks such as the DPR model and the PPs, practitioners can enhance their ability to navigate challenging situations, forge meaningful connections with clients and facilitate positive outcomes in probation supervision. Further research should be conducted on the applicability of the model for probation practice and any potential impacts it may have on the therapeutic alliance between practitioner and person on probation.

Reflective prompts

- How has your understanding of the theoretical skills and approaches used in probation practice (declarative knowledge) impacted on your daily interactions with the individuals under your supervision?
- Think of a specific skill you have developed through practice and feedback (procedural knowledge) throughout your time as a probation practitioner. What was the impact of using this skill on the interaction with your person on probation?

- Consider a recent supervision session with your senior probation officer. How did critically exploring your experiences, emotions and feedback from your senior probation officer enhance your self-awareness and professional growth?
- Reflect on how your professional interactions may have been influenced by your personal beliefs, biases and natural emotional responses in a recent session which did not go as planned.
- Think about the last difficult session you had with a person on probation. How did your emotional state impact on this? Which personal practices could you have practised to manage this and alleviate its impact on your practice?

References

Ainslie, S. (2020) A time to reflect? *Probation Quarterly*, 17: 9–12.

Ainslie, S., Fowler, A., Phillips, J. and Westaby, C. (2022) 'A nice idea but …': Implementing a reflective supervision model in the National Probation Service in England and Wales, *Reflective Practice*, 23(5): 525–538. https://doi.org/10.1080/14623943.2022.2066075

Ashley, G.C. and Reiter-Palmon, R. (2012) Self-awareness and the evolution of leaders: The need for a better measure of self-awareness, *Journal of Behavioral and Applied Management*, 14(1): 2–17. https://doi.org/10.21818/001c.17902

Bennett-Levy, J. (2006) Therapist skills: A cognitive model of their acquisition and refinement, *Behavioural and Cognitive Psychotherapy*, 34: 1–22. https://psycnet.apa.org/doi/10.1017/S1352465805002420

Bennett-Levy, J. (2019) Why therapists should walk the talk: The theoretical and empirical case for personal practice in therapist training and professional development, *Journal of Behavior Therapy and Experimental Psychiatry*, 62: 133–145. https://doi.org/10.1016/j.jbtep.2018.08.004

Bennett-Levy, J. and Thwaites, R. (2007) Self and self-reflection in the therapeutic relationship: A conceptual map and practical strategies for the training, supervision and self-supervision of interpersonal skills, in P. Gilbert and R. Leahy (eds) *The Therapeutic Relationship in the Cognitive Behavioural Therapies*, Routledge, pp 255–281.

Bennett-Levy, J. and Finlay-Jones, A. (2018) The role of personal practice in therapist skill development: A model to guide therapists, educators, supervisors and researchers, *Cognitive Behaviour Therapy*, 47(3): 185–205. https://doi.org/10.1080/16506073.2018.1434678

Bennett-Levy, J., Thwaites, R., Chaddock, A. and Davis, M. (2009) Reflective practice in cognitive behavioural therapy: The engine of lifelong learning, in J. Stedmon and R. Dallos (eds) *Reflective Practice in Psychotherapy and Counselling*, Open University Press, pp 115–135.

Burgess, S., Rhodes, P. and Wilson, V. (2013) Exploring the in-session reflective capacity of clinical psychology trainees: An interpersonal process recall study, *Clinical Psychologist*, 17: 122–130. https://doi.org/10.1111/cp.12014

Burrell, A. (2022) The reflective practitioner in transition: Probation work during reintegration of probation services in England and Wales, *Probation Journal*, 69(4): 434–451. https://doi.org/10.1177/02645505221117537

Carden, J., Jones, R.J. and Passmore, J. (2022) Defining self-awareness in the context of adult development: A systematic literature review, *Journal of Management Education*, 46(1): 140–177. https://doi.org/10.1177/1052562921990065

Chaddock, A., Thwaites, R., Bennett-Levy, J. and Freeston, M.H. (2014) Understanding individual differences in response to self-practice and self-reflection (SP/SR) during CBT training, *The Cognitive Behaviour Therapist*, 7(14): 1–17. https://psycnet.apa.org/doi/10.1017/S1754470X14000142

Chant, R.H., Heafner, T.L. and Bennett, K.R. (2004) Connecting personal theorising and action research in preservice teacher development, *Teacher Education Quarterly*, 31(3): 25–42. Available from: https://files.eric.ed.gov/fulltext/EJ795251.pdf

Coley, D. (2020) Probation staff supervision: Valuing 'me time' within congested spaces, *Probation Journal*, 67(3): 228–245. https://doi.org/10.1177/0264550520926581

Davis, M.L., Thwaites, R., Freeston, M.H. and Bennett-Levy, J. (2015) A measurable impact of a self-practice/self-reflection programme on the therapeutic skills of experienced cognitive-behavioural therapists, *Clinical Psychology and Psychotherapy*, 22: 176–184. https://doi.org/10.1002/cpp.1884

Eckroth-Bucher, M. (2010) Self-awareness: A review and analysis of a basic nursing concept, *Advances in Nursing Science*, 33(4): 297–309. http://dx.doi.org/10.1097/ANS.0b013e318 1fb2e4c

Eurich, T. (2018) What self-awareness really is (and how to cultivate it)?, *Harvard Business Review*, 4 January. Available from: https://membership.amavic.com.au/files/What%20s elf-awareness%20is%20and%20how%20to%20cultivate%20it_ HBR_2018.pdf

Ferguson, H. (2018) How social workers reflect in action and when and why they don't: The possibilities and limits to reflective practice in social work, *Social Work Education*, 37(4): 415–427. https://doi.org/10.1080/02615479.2017.1413083

Fowler, A., Phillips, J. and Westaby, C. (2018) Understanding emotions as effective practice in English probation: The performance of emotional labour in building relationships, in P. Ugwudike, P. Raynor and J. Annison (eds) *Evidence-based Skills in Criminal Justice: International Research on Supporting Rehabilitation and Desistance*, Bristol University Press, pp 243–262.

Goldhill, R. (2010) Reflective practice and distance learning: Problems and potentials for probation training, *Reflective Practice*, 11(1): 57–70. https://doi.org/10.1080/14623940903500085

Haarhoff, B. and Thwaites, R. (2016) *Reflection in CBT*, SAGE.

Hochschild, A.R. (1983) *The Managed Heart: Commercialization of Human Feeling*, University of California Press.

Knight, C. (2014) *Emotional Literacy in Criminal Justice: Professional Practice with Offenders*, Palgrave Macmillan.

Knight, C. and Modi, P. (2014) The use of emotional literacy in work with sexual offenders, *Probation Journal*, 61(2): 132–147. https://doi.org/10.1177/0264550514523817

Osterman, K.F. and Kottkamp, R.B. (2004) *Reflective Practice for Educators: Professional Development to Improve Student Learning* (2nd edn), Corwin Press.

Phillips, J., Westaby, C. and Fowler, A. (2016) 'It's relentless': The impact of working primarily with high-risk offenders, *Probation Journal*, 63(2): 182–192. https://doi.org/10.1177/026455051 7692058

Phillips, J., Westaby, C. and Fowler, A. (2020) Emotional labour in probation, HM Inspectorate of Probation. Available from: https://www.justiceinspectorates.gov.uk/hmiprobation/wp-content/uploads/sites/5/2020/04/Emotional-Labour-in-Probation.pdf

Rasheed, S.P. (2015) Self-awareness as a therapeutic tool for nurse/client relationship, *International Journal of Caring Sciences*, 8(1): 211–216. Available from: https://www.internationaljournalofcaringsciences.org/docs/24-%20review-parveen.pdf

Rasheed, S.P., Younas, A. and Sundus, A. (2019) Self-awareness in nursing: A scoping review, *Journal of Clinical Nursing*, 28(5–6): 762–774. https://doi.org/10.1111/jocn.14708

Schön, D.A. (1991) *The Reflective Practitioner: How Professionals Think in Action*, Ashgate.

Sutton, A., Williams, H.M. and Allinson, C.W. (2015) A longitudinal mixed method of self-awareness training in the workplace, *European Journal of Training and Development*, 39(7): 610–627. http://dx.doi.org/10.1108/EJTD-04-2015-0031

Webster, N., Doggett, L. and Gardner, S. (2020) If you want to change the world you have to start with yourself: The impact of staff reflective practice within the offender personality disorder pathway, *Probation Journal*, 67(3): 283–296. https://doi.org/10.1177/0264550520939180

Westaby, C., Phillips, J. and Fowler, A. (2016) Spillover and work–family conflict in probation practice: Managing the boundary between work and home life, *European Journal of Probation*, 8(3): 113–127. https://doi.org/10.1177/2066220316680370

Westaby, C., Fowler, A. and Phillips, J. (2020) Managing emotion in probation practice: Display rules, values and the performance of emotional labour, *International Journal of Law, Crime and Justice*, 61: 1–11. https://doi.org/10.1016/j.ijlcj.2019.100362

Wood, D. (2020) Maintaining professional standards and reflective practice, in I. Pepper and R. McGrath (eds) *Introduction to Professional Policing*, Routledge, pp 7–26.

PART II

The organisational space for reflection

5

Fostering reflective practice as part of leadership

Jennifer Grant

Since the late 20th century, the Probation Service has increasingly been held accountable for its outcomes and performance, resulting in a managerialist approach to its staff and workload (Burrell, 2022). As discussed in Chapter 2, probation practice and culture have been subject to transformational change, significantly affecting senior leadership and management roles. The senior probation officer (SPO) role is distinct in its approach to middle management within the public sector, because it is placed to meet both organisational and fieldwork priorities (His Majesty's Inspectorate of Probation [HMIP, 2024]). The sustainability of this role is of concern and has become a clear focus for both HMIP and His Majesty's Prison and Probation Service (HMPPS).

There are numerous SPO roles within the Probation Service due to the number of contexts it operates within. This chapter will focus on the sentence management SPO role, which is especially applicable to recent directives including Skills for Effective Engagement, Development and Supervision (SEEDS) and Reflective Practice Supervision Standards (RPSS) (Westaby et al, 2021). Sentence management SPOs have varied responsibilities, but this chapter is focused on the task of supervision, which refers to the regular formal meetings held between SPOs and individual practitioners (HMIP, 2024). These meetings should generally include reflective casework discussions, but also address other issues such as performance and well-being. Effective supervision is perceived by both practitioners and SPOs as having several benefits, including enhancing confidence in decision-making (Coley, 2020) and promoting continuous professional development (Ruch, 2009). Thus, it is an important space to foster reflective practice within the Probation Service.

This chapter will first consider the aims and outcomes of reflective supervision, with a focus on its benefits to demonstrate its importance. The policy directives of SEEDS and RPSS will then be explored, due to their recent impact on the supervision space. Management oversight, workload and the influence of senior leaders will be investigated as potential pitfalls to effective supervision. This chapter will then identify three barriers to fostering reflective practice in leadership. It will explore the dual and often contested role of supervision; the impact of emotional labour and the effect of SPO bias on their relationship with practitioners. These barriers will be illustrated by reflective accounts. Finally, conclusions will be made as to how these barriers can be overcome, with an emphasis on the use of a whole systems approach.

Supervision

The rise of the 'risk society' and a politically driven public protection agenda (Beck, 1992), coupled with the need for financial efficiencies in the public sector (Goldhill, 2010), has resulted in increased bureaucracy within the Probation Service (Tuddenham, 2000). What takes place within staff supervision has been influenced by the changing organisational climate. Over the last 50 years, supervision has evolved from being a space wherein reflection and professional development are prioritised, to a 'muddled' space where surveillance and performance management must also be undertaken (Coley, 2020: 233). One-to-one supervision sessions must prioritise reflective clinical case discussions; implement performance management; explore staff's emotional well-being and support their continuous professional development (Coley, 2020). This means that reflective case discussions, requiring practitioners to be open and vulnerable, must also be balanced with the performance management and monitoring needs of the organisation.

Supervision as a reflective 'safe space' has therefore not been insulated against a neoliberal, risk management agenda (Noble and Irwin, 2009). This is despite evidence that reflective supervision increases staff's confidence in their own decision-making (Rex and Hosking, 2013) and is an important tool for professional development (Ruch, 2009). The recently implemented Community Policy Framework acknowledges that SPO-led reflective supervision is 'in support of their ongoing professional development' and 'enables emotionally informed practice' (Ministry of Justice, 2023: 12 and 61). In fact, ineffective supervision can distress practitioners and result in them leaving their roles (Westaby et al, 2021). This chapter therefore posits that reflective supervision is an important facet to consider in addressing retention. At a time when the probation workforce is in turmoil (Tidmarsh, 2024) due to high numbers of turnover and new staff (HMPPS, 2023), reflective supervision provides one solution to supporting and retaining practitioners. It also emphasises the organisation's commitment to its staff. Thus, the importance of reflective supervision as a space for reflective practice cannot be underestimated.

Reflective practice in supervision

The Probation Service acknowledges the significance of reflective practice and has formalised it within the SEEDS framework. SEEDS was initially intended to enhance the organisation's reflective culture by increasing practitioner's engagement skills, in order to reduce reoffending. The pilots for SEEDS in 2011/2012 highlighted the importance of the SPO role in securing a whole systems approach to this organisational culture change, given its link between strategic direction and fieldwork practice (Rex and Hosking, 2013). A whole systems approach acknowledges the holistic nature of systems which try to effect change (Pycroft, 2014) and is relevant to embedding reflective practice in probation due to the complexity of the actors required to be involved with this. The wider context is also relevant to this whole systems approach, given the Probation Service is also part of the wider Civil Service.

Moreover, the SEEDS framework formalised regular, structured one-to-one reflective supervision, acknowledging the importance of this space for professional development (Robinson, 2014). Unfortunately, the effectiveness of SEEDS was difficult to review due to being disrupted by Transforming Rehabilitation. That being said, a small-scale study of 55 ongoing staff evaluations highlighted that practitioners received SEEDS positively (Sorsby et al, 2013).

Just prior to reunification, the Probation Service launched SEEDS2. This framework has revived the intention to increase practitioner's skills and create a reflective culture. The accompanying RPSS consolidate the importance of reflective staff supervision delivered by trained SPOs, who also undertake regular observations of practice (Westaby et al, 2022). SEEDS2 appears to represent a return to a more traditional SPO role, wherein reflective supervision is prioritised over performance management and surveillance (Burrell, 2022). As previously considered in Chapter 3, the realisation of RPSS is impacted on by several issues within the current Probation Service.

Time has been identified as one barrier to reflective supervision by both probation officers and SPOs (Westaby et al, 2021; Ainslie et al, 2022). In fact, the endemic workload issues in the Probation Service (HMIP, 2021) appear to mean that the RPSS's ambitions are not currently being realised. Nationally, only 7 per cent of practitioners received reflective supervision in the 12 months prior to June 2023, despite SPOs reporting that they acknowledge the benefits of this for professional development (HMIP, 2024). Moreover, staff have reported that they were not receiving completed feedback following observations of their practice (Westaby et al, 2021). Without this, they cannot effectively reflect on and develop their casework decision-making skills with people on probation. I know from experience that delivering feedback on observations requires space for the SPO to reflect on the observation and then clearly allotted time to provide feedback to the practitioner. It is not a quick process, nor should it be given the importance of feedback to staff development (Ainslie et al, 2022). These difficulties implementing the RPSS are concerning and highlight unmanageable workloads within the Probation Service. They also suggest that a whole systems approach to a reflective culture is not yet in place.

Senior leadership

A whole systems approach requires the buy-in of senior leaders, as they are an integral part of facilitating a culture of reflective practice within the Probation Service. Ainslie et al (2022) found that senior leaders are not modelling the reflective supervision approach prescribed to SPOs through the RPSS. This is arguably a missed opportunity to instil reflective practice as part of staff supervision within all roles. The same study also found that senior leaders are not always facilitating the implementation of the RPSS within their regions. This is surprising, given that the Community Policy Framework encourages reflective staff supervision as part of quality assurance, as well as continuous professional development for practitioners (Ministry of Justice, 2023). Moreover, other evidence suggests SPOs are positive about their own line management, despite this often having a strong focus on performance issues (HMIP, 2024). Still, the reasons for inconsistencies in promoting a reflective culture within senior leadership nationally is unclear.

Information regarding the views of senior leaders is an ongoing vacuum in the probation research space. That being said, a recent study has captured the views of 12 senior leaders. Robinson et al (2023) found that Regional Probation Directors are aware of a demoralised and overworked workforce, and have clear intentions to support and encourage their staff. This is being addressed at a national level through the Rehabilitating Probation project. Given the large scope of the regions they are responsible for (Robinson et al, 2023), it can be assumed that senior leaders also have workloads that are difficult to manage. Time therefore may also impact their ability to both undertake and promote reflective practice. However, a lack of support for the RPSS framework is a reminder that senior leaders are also directly tied to the managerialist demands of a service that is held publicly accountable when things go wrong and serious further offences (SFOs) occur.

Management oversight

The organisational fear of public scrutiny when SFOs occur has led to defensive policies and decision-making within the

Probation Service (Calder, 2024; HMIP, 2024). Bureaucratic tasks now infiltrate all aspects of the SPO role (Westaby et al, 2021). Despite this, the same areas of concern continue to be identified when SFOs are subject to public inquiry. One of these areas is management oversight, defined by HMIP as assurance that 'operational delivery is undertaken consistently and to the required standard' (2024: 10). Management oversight is a key feature of staff supervision but permeates many SPO responsibilities, including countersigning risk assessments and overseeing the processes relevant to public protection (HMIP, 2024). The varied nature of management oversight means there are several conflicting policies that guide this responsibility (HMIP, 2024). This is problematic, as a recent inspectorate-led thematic highlighted that 72 per cent of 1,721 cases inspected between 2021 and 2023 had insufficient management oversight (HMIP, 2024).

The scope of the oversight task is arguably a key reason for this. The author's anecdotal evidence suggests that each practitioner supervises at least 40 people on probation, with sentence management SPOs overseeing at least ten practitioners. These conservative estimates mean that relevant SPOs are expected to have oversight of over 400 people on probation. Some will be long-term prisoners, so not all will require regular management oversight, yet that figure remains startling. SPOs have to prioritise where they provide management oversight, and it appears that SFOs have an influence here as the most effective management oversight is evidenced within high risk of serious harm cases (HMIP, 2024).

It is inconceivable for SPOs to achieve regular management oversight across their practitioners' caseload, especially as it is just one responsibility within their overburdened role. The workload of SPOs is an ongoing organisational risk, especially as they regularly manage more than ten practitioners (HMIP, 2024). Though a strong correlation has not been found between insufficient management oversight and team size (HMIP, 2024), it can be assumed that the weight of the management oversight task affects other parts of the SPO role. One of these is likely to be supervision, given that management oversight often falls into this space (HMIP, 2024). This is a reminder that SPOs are expected to meet the sometimes dissonant needs of both senior leadership and practitioners (Harding et al, 2014). The tension apparent within this dual role is the first specific barrier to fostering reflective practice as part of leadership to be discussed.

Barrier 1: The dual role

Traditionally, the sentence management SPO occupied roles including that of the adviser, organiser and expert (Boswell, 1986, as cited in Westaby et al, 2022). However, this role is now a balancing act between strategic directives and practitioner support. This tension is apparent in casework supervision, which was initially described as a contested space in the 1980s (Davies, 1984, as cited in Westaby et al, 2022). The purpose of supervision, and what to include within it, has therefore been a 'dilemma' for some time (Ainslie et al, 2022: 531). Yet, it is clear that practitioners support effective supervision spaces. Coley's (2020) large-scale study demonstrated that practitioners want supervision to focus on collaborative reflection and problem solving, rather than performance management and monitoring. Unsurprisingly, given the benefits of reflective supervision, SPO views are highly similar. They want to create a reflective and emphatic culture within supervision, rather than utilise this for surveillance (Beddoe, 2010; Westaby et al, 2022). Supervision should be a 'safe space' which is not obscured by organisational pressures (Revell and Burton, 2016). Despite this, the staff experience of supervision has largely involved performance management and monitoring (Eadie et al, 2013). It appears that in trying to balance the dual needs of the organisation and their staff, SPOs are perhaps prioritising managerialist priorities:

> My own experience reflected the dichotomy of staff supervision. I was encouraged to provide practitioners with a safe and reflective supervision space. However, I was also expected to capture headlines about performance management and other HR processes. This felt like an unsustainable balancing act. On reflection, this was because the practitioners who were performing well received regular reflective casework discussion, as they didn't have outstanding

risk assessments (or the like) that I needed to monitor. Contrastingly, anyone who wasn't performing well received less collaborative casework discussion in supervision sessions. Even though their emotional well-being was always discussed, this lack of regular reflective casework discussion was to the detriment of their continuous professional development.

The prioritisation of strategic priorities highlighted within this reflection is unsurprising, given that SPO's outcomes are scrutinised. A performance management approach to supervision is not beneficial for staff morale and performance, as practitioners who experience supervision as a monitoring exercise feel unsupported and frustrated (Newcombe, 2022). At the present time, SEEDS2 and the RPSS have attempted to disperse these conflicts. Both frameworks have formalised reflective supervision, observations of practice and professional development as key responsibilities for sentence management SPOs (Westaby et al, 2021).

The RPSS has been received well by relevant SPOs, as they want to be 'person centred' and improve staff well-being (Westaby et al, 2021: 14). As previously highlighted, however, staff are not experiencing the RPSS as designed (Westaby et al, 2021). This mirrors the conflicts between these expectations of the PS and the needs of its staff, which SPOs have to attempt to balance. The RPSS suggests that SPOs review two cases in supervision, which presumably would enable time for reflective discussion. However, this is at odds with the organisation's expectation that SPOs have management oversight of the full caseload of each practitioner they supervise (Westaby et al, 2021). It seems clear that the sentence management role has too many responsibilities and could be split into two roles, so some SPOs can be practice-focused and others more performance-focused (Ainslie et al, 2022). This could also help reorganise the contested supervision space as, despite its best intentions, the RPSS does not address the tensions inherent within this space.

The RPSS has not addressed the wider context of a managerialist culture and defensive approach to risk management in the Probation Service (Ainslie et al, 2022). It has arguably exacerbated the tensions in positing reflective supervision as both a tool which supports staff and provides quality assurance (Ministry of Justice, 2023). Given the continued difficulties putting the RPSS into practice, Westaby et al (2021) suggested that the framework should review its approach to reflective supervision. This is one solution to implementing reflective supervision which results in continuous professional development for all staff. However, the RPSS cannot affect cultural change without the buy-in of senior leadership to enable a whole systems approach. Thus, senior leadership should be trained in, and undertake, regular reflective supervision with its SPOs. This recommendation is reiterated by the further two barriers explored in this chapter, the next being concerned with SPO's potential biases.

Barrier 2: Senior probation officer bias

For reflective supervision to be effective, staff must feel able to be vulnerable during case discussions. This is necessary for SPOs to support practitioners in identifying and understanding the impact of feelings, assumptions and biases on their decision-making (Morrison, 2007). Building on this, Tuddenham's (2000) concept of reflexivity asks what impact the individual and wider context has on their casework decisions. Thus, it enables practitioners to consider the effect of their organisational culture and on their decision-making. Enabling reflexivity therefore requires SPOs to have the time and ability to 'conduct supervision within a spirit of enquiry' (Tuddenham, 2000: 180). As further explored in the next section of this compendium, critical reflection and reflexivity are paramount to reducing the impact of conscious and unconscious biases in casework practice.

SPO bias has been less widely discussed in the literature, despite this role also requiring interpersonal relationships. Having had experience of casework, SPOs bring their own assumptions and experiences to supervising their staff. Their mood, values and unconscious biases affect the decisions they make. The relationships with their practitioners are also impacted on by power dynamics (Burrell, 2022), given managers can place their staff on performance management and other human resources measures. SPO decision-making is also more acutely affected by the organisational context (Ainslie, 2020), due to their dual role. Yet, the probation strategies and directives explored in this chapter do not consider how SPOs navigate the conscious and unconscious dynamics in the relationships with their practitioners (Revell and Burton, 2016). Organisationally, SPO bias has not been identified as a risk to a reflective culture, or staff morale and retention. In my experience:

> Receiving reflective supervision as an SPO highlight my biases. In one session, I raised that I felt a member of staff was not valuing my time. They were leaving assessments to the last minute and this sometimes meant I had to work late or do some of their work for them. After having a productive discussion with the practitioner about this, I felt frustrated and disappointed when it happened again. In reflective supervision, it became apparent that I was measuring them against my own values and working practices. Rather than consider how I could support them with their own ways of working, I was willing them to be a practitioner in the same way I had been. Without reflective supervision, I would have continued to see their practice as being reflective of their attitude towards me, rather than being personal to them.

This reflection demonstrates the potential impacts of SPO bias and the benefits of SPOs receiving reflective supervision. The relationship between SPO and practitioner is a significant strategic oversight in terms of building a reflective culture, but also management oversight. The formalised arena to seek management oversight, and build interpersonal relationships between SPOs and their staff, is supervision. Ainslie et al (2022) identified that practitioners' perceptions of this relationship as negative can be a barrier to effective supervision. This is understandable, as if a practitioner does not feel comfortable or is concerned that their competence is being evaluated, they are unlikely to be vulnerable (Newcombe, 2022). Thus, it can be assumed that practitioners who feel positive about the relationships with their SPOs seek more frequent management oversight. When SFO reviews highlight important stages of casework supervision where practitioners did not seek management oversight (for example, setting licence conditions), they have not yet considered whether the relationship between SPO and probation officer was a barrier to asking for oversight (HMIP, 2023).

Barrier 3: Emotional labour

These working relationships are one of the SPO responsibilities which have an emotional impact. Thus, well-being is arguably another barrier to the effectiveness of casework supervision. SPO's responsibilities require them to display a range of emotions, which are not always genuine. The resulting emotional labour reflects how staff manage their authentic emotions to attain organisational goals (Hochschild, 1983). Westaby et al's (2022) recent study explored surface and deep acting as two ways in which SPOs manage their emotional displays. The first, surface acting, requires a display of emotions which are not authentic to one's actual feelings (Hochschild, 1983). This is applicable to middle management specifically given the tensions inherent within the dual role. An example of this would be an SPO embedding organisational directives without displaying their true feelings about these, even if they are negative (Westaby et al, 2022).

Regular surface acting is significant because it has an emotional toll (Phillips et al, 2020). Westaby et al (2022) found that when SPOs repress their emotions towards implementing a policy via surface acting, this can result in frustration towards their staff and the organisation. Feelings of frustration and low morale may be part of the reason the number of SPOs leaving the service has recently increased (Webster, 2022). Moreover, surface acting is argued to have a relationship with burnout (Phillips et al, 2020), which is significant to retaining and supporting SPOs. I reflect that:

> Surface acting regularly featured in my discussions about performance management. I felt accountable for any financial losses that might occur from missed targets, despite staff's high workloads. There were times I knew that staff completing multiple risk assessments in a week was not only unfair, but also futile given

that the quality would be insufficient. Despite this, I would try to appear positive and motivational about practitioners' ability to complete their own risk assessments. I was expected to start each morning highlighting staff's targets to them, despite often feeling demotivated about having to chase staff when I knew the pressure they were under. It never felt like there was any alternative to this approach available within a managerialist organisation.

Arguably, there is less emotional toll in deep acting, which is when one tries to align their feelings to others by using their own experiences (Hochschild, 1983). SPOs regularly undertake deep acting because their professional experience provides them with empathy towards the emotional labour of fieldwork (Westaby et al, 2022). This appears to be beneficial, as such emotional labour can actually promote the well-being of their practitioners. However, Westaby et al's (2022) study highlighted the emotional impact of deep acting. Whether this be when SPOs persuade themselves that implementing a directive is justified, or the emotions they take on internally when supporting practitioners with challenging casework, they are still regulating their emotions. An example of this is:

> One staff member's reflective supervision regularly involved reflective casework discussions about a young, suicidal man with multiple disadvantages. In trying to support the practitioner with the resulting emotional toll, I engaged in deep acting to repress my own feelings of worry about both the young man and practitioner's emotional well-being. I would think of this situation outside of work hours and it affected my sleep. Unfortunately, the opportunities to discuss the emotional impact casework supervision was having at this time were limited. We were in the COVID-19 pandemic, so I was no longer receiving reflective supervision.

The two reflective examples highlight the emotional labour involved within the SPO role, specific to reflective supervision.

They illustrate that SPOs may regularly undertake emotional labour for wider reasons than supporting the organisation, including to improve outcomes for people on probation and to emotionally support their staff. Thus, middle management roles require safe spaces to protect their own emotional well-being (Revell and Burton, 2016). Embedding reflective supervision to support SPOs with the emotional labour they experience is one clear solution to supporting their morale and retention rates, given supervision has a positive impact on emotional well-being for both probation officers and SPOs (Webster et al, 2020).

Conclusion

This chapter has demonstrated that reflective supervision is beneficial to both practice and continuous professional development. Supervision also benefits emotional well-being (Webster et al, 2020) and morale (Coley, 2020), which are important focuses for the current Probation Service (Webster, 2022; HMPPS, 2023). However, the integral task of reflective supervision (Ministry of Justice, 2023) is not straightforward to implement. Sentence management SPOs are expected to meet managerialist priorities, monitor performance management and enable a reflective culture. It has been reiterated within this chapter that a whole systems approach to reflective practice and supervision is integral to the RPSS, as the support of senior leadership is necessary to facilitate cultural change.

Positive relationships with staff are also necessary to foster reflective practice, yet the potential impact of SPO bias on this has been overlooked. SPOs have their own assumptions and experiences of practice, so alike practitioners would benefit from reflective supervision. SPOs are expected to be an 'emotional buffer' between practitioners and senior leaders and their dual role can result in emotional labour and burnout (Westaby et al, 2021). There has been a lack of attention paid to this, despite its potential impact on retention. Receiving regular supervision represents a whole systems approach to reflective practice, which could improve the effectiveness of the reflective supervision they deliver, and enhance SPO's emotional well-being. Paying attention to the latter may also address HMIP's (2024) concern about the levels of effective management oversight.

Management oversight is just one of several bureaucratically driven responsibilities for sentence management SPOs. This dual role is negatively affecting SPO's ability to prioritise reflective discussions within the congested supervision space, even with the implementation of SEEDS2 and the RPSS (Westaby et al, 2021). The current HMPPS action plan for the SPO role seeks to provide a single framework for management oversight and enhance training opportunities. It also considers a whole system approach to the implementation of a probation learning culture through the human factors approach (HMPPS, 2024), which is an interesting development. However, this does not address suggestions that the sentence management SPO role needs to be split (Westaby et al, 2021; Ainslie et al, 2022). Arguably, there is still more to be done to support SPOs in fostering reflective practice.

Reflective prompts

- How can I try to balance reflective discussion and the organisation's needs in this supervision session?
- Are there any aspects of this session which I am feeling uncomfortable about, and why?
- To what extent am I feeling confident about this practitioner's professional practice, and why?
- What are the risks of emotional labour (deep and surface acting) in this supervision session?
- What opportunities for reflection can I take after leading this supervision session?

References

Ainslie, S. (2020) 'A time to reflect?', *Probation Quarterly*, 17: 9–12.

Ainslie, S., Fowler, A., Phillips, J. and Westaby, C. (2022) 'A nice idea but ...': Implementing a reflective supervision model in the National Probation Service in England and Wales, *Reflective Practice*, 23(5): 525–538. https://doi.org/10.1080/14623943.2022.2066075.

Beck, U. (1992) *Risk Society Towards a New Modernity*, SAGE.

Beddoe, L. (2010) Surveillance or reflection: Professional supervision in 'the risk society', *British Journal of Social Work*, 40: 1279–1296. https://doi.org/10.1093/bjsw/bcq018.

Burrell, A. (2022) The reflective practitioner in transition: Probation work during reintegration of Probation Services in England and Wales, *Probation Journal*, 69(4): 434–451. https://doi.org/10.1177/02645505221117537

Calder, S. (2024) *Serious Further Offence Reviews: Understanding the Perceptions of Probation Practitioners and Policy Makers*, Master's Thesis, University of Cambridge. Available from: https://www.crim.cam.ac.uk/files/calder_steven.pdf

Coley, D. (2020) Probation staff supervision: Valuing 'me time' within congested spaces, *Probation Journal*, 67(3): 228–245. https://doi.org/10.1177/0264550520926581

Eadie, T., Wilkinson, B. and Cherry, S. (2013) 'Stop a minute': Making a space for thinking in practice, *Probation Journal*, 60(1): 9–23. https://doi.org/10.1177/0264550512470188

Goldhill, R. (2010) Reflective practice and distance learning: Problems and potentials for probation training, *Reflective Practice*, 11(1): 57–70. https://doi.org/10.1080/14623940903500085

Harding, N., Lee, H. and Ford, J. (2014) Who is 'the middle manager', *Human Relations*, 67(10): 1213–1237. https://doi.org/10.1177/0018726713516654

HMIP (HM Inspectorate of Probation) (2021) Caseloads, workloads and staffing levels in probation services. Available from: https://www.justiceinspectorates.gov.uk/hmiprobation/wp-content/uploads/sites/5/2021/03/Caseloads-and-Workloads-RAB-LL-designed-RM-amends-Mar-21.pdf

HMIP (2023) Independent serious further offence review of Jordan McSweeney. Available from: https://www.justiceinspectorates.gov.uk/hmiprobation/wp-content/uploads/sites/5/2023/01/FINAL-JM-report-HMI-Probation.pdf

HMIP (2024) The role of the senior probation officer and management oversight in the probation service. Available from: https://www.justiceinspectorates.gov.uk/hmiprobation/wp-content/uploads/sites/5/2024/01/The-role-of-the-senior-probation-officer-and-management-oversight-in-the-Probation-Service.pdf

HMPPS (HM Prison and Probation Service) (2023) Probation workforce strategy (2023–25). Available from: https://assets.publishing.service.gov.uk/media/63db90938fa8f57fbfff3da2/Probation_Workforce_Strategy__2023-2025_.pdf

HMPPS (2024) A response to: A thematic inspection on the role of the senior probation officer and management oversight in the probation service. Available from: https://www.gov.uk/government/publications/a-thematic-inspection-on-the-role-of-the-senior-probation-officer-management-oversight-in-the-probation-service

Hochschild, A.R. (1983) *The Managed Heart: Commercialization of Human Feeling*, University of California Press.

Ministry of Justice (2023) *Sentence Management and the Community Policy Framework*. Available from: https://assets.publishing.service.gov.uk/media/64f07b539304010013fd9ab7/sentence-management-pf.pdf

Morrison, T. (2007) Emotional intelligence, emotion and social work: Context, characteristics, complications and contribution, *British Journal of Social Work*, 37(2): 245–263. https://doi.org/10.1093/bjsw/bcl016.

Newcombe, M. (2022) Supportive social work supervision as an act of care: A conceptual model, *British Journal of Social Work*, 52: 1070–1088. https://doi.org/10.1093/bjsw/bcab074.

Noble, C. and Irwin, J. (2009) Social work supervision: An exploration of the current challenges in a rapidly changing social, economic and political environment, *Journal of Social Work*, 9(3): 345–358. https://doi.org/10.1177/1468017309334848

Philips, J., Westaby, C. and Fowler, A. (2020) Emotional labour in probation, HMIP. Available from: https://www.justiceinspectorates.gov.uk/hmiprobation/wp-content/uploads/sites/5/2020/04/Emotional-Labour-in-Probation.pdf

Pycroft, A. (2014) Probation practice and creativity in England and Wales: A complex systems analysis, in A. Pycroft and C. Bartollas (eds) *Applying Complexity Theory*, Policy Press, pp 199–220.

Revell, L. and Burton, V. (2016) Supervision and the dynamics of collusion: A rule of optimism?, *British Journal of Social Work*, 46: 1587–1601. https://doi.org/10.1093/bjsw/bcv095.

Rex, S. and Hosking, N. (2013) A collaborative approach to developing probation practice: Skills for effective engagement, development and supervision (SEEDS), *Probation Journal*, 60(3): 332–338. https://doi.org/10.1177/0264550513499002

Robinson, G., Annison, H., Burke, L., Carr, N., Millings, M. and Surridge, E. (2023) Whose confidence? Regional leaders' perspectives on building confidence in a reconfigured Probation Service, *Criminology and Criminal Justice*: 1–20. https://doi.org/10.1177/17488958231218571

Robinson, Z. (2014) *Changing Probation Practice: Frontline Perspectives on a New Model for Supervising Offenders*, PhD Thesis. University of Portsmouth, Available from: https://researchportal.port.ac.uk/files/5623624/Zoe_Robinson_changing_probation_practice_frontline_perspecti.pdf

Ruch, G. (2009) Reflective practice and reflective spaces, in G. Ruch (ed) *Post-qualifying Childcare Social Work: Developing Reflective Practice*, SAGE, pp 19–30.

Sorsby, A., Shapland, J., Farrall, S., McNeill, F., Priede, C. and Robinson, G. (2013) Probation staff views of the Skills for Effective Engagement Development (SEED) Pilot, National Offender Management Service. Available from: https://assets.publishing.service.gov.uk/media/5a7c80e0ed915d48c24

Tidmarsh, M (2024) Legacies of change: Probation staff experiences of the unification of services in England and Wales, *British Journal of Criminology*, 64(2): 468–486. https://doi.org/10.1093/bjc/azad042

Tuddenham, R. (2000) Beyond defensible decision making: Towards reflexive assessment of risk and dangerousness, *Probation Journal*, 47(3): 173–183. https://doi.org/10.1177/026455050004700302

Webster, N., Doggett, L. and Gardner, S. (2020) If you want to change the world you have to start with yourself: The impact of staff reflective practice within the Offender Personality Disorder pathway, *Probation Journal*, 67(3): 283–296. https://doi.org/10.1177/0264550520939180

Webster, R. (2022) Prison and probation officers leaving in droves [blog], 19 August. Available from: https://www.russellwebster.com/prison-and-probation-officers-leaving-in-droves/

Westaby, C., Fowler, A., Phillips, J. and Ainslie, S. (2021) An evaluation of the implementation of reflective practice supervision standards in the national probation service, Sheffield Hallam University. Available from: https://shura.shu.ac.uk/28842/1/SEEDS2%20RPSS%20Report%20Final.pdf

Westaby, C., Phillips, J., Ainslie, S. and Fowler, A. (2022) 'Pushed from above and pushed from below': Emotional labour and dual identities amongst senior probation officers in England and Wales, *European Journal of Probation*, 15(1): 40–59.

6

Thinking about safeguarding

Mike Nash

Those joining the Probation Service will undoubtedly spend time reflecting on their future role and responsibilities. It is highly likely that working with offenders, managing their supervision, assessing and managing the risks they pose, working with them on ways to desist from offending and working closely with partner agencies will feature highly. It is perhaps less likely, at least at the beginning of training, that safeguarding will feature prominently on the list. Safeguarding is a broad term and is one which very much includes child protection and welfare. Some might ask, however, isn't that a role for social services departments? Others, who may have examined a little of probation history before joining, may recall that home secretaries Michael Howard (Conservative) and Jack Straw (Labour) made great efforts in the 1990s to separate probation from any association with social work (including work with children) in their push to create a more controlling and punitive Probation Service (see, for example, Dunbar and Langdon, 1998; Raynor and Vanstone, 2007; Canton and Dominey, 2018). Indeed, a separate organisation, the Children's Family Court Advisory and Support Service, was established in 2001, very much sending out the message that this type of work was not part of mainstream probation activity. Yet by 2021, a serious further offence case (HMIP, 2022) had seen probation officers accused of 51 failings, many of which directly related to the safeguarding of children and women. In this chapter we will explore the varying degrees of importance attached to this work since the 1990s but at this point would ask trainees and new in post staff to reflect upon the question – do I really have a role with children and families and, if so, what is it?

No one would dispute the role of probation in working with crime and offenders (and victims of course), but it appears at times as if crime against women and children, notably but not exclusively in the domestic context, is somehow seen as outside of mainstream crime, an experience replicated across the police service, courts, prisons and frequently the media. Yet this is a serious crime problem and rightly falls into the domain of probation staff. According to the National Police Chiefs' Council (2024), violence against women and children amounts to 3,000 police recorded crimes each day, making it 20 per cent of all police recorded crime. These figures increased by 37 per cent between 2018 and 2023, with child sexual abuse and exploitation increasing by more than 400 per cent from 2013 to 2022. One in six of all murders recorded in 2022–2023 were related to domestic abuse. With an exceptionally high non-reporting rate of over 75 per cent (National Centre for Domestic Violence, nd), these are very serious crimes hidden from view but are ones which probation officers might come across in their daily practice with offenders. This situation has led the government to declare violence against women and girls as both a national threat and national emergency. Indeed, in line with this terminology, the *Sunday Times* (Wheeler, 2024), reported that the government would adopt counter-terrorism style tactics to monitor the country's 1,000 most dangerous abusers (further discussion later in this chapter). So, in the face of such a serious and dangerous crime problem, why is it that the Probation Service could be accused of 51 failings in the Damian Bendall serious case review noted earlier (HMIP, 2022)? It appears as if safeguarding and crime work receive a differentiated approach or different priorities.

So, what exactly is it that probation officers are meant to be doing that allegedly they are not? Public protection is a core task (Nash, 1996a; 1996b; 2006; Kemshall and Maguire, 2001), but is this automatically thought to include child protection and safeguarding adults? Of course, it should; protecting lives and well-being is a key responsibility of many public servants, but somehow and too often, the lives of women and children are seen as outside of the main public protection brief; it is an 'add on'. In the case of children, child protection concerns those for whom there is a plan in place and safeguarding is for those who may become 'at risk' (Ansbro, 2014). The latter group would include those who may witness domestic abuse or sexual violence, drug or alcohol abuse or other forms of abusive or criminal behaviour. One or many of these behaviours may be present in the families and homes of offenders and therefore bring probation staff into direct contact with protection and safeguarding issues. It goes without saying that undertaking home visits is central to these tasks (Ministry of Justice, 2021). Moreover, it involves a change of mindset, where safeguarding should be core to the work of public protection and therefore of probation officers (Nash and Williams, 2025).

In a way, what has just been described is a form of 'boxing off'. By this we mean that responsibilities or actions are segregated into different boxes, such as, that is not my responsibility, it is theirs, or this is serious but not as serious as that, therefore I will give it less attention. This may sound like a crude distinction but it is something we all do in everyday life. For example, ask yourself a question about relative harms and risks. If you were preparing a report on a man accused of violently assaulting his wife and another accused of violently assaulting a woman unknown to him, would you regard one as more serious than the other? Why might this be and in what ways? There is no doubt that this differentiation has been made for years, indeed probably for as long as anyone can remember. Priorities and risks have to some extent been reconfigured over the years and yet, in many ways, nothing has changed at all. A brief delve into history might help explain some of these points.

In the 19th century, there was less worry about violent and sexual offending. There was much more concern with crimes against property and wealth, attacks which were regarded as striking at the very heart of society (Pratt, 1997). Crimes against the person were regarded less seriously; they were seen as having been committed in 'hot blood', a result of human emotions and passions. Human characteristics such as anger, envy, lust and jealousy were felt to be behind most crimes of violence. They were regarded as localised and not presenting a wider threat to the public – importantly, most of these were regarded as unpreventable. Even the notorious murders committed by Jack the Ripper were seen as posing a risk to a 'certain kind' of woman in a specific part of London (Anderson, 1907). His murderous actions were not regarded as a wider threat. Punishments for seriously violent crimes were, on average, consistently less than for property crimes. If we leap forward to the present day, then it is clear that the sentences available for serious violence are extremely punitive and in a number of cases have been steadily becoming longer and longer. Indeed, for a number of offences involving murder, the punishment could not be any longer, with the current expansion in the use of whole life orders becoming mandatory in a number of situations (Ministry of Justice, 2023). Yet, we can consistently see lower sentences and a less hostile public reaction when behaviour with the same outcome, violence, death or rape, arises from what can be described as a relationship, no matter how loose or short-lived it may be. Is it the case then, that in these so-called domestic incidents, we still regard violence as arising from basic human emotions of anger or jealousy or sexual arousal and this is somehow seen as less serious if there is a degree of consent (traditionally regarded as the marriage certificate for example) or relationship? Why is it that a young person leaving a nightclub with a stranger, with whom they have danced or had a drink and is then attacked, has somehow, even in a small way, 'consented' to a sexual encounter by that behaviour? Think back to the public views expressed about Jack the Ripper and ask if it is so different well over a hundred years later.

Indeed, enduring stereotypical attitudes such as this have seen the Sentencing Council (2018) advise that domestic abuse should be punished more severely than non-domestic because it is rarely a one-off incident; it is likely to become increasingly frequent and more serious the longer it continues. Hessick (2007) argues that treating violence within relationships just as seriously as violence between strangers will reinforce the message that non-stranger violence is entirely unacceptable behaviour. Somewhat conversely, Cooney and Burt (2008: 491) argue that 'all else being equal, where a particular crime is frequent, any punishment applied to it is likely to be mild; conversely where a crime is infrequent, its punishment ought to be severe'. Aside from suggestions put forward in this chapter about historic perceptions of domestic related crimes, these authors argue that frequency of offending sees a lower response. This appears to fit the response to domestic abuse in this and many other countries. It is therefore important that probation officers are not sucked into the argument that a narrow domestic context – implying an absence of wider risk – should automatically mean that the crime is both less serious and responded to less seriously. Equally it would be foolish to think that offending in one context cannot be repeated in another, quite different context.

Safeguarding activities may therefore suffer from a range of assumptions leading to non or limited action, not only from criminal justice professionals, but from victims themselves (see Gurm and Marchbank [2020] for a good summary and Hopkins [2023] for a detailed study of victim retraction statements in domestic violence and abuse cases). We have already briefly discussed the notion that criminal justice staff, including probation officers, may be influenced by commonplace assumptions about the severity of domestic cases as compared with stranger assaults, for example. This may be reinforced by lesser sentences being imposed despite guidelines such as those mentioned earlier. There may be an assumption that it is someone else's responsibility and probation officers could be forgiven for thinking this given the brief history already outlined. It may also be easier to think about direct and obvious risks related to specific criminal behaviours but perhaps less obviously about the referred impact of any abusive behaviour on children in the home. For example, if you were visiting the home of an offender charged with an assault on another man in a public place, would your initial thoughts be concerned with any risks to children? Would officers think about harmful behaviour to the wife or partner as well and whether that violence might be witnessed by children – or indeed they become a victim of it? Of course, it goes without saying that staff should not focus solely on the instant offence, but on previous offences and behaviours and the context in which they occurred. It is also very important to consider if the instant behaviour is transferable to other victim types, different genders or ages. A personal reflection of the author might illustrate the point. Both of the following cases were of prisoners serving life sentences.

Case 1

The prisoner was serving a life sentence for the rape and murder of a young woman. The perpetrator was in his early 20s at the time. He had for some time observed the victim walking her dog near his home. He plotted her walking times and killed her when the area was quiet. In assessing this man's risk of committing a further serious offence, however, something got in the way. This was the fact that during the hours of darkness, he had broken into a mortuary where he worked and had sex with the corpses of two elderly people. He was charged with two counts of necrophilia. For staff assessing this prisoner it appeared as if the necrophilia charges took precedence over the murder. It was such an unusual and for many people bizarre and awful crime that it served to define him. In other words, many professionals working with him appeared to struggle with their own repugnance over the necrophilia with less attention paid to the reasons for committing the murders. These were of course many, but in this case, the prisoner was the younger brother of a brilliant musician and was always in his shadow, his brother being his parents' favourite. He struggled with severe jealousy and a need to prove himself; he had a very poor self-image. What has this to do with safeguarding, readers may ask? Well, of course, work with this prisoner should very much have been about protecting possible future victims. The 'other' matter however got in the way of a clear focus on the murder and the reasons for it. It is not unusual for professionals to be sucked into an alternative narrative, or indeed false trails laid by the offender. Case 2 offers an example of this.

Case 2

This might be regarded as a less complicated example than the previous case, reflecting a period in time where this was viewed as a less serious crime. A middle-aged man had murdered his wife by strangulation, put her body into the boot of his car and buried her body in waste ground. He received a tariff of eight years (think about the message that would send out today!). During his parole assessments in prison he was regarded as a very low risk. In simple terms, he was not regarded as posing a wider risk as his wife was dead and therefore any risk was either non-existent or extremely limited. Indeed, the perception of lower risk was shared by some members of the author's family. When told that he was to work in a lifer's prison they said, in essence, no worries, they're only domestics. Alongside what the author considers to be a very flawed perception of risk, the prisoner worked extremely hard to create an alternative persona. He was helpful on the wing, always making tea for officers, buying biscuits out of his allowance and became a trusted wing orderly. In this scenario, his risk was rarely discussed. It was more the case of *when* not *if* he would be released. He received favourable parole reviews, aided by forming a friendship with a female prison visitor from a local church whom he married just prior to his release. He had been released at his first application. It might be interesting to ask readers what they think happened next – but this may be too obvious. Within months of his release, he strangled his new wife and made to bury her body in waste ground. He put her in the boot of his car and drove towards waste ground to bury her. Fortunately for her, the boot lock was either broken or not fastened correctly. His wife was able to make her escape and he received a second life sentence. In the author's view this case represented a failure of safeguarding. The motivation for his offending, which in subsequent assessments was seen to be pathological jealousy (a condition felt to be impossible to treat [Prins, 1988]) meant that any woman with whom he had a relationship was at very high risk of harm. As he was not assessed in risk terms for his first murder (for the reasons given), it was felt unlikely that there would be a second victim. His well-crafted, nice guy persona and outmoded views of the nature of domestic murder left him free to kill again.

What both of these cases demonstrate is a need to go beyond the obvious, or what might be considered to be staring you in the face. This process has become widely known as displaying professional curiosity. In its latest guidance on Multi Agency Public Protections Arrangements level 1 management, the Ministry of Justice (2024: 10) describes this as 'adopting a healthy scepticism and taking an investigative approach to casework. It involves asking direct questions, active listening and seeking independent verification of the information that is obtained where possible, not making assumptions, further exploration and reflective practice'.

The same document referred to the importance of information-sharing utilising Multi-Agency Risk Assessment Conferences, Multi-Agency Safeguarding Hubs and Victim Services.

Legal responsibilities

Despite what might be described as mixed messaging over child safeguarding and protection for many years, there is a clear, legal duty in this regard. The 2004 Children Act articulated in law, for the first time, the responsibility for the Probation Service in safeguarding children at risk of harm and for promoting the welfare of children (under s47 of the 1989 Children Act). Statutory Guidance from 2007 said that the Probation Service contributes to safeguarding through the management of adult offenders in ways that will reduce the risk of harm they may present to children through skilful assessment, the delivery of well-targeted and quality interventions and risk management planning (Burke and Collett, 2010: 243). A joint Ministry of Justice and Department for Children, Schools and Families document in 2009 demanded that probation officers play a part in the lives of offenders' children. However, an inspection of child protection practice (HMIP, 2014), although identifying some good practice, also found that there were too few home visits, failures to attend child protection conferences and ineffective referral of concerns. Again, we might pause here and ask why these core tasks have not been carried out as well as they should. Can readers identify factors which might get in the way? We have already identified a number of possibilities, but of course time (or a lack of) is very frequently cited as a causal factor why job requirements are not carried out satisfactorily.

It is clear that probation staff need time to do their difficult job successfully and it may just be the case that, at an earlier stage in the organisation's history, more time was available. As a former practitioner the author can confirm that caseloads were very high a number of years ago – so what has changed? Is it the case that offenders and offending has become more serious and dangerous? Somehow this appears to be unlikely. A rape has always been a rape and a murder has only one outcome. Of course, there are elements that are different to earlier times, most notably the ubiquity of the internet and a greater freedom to travel, meaning offenders can be far more mobile than ever before. Yet, fundamentally, offenders are the same. It remains the case that to properly understand the risks they pose they do have to be *known*. This means that there has to be consistent contact, there need to be home visits or prison/hostel visits. They must be understood in the context of their background and circumstances, and their families should be engaged to gain more knowledge and, if possible, involved in supervision. Importantly, information held by partner agencies needs to be obtained, not just previous convictions but also previous allegations and reports of incidents which had not resulted in convictions. Space needs to be created to allow staff to work with their partners to build trust, a necessary requirement for the most effective sharing of information. Co-location developments in areas such as mental health (Skett and Lewis, 2019) and counter-terrorism (Hall, 2020; Wong, 2022) have shown a positive impact on probation officers' confidence and skill sets. Effective safeguarding and public protection require effective multi-agency collaboration; it is an impossible task for any one agency. So how can the situation be improved? Each serious further incident or offence inevitably leads to calls for change and new developments in practice, but how many times can this keep repeating itself? If each new incident leads to fresh calls for change, the inevitable outcome is a service which faces constant upheaval, with new procedures which staff then have to learn rather than having the time to do the job properly. There may be an argument that rather than change what is needed is doing things better in the first place. New staff might like to reflect as they enter the workplace on what might be done more efficiently or, indeed, not done at all. It may be a case that decisions need to be taken over what has to be done now and what can wait. In the field of safeguarding, people's lives may be at risk and this surely takes priority.

Good safeguarding practice?

In a safeguarding overview, HMIP (2023) spoke of the need for probation staff to develop trusted and supportive relationships, suggesting that children needed practitioners to be friendly, flexible, persevering and non-judgemental. Readers might ponder what Michael Howard would have made of these words. Probation's role is the protection of children from harm in all its forms, including harms not yet manifest. This would include the witnessing of domestic violence and abuse, sexual exploitation and bullying, for example, along with alcohol and drug use. It is difficult to see these activities and responsibilities as anything other than protecting the public, a key probation task – so why has it been apparently sidelined for so long? Burke and Collett (2010: 243) had noted 'the correctional drift ... encouraged probation's withdrawal, on a day-to-day basis, from offenders families, their communities and until recently, their partnership arrangements in communities at the local level'. The COVID-19 pandemic has undoubtedly not helped in this regard, but it is likely that this was the direction of travel before the epidemic sent everyone into their homes and behind their computer screens. It is worth briefly examining what HMIP (2023) described as key practice and themes and principles for safeguarding, while asking the question is it so different from what probation officers do in work with offenders on a daily basis? The following points were listed:

- Understand what the child's daily life is like (*it is hard to see how this understanding can be gained unless regular home visits are undertaken*).
- Work with families where their engagement is reluctant and sporadic (*be professional and demonstrate zeal – the latter being a key quality for probation practitioners first identified in 1909*). (Readers might be interested in the qualities said to be necessary for the embryonic Probation Service: 'It is a system in which rules are comparatively unimportant, and that personality is everything. The Probation Officer must be a picked man or woman, endowed not only with intelligence and zeal, but, in a high degree, with sympathy, tact and firmness. On his or her individuality the success or failure of the system depends. Probation is what the officer makes it' [Hanson, 2014].)
- Apply critical thinking and challenge (*a persistent theme in serious further offence inquiry reports*).
- Respond to changing risk and need (*a core quality for probation officers in all their work*).

- Share information in a timely and appropriate way (*blockages to this process were touched on earlier*).
- Recognising the importance of effective organisational leadership and culture (*safeguarding has to be held as a priority by management at all levels*).

It is highly likely that, on a daily basis, probation practitioners encounter a range of factors identified for children at risk: parental mental health, substance abuse, domestic violence, housing security, drugs and alcohol in the neighbourhood, poverty, social isolation and disabilities. Just as with risk of harm assessments, HMIP (2023) note that in safeguarding, the higher the risks and the lower the protective factors, the more likely intervention is required. This sounds very much like basic probation practice, so the question has to be asked, why isn't it being done on a more regular basis in safeguarding contexts?

A better question, however, might be do new in post probation staff *expect* to be involved in safeguarding? Although it is detailed in official documentation as noted earlier, it would appear to have a low profile in recruitment and role expectation literature. For example, the probation officer (band 4) role descriptor mentions managing low to high risk offenders, assessing and managing the risk they pose to the public and victims of crime, and providing high quality advice to courts to inform sentencing decisions (HM Prison and Probation Service, 2022) – there is no mention of safeguarding. At an earlier stage, recruitment agencies also appear to play down or completely omit discussion of safeguarding. Take, for example, this list of responsibilities from a recruitment agency:

> [M]eeting with and supervising offenders, reviewing reports and compiling assessments and liaising with other agencies such as social workers (the nearest perhaps to a safeguarding reference), writing pre-sentence and parole reports, collaboration with other parts of criminal justice, such as courts and prisons, to protect the public, carrying out risk assessments, working with offenders to motivate them towards positive change, working with victims of violent and sexual crime and attending court. (Indeed, 2024)

There is no specific mention of safeguarding here and absolutely no reference to child protection. To refer back to the question posed earlier in this chapter, do new trainees expect to work in a way which protects children? If it is not suggested early in the recruitment process, then the 51 faults from the Bendall review may, at least in part, be more explainable. This situation might be seen as somewhat opposite to that described by Charman (2018) in her research in new entrant police officers. Here she describes initial expectations from new recruits that crime fighting would be a key role for them (86 per cent in agreement at the beginning of their service), while safeguarding began with 17 per cent in agreement, but rose to 85 per cent after four years in post. In other words, safeguarding became the reality of police work but was not the expectation. Probation officers, it seems, have been criticised for something they maybe did not anticipate doing.

Conclusion

We mentioned earlier that the newly elected Labour government have made strong statements about the protection of women (and children) from domestic abuse. The adoption of counter-terror methods of policing against the most prolific and serious domestic abuse offenders sends out a sharp message and underpins the importance given to the task. Information sharing between agencies will undoubtedly be a key feature of this approach. Indeed, in a significant move, it was announced that promotion for police officers would require the completion of compulsory work experience in a child protection or domestic violence unit. This is a bold and encouraging plan. There is no such plan for probation as yet, although it is worth mentioning that for many officers who undertook the earlier social work-based qualification, a placement in child care or social services more generally was a requirement *before* qualification.

Clearly, the Ministry of Justice has had to respond to the findings in the Bendall review and has produced an action plan (HM Prison and Probation Service and Ministry of Justice, 2023) with a number of points targeted at improving safeguarding practice. Among these are a range of new procedures and checks, alongside training and what might be regarded as attempts to change philosophy. However, questions might be raised over the appointment of newly funded civilian staff employed to obtain information from the police in appropriate cases; this approach surely does not encourage the skills of practitioners or improve their ability to communicate with police officers. A similar approach is envisaged for children's services. It is evident from examples already cited in this chapter that a better understanding between agencies, and therefore better communication, arises from closer working and even co-working. The addition of a new civilian layer between these agencies hardly seems to be a good step to encouraging improvements and effective inter-agency working. Readers might wish to consult the action plan to understand how many changes can arise from one case and think about what can happen if there is a similar response to repeated cases. The potential is for a succession of changes, requiring more learning, more administration and more compliance oversight. The prize is finding ways of nipping this recurrent process in the bud. Finally, it is worth commenting on one action point in particular which reflects much of what this chapter has been about. This concerns the requirement for practitioners to undertake a new advanced level child safeguarding course, much of it delivered face-to-face and taking a child-centred approach. Somehow one doubts if this has been heard of in probation circles for decades – not since working with children was said to be nothing to do with probation!

Reflective prompts

- What is the role of the probation practitioner in safeguarding adults and children?
- Consider your experience of working with safeguarding cases; what challenges have you encountered? What has worked well?
- How can reflective practice help you manage the emotions evoked within this type of work?
- How can reflective practice enhance your confidence in working with safeguarding cases?

References

Anderson, R. (1907) *Crime and Criminals*, James Nisbet and Co.

Ansbro, M. (2014) Probation officers and child protection work: What does think family look like in practice?, *Probation Journal*, 61(4): 381–396. doi: https://doi.org/10.1177/0264550514548254

Burke, L. and Collett, C. (2010) People are not things: What New Labour has done to probation, *Probation Journal*, 57(3): 232–249. doi: https://doi.org/10.1177/0264550510373957

Canton, R. and Dominey, J. (2018) *Probation*, Routledge.

Charman, S. (2018) From crime fighting to public protection: The shaping of police officers' sense of role, *Police Foundation, Perspectives on Policing, Paper 3*. Available from: https://www.police-foundation.org.uk/wp-content/uploads/2018/01/perspectives_on_policing_officers_sense_of_role-FINAL.pdf

Cooney, M. and Burt, C.H. (2008) Less crime, more punishment, *American Journal of Sociology*, 114(2): 491–527. doi: https://doi.org/10.1086/592425

Dunbar, I. and Langdon, A. (1998) *Tough Justice: Sentencing and Penal Policies in the 1990s*, Blackstone Press.

Gurm, B. and Marchbank, J. (2020) *'Why Survivors don't Report': Making Sense of a Global Pandemic: Relationship Violence and Working Together towards a Violence Free Society*, KPU Press Books, Simple Publishing.

Hall, J. (2020) *Terrorist Risk Offenders: Independent Review of Statutory Multi-Agency Public Protection Arrangements*, Ministry of Justice.

Hanson, C. (2014) 'A short history of the probation service', *Inside Time*, 1 February. Available from: https://insidetime.org/newsround/a-short-history-of-the-probation-service/#:~:text=The%20probation%20service%20has%20its,who%20came%20before%20the%20courts

Hessick, C.B. (2007) Violence between lovers, strangers and friends, *Washington Law Review*, 85(2): 344–402. Available from: https://openscholarship.wustl.edu/law_lawreview/vol85/iss2/3

HMIP (HM Inspectorate of Probation) (2014) An inspection of the work of probation trusts and youth offending teams to protect children and young people. Available from: https://www.justiceinspectorates.gov.uk/hmiprobation/wp-content/uploads/sites/5/2014/08/Protecting-Children-Thematic-Report1.pdf

HMIP (2022) Independent serious further offence review of Damien Bendall, Ministry of Justice. Available from: www.justiceinspectorates.gov.uk

HMIP (2023) Safeguarding overview. Available from: https://www.justiceinspectorates.gov.uk/hmiprobation/research/the-evidence-base-youth-offending-services/specific-types-of-delivery/safeguarding-overview/

HM Prison and Probation Service (2022) Statutory guidance: Core probation roles and qualifications requirements. Available from: https://www.assets.publishing.service.gov.uk

HM Prison and Probation Service and Ministry of Justice (2023) Damien Bendall independent review action plan. Available from: https://www.gov.uk/government/publications/damien-bendall-independent-review-action-plan

Hopkins, A. (2023) Examining reasons for victim retraction in domestic violence and abuse: A qualitative analysis of police retraction statements in the UK, *The Police Journal: Theory, Practice and Principles*, 97(2). doi: https://doi.org/10.1177/0032258X231159807

Indeed (2024) What does a probation officer do. Available from: uk.indeed.com/career-advice/finding-a-job/what-does-probation-officer-do

Kemshall, H. and Maguire, M. (2001) Public protection, punishment and risk penalty: The multi-agency risk management of sexual and violent offenders, *Punishment and Society*, 3(2): 237–264. doi: https://doi.org/10.1177/14624740122228

Ministry of Justice (2021) Home visits policy framework. Available from: https://www.gov.uk/government/publications/home-visits-policy-framework

Ministry of Justice (2023) Sentencing bill fact sheet. Available from: https://www.gov.uk/government/publications/sentencing-bill-2023/sentencing-bill-factsheet-short-sentences#:~:text=Headline%3A%20The%20Sentencing%20Bill%20(the,are%20locked%20up%20for%20longer

Ministry of Justice (2024) Probation service management of MAPPA level 1 cases: Policy framework. Available from: www.assets.publishing.probation.service.gov.uk

Ministry of Justice and Department Children, Schools and Families (2009) Reduce reoffending, supporting families, creating better futures: A framework for improving the local delivery of support for the families of offenders. Available from: https://dera.ioe.ac.uk/id/eprint/207/7/reducing-reoffending-supporting-families_Redacted.pdf

Nash, M. (1999a) *Police, Probation and Protecting the Public*, Blackstone Press.

Nash, M. (1999b) Enter the polibation officer, *International Journal of Police Science and Management*, 1(4): 360–368. doi: https://doi.org/10.1177/146135557990010040

Nash, M. (2006) *Public Protection and the Criminal Justice Process*, Oxford University Press.

Nash, M. and Williams, A. (2025) *Politics and Public Protection*, Emerald Publishing.

National Centre for Domestic Violence (nd) Domestic abuse statistics UK. Available from: https://www.ncdv.org.uk/domestic-abuse-statistics-uk/#:~:text=It%20is%20estimated%20that%20less,is%20reported%20to%20the%20police

National Police Chiefs' Council (2024) Call to action as VAWG epidemic deepens, 23 July. Available from: www.news.npcc.police.uk

Pratt, J. (1997) *Governing the Dangerous*, Federation Press.

Prins, H. (1988) 'Dangerous clients: Further observations on the limitation of mayhem, *British Journal of Social Work*, 18: 593–609. Available from: http://www.jstor.org/stable/23709038

Raynor, P. and Vanstone, M. (2007) Towards a correctional service, in L. Gelsthorpe and R. Morgan (eds) *Handbook of Probation*, Routledge, pp 51–89.

Sentencing Council (2018) Overarching principles: Domestic abuse. Definitive guidelines. Available from: https://www.sentencingcouncil.org.uk/overarching-guides/magistrates-court/item/domestic-abuse/

Skett, S. and Lewis, C. (2019) Development of the offender disorder pathway: A summary of the underpinning evidence, *Probation Journal*, 66(2): 167–180. doi:https://doi.org/10.1177/0264550519832370

Wheeler, C. (2024) Counterterror plan to monitor domestic abuse, *Sunday Times*, 18 August. Available from: https://www.thetimes.com/uk/politics/article/police-use-counterterrorism-skills-to-tackle-domestic-violence-8qj76wlhm

Wong, J. (2022) Sharing terrorism intelligence: Insights from the UK law enforcement agencies, *Journal of Policing, Intelligence and Counter-Terrorism*, 12(2): 218–228. doi: https://doi.org/10.1080/18335330.2021.2016898

7

A relational role in the prison environment

Lauren Stevens

Prisons adopt a wide range of methods and approaches to rehabilitate offenders for the purposes of reducing reoffending. Rehabilitation in prison is a multifaceted and complex concept which encompasses a focus on facilitating a positive change in individuals and applying a range of treatment programmes and interventions (Klingele, 2019) – alongside the support given from others. The success of rehabilitation and resettlement hinges, in part, on individuals' ability to establish a positive sense of connectedness within a social network. The Ministry of Justice (MoJ) and HM Prison and Probation Service (HMPPS) (2019) advocate that familial support and the preservation of family connections are crucial for the welfare of prisoners, while contributing to successful reintegration back into the community on release from prison.

Imprisonment can cause significant mental health issues and rupture an individual's social ties and family relationships with the 'outside' (Scott and Codd, 2010). Strong family relationships are linked to a decreased risk of self-harm and suicide, as well as increased likelihood of desistence and successful resettlement back into the community (Social Exclusion Unit, 2002). However, maintaining family links has traditionally been treated as an unimportant aspect of prison policy in England and Wales, because the historical idea of isolation and deprivation of liberties were seen as fundamental for punishment (Coyle, 2005). Prison visitations, custodial and non-custodial staff all play a valuable role in the maintenance of family links, reduce stress and anxiety associated with their separation (Dixey and Woodall, 2012), provide support for the family unit (Woodall et al, 2009), enhance the therapeutic relationships between prisoner and staff (Mills, 2005) and provide visits to 'normalise' the prison environment for the purposes of representing the 'outside world' and its associated responsibilities (Dixey and Woodall, 2012).

This chapter examines the vital role played by the relationships and inter-connectedness between prisoners and their families in initiating the rehabilitative journey within the prison environment. The chapter emphasises the indispensable nature of multi-agency working (both in custody and community) in implementing the 'transform through partnerships' strategy to reduce reoffending outcomes. In addition to this, the chapter provides an in-depth reflective analysis of how to navigate the challenges in multi-agency working within the prison setting – and to be applied within the probation context.

Relationships, desistance and the prison environment
Family relationships and desistance

Familial relationships are a significant source of support for prisoners during imprisonment and in promoting desistance efforts in preparation for resettlement (Kazemian, 2019). However, imprisonment can also be the cause of their deterioration, especially for those serving long sentences (Bales and Mears, 2008). There is a plethora of research that evidences the negative impact of imprisonment on all areas of social bonds, including those in the context of family, work, school and the local community (National Research Council, 2014). Although one of the 'pains of imprisonment' is intended to be the 'deprivation of liberties' – or more appropriately phrased – being 'cut-off' from family as part of the offender's punishment (Sykes, 1958: 65), the consequences are arguably extended to the family who suffer loss and are punished socially, psychologically, emotionally and financially, alongside the prisoner (Codd, 2008). However, the 'Pathways to Resettlement' – approaches to successful offender management and the reduction of recidivism – incorporates the importance of maintaining family relationships as a useful mechanism for the Prison Service to be able to encourage behavioural change at the start of their desistance journey, which highlights the significance of visitation (National Offender Management Service, 2015).

The desistance journey is a complex and multifaceted process that requires support from multiple sources over an extended period (Fortune et al, 2012). Strong and consistent familial relationships are one of the most influential factors in the transformative journey, providing emotional support, fostering a sense of belonging and assisting in facilitating the conditions for successful rehabilitation (Mills, 2005; Scott and Codd, 2010). Research supports that identity theories of desistance and the 'hook for change' is strengthened by the family during a prisoner's transition from prison to the community (Maruna, 2001; Giodano et al, 2002).

The significance of social bonds in serving as a source of social control for desistance is commonly asserted (see Bersani and Doherty, 2018; Laub et al, 2018). Social bond theory claims that the strength of an individual's bond to society plays a crucial role in determining their likelihood of engaging in criminal behaviour (Hirschi, 1969). Social bond theory suggests that family ties, employment and education programmes (particularly during early adulthood) can explain positive changes in criminal behaviour, through the process of 'maturing' (Maruna, 2001; McNeill, 2006). However, desistance theorists and prisons have been criticised for using families only as a resource to reduce reoffending – rather than providing due care and support as the priority (Codd, 2008). This reinforces the need for a multi-agency approach to criminal justice as it demonstrates the different roles, responsibilities and objectives vital to achieving the purposes of the prison environment.

Multi-agency working and third sector partners

Multi-agency working is a collaboration involving the coordination of different agencies and organisations to collectively assist individuals – for the purposes of addressing their criminogenic needs and promoting desistance from crime (Hilder and Kemshall,

2013). The key principles of multi-agency working are reliant upon different agencies pursuing the core attributes of effective practice in partnerships. These attributes are: (1) establishing a clear purpose and achievable outcomes; (2) being committed to achieving these outcomes; (3) being clear about the roles and responsibilities; (4) coordination; (5) modelling professional curiosity; (6) effective communication; and (7) fostering positive relationships between professionals and individuals (Criminal Justice Inspectorates, 2023). Multi-agency working within the criminal justice system is an approach to offender supervision and management that requires different agencies to work collaboratively to achieve a shared purpose – that of reducing reoffending (Hilder and Kemshall, 2013; Canton and Dominey, 2017). There is a plethora of research addressing the multi-agency approaches with different organisations working with probation and offenders in the community. Multi-agency is integral to the work of probation in the management of risk, responding to criminogenic needs and protecting the public (Kemshall and Wood, 2007) – all of which are most effective using the various expertise and resources of different agencies. However, effective partnerships in prison are equally as integral and foundational as those partnerships in the community setting (Mills et al, 2012).

There is recognition from the MoJ, HMPPS and academics that offending behaviour cannot be effectively addressed by any one individual agency, but rather the effort to reduce reoffending would benefit from collaborative partnerships between the criminal justice system and the third sector (Home Office, 2005). The MoJ and National Offender Management Service stated that: '[t]he third sector has a crucial role to play as advocates of services users and communities, as partners in strategy and service development, and as service providers. We value their role as enablers of effective community engagement, volunteering, and mentoring' (MoJ and NOMS, 2008: 7).

Although policy makers appear to be enthusiastic about the effective partnerships with third sector organisations, there are potential challenges when working in the secure environment of a prison. One such problem is that the priorities and practices of the agencies are likely to differ (Mills et al, 2012), given the dichotomous nature of their being either rehabilitative- or risk- and security-focused. However, charitable volunteers and organisations have traditionally been criticised as being naive 'do-gooders' within the prison setting and may be subject to substantial scepticism by criminal justice staff, either due to fears that these charitable entities could replace paid labour (Neuberger, 2009) or that they would diminish the creative aspects of their work (Bryans et al, 2002). Relationships between prisoners, custodial and non-custodial staff (in both the private and volunteer sectors) are pivotal in laying the foundations for a transformative prison environment (Lewis, 2019). The effectiveness of multi-agency working hinges on the strength of these relationships and being critical of their limitations, as this can offer valuable insight for improving practice in multi-agency collaborations.

Therapeutic relationship

Relationships can be a powerful instrument for invoking change and creating conditions for growth (Copsey, 2011). Creating a prosocial, rehabilitative environment between all parties within prisons fosters the necessary conditions for the prisoner to reconsider their responsibilities (of their own actions and towards their respective families), focus on the rehabilitative process and evaluate their self-identity as part of their desistance journey (Lewis, 2019). A desistance-focused approach which starts in the prison setting assists prisoners to form meaningful therapeutic relationships with practitioners (Ross et al, 2008) – although not all these interactions are easily 'therapeutic' by nature, given the power dynamic between practitioner groups. As the HMPPS *Offender Management in Custody Model* (2019) indicates, the practitioner's role is to establish constructive and motivational relationships with prisoners to support their decisions in making positive choices for their future, taking responsibility and giving them hope. Similarly, establishing a therapeutic relationship is crucial in the community setting between probation officers and individuals on probation. Probation officers utilise this working alliance in a collaborative and motivating approach to establish goals which meet individual needs, maintain boundaries in accordance with licensing conditions, assist with set goals, and encourage a sense of responsibility and change (HM Inspectorate of Probation, 2023). Therefore, the therapeutic relationship is a strong predictor of clinical outcomes and successful desistance for people in the criminal justice system from custody through to probation (Martin et al, 2000).

The dynamic model of therapeutic relationships within the prison setting is a conceptual framework that outlines the evolving and interactive nature between prison institutions and therapeutic entities (usually third parties). This model recognises these relationships are not static; rather, they are subject to continuous change, adaptation and mutual influence (Lewis, 2016). In addition to this, the model highlights the importance of clear and open lines of communication between custodial staff, non-custodial staff and prisoners to ensure effective therapeutic relationships can be established and maintained (Safran and Muran, 2003). In the context of a prison environment, effective communication systems among all staff groups are indicative of a well-operated institution (Coyle, 2002). Information channels play a crucial role in facilitating the exchange of knowledge and managing intricate processes within the prison system (Hancock and Raeside, 2009). It is a common challenge within prison that custodial staff lack communication with third sector organisations about relevant and valuable updates (Mills et al, 2012). This can be a particular issue when changes to regime and security during visitation occur and can consequently affect the smooth running of the prison regime and hinder the positive working relationship external organisations have with the prison (Vangen and Huxham, 2003).

The importance of relationships between different staff groups can be just as complex as prisoner–staff relationships and be detrimental to establishing and maintaining a rehabilitative culture within the prison setting (Lewis, 2019). Inclusion, trust, communication, empowerment and appreciation are all characteristics that are integral to building these relationships and are valuable to maintaining effective multi-agency working (Vangen and Huxham, 2003). A rehabilitative culture is most evident in the interactions between prison staff and those under their care. This foundation provides essential support for additional targeted rehabilitative efforts or initiatives, and when conducted within a rehabilitative environment, such efforts can result in more significant effects (Cullen et al, 2012).

The relationships fostered in the prison environment are an essential factor in establishing a rehabilitative culture, creating an effective multi-agency arrangement between staff groups, and maintaining a functional environment for prisoners and their families to support the desistance journey (Mills et al, 2012). The following section of this chapter seeks to reflect on the concepts that have been addressed in this literature review.

The role of visitor centre staff in promoting relational connections

The author's non-custodial role was as a visitor centre's coordinator for a charity that was commissioned by HMPPS to provide support services to families and prisoners during visitations on a prison site. The visitor centre's role is not limited to just a building, but a mechanism that encourages support for families and should be used to lessen the impact of imprisonment by maintaining family relationships (Maguire et al, 2010). According to Woodall et al (2009) families recognised and valued the four different types of support that visitors' centres provide, such as: *bureaucratic support* where relevant forms are provided for visitation; *functional support* for providing refreshments and shelter; *stress reducing support* through peer encouragement and additional service provision support. The following reflections are on the author's experiences and skills used during their employment to navigate the challenges of a non-custodial staff member working in the prison environment.

Bureaucratic support

Bureaucratic support is a key service provided by the third-party organisation to the families on visitations days. As coordinator, it was my role to provide administrative assistance and knowledge of the prison's complex visiting regulations and rules. These rules quite often caused much anxiety and frustration – especially for first time or non-frequent visitors. When the prison changed its visiting and search procedures, I observed how stressful it was on the families to experience unfamiliar procedures and regulations. One example would be when I supported a young vulnerable adult who was autistic – who had only visited the prison a couple of times over the past year. Visitation was an anxious time for him – especially in relation to locking his items away in a locker and the 'pat-down' searches undertaken before a visit. On one such visit, there was a change of procedure location to an unfamiliar room due to an unforeseen technological failing at the main gate. This situation required my role to be more responsive and adapt to unexpected changes. The change led to the visitor experiencing sensory overload, and rendered them anxious, irritable and finding it difficult to communicate with prison staff. I interceded between the prison officer and visitor in relaying key information about the visitor's additional needs. I provided additional support to both visitor and prison staff in recognising the vulnerabilities and attempted to create a more enabling environment, to allow a smoother time for the visitor to see their loved one and to adhere to the necessary security procedures.

By applying a more inclusive environment and sharing key information with the prison security team, this assisted in making the visitor's time a more enjoyable experience, while demonstrating good practice in multi-agency working. As Mills et al (2011) argue, the focus for either organisation tends to differ – that is, risk-focused custody staff and person-centred third-party staff – so it is essential to find a 'middle-ground' to ensure dignity and respect are upheld towards the visitor and security procedures. When there is not coherence in the approach to visitors, this can affect communication between agencies. In this situation, because of communication shortcomings, the prison did not effectively communicate procedural challenges promptly, leading to limited time to prepare to offer the necessary bureaucratic support, and to ensure vulnerable visitors had a pleasant visit. Additionally, more staff training is required on neurodiversity to ensure awareness of the needs and challenges of visitors. As argued by the Criminal Justice Joint Inspection (2021), there is limited training on effective practice around neurodivergence, and thus custodial staff are often not well-equipped to work effectively with neurodivergent residents in both prison and probation contexts.

The relational barriers between staff groups caused much frustration and were exacerbated by the lack of communication.

It often appeared that the visitor centre was not regarded as a significant department of the prison, but merely as the 'hut outside'. The common challenge in these situations is that the service was rarely informed when the visitation regulations changed. This can become particularly problematic when first-time visitors arrive and ask the centre for information. This demonstrates the difficulties in communication between agencies (custodial and non-custodial staff) and damages the collaborative nature of our professional relationship. In relation to probation settings, it is a common challenge for agencies to fail to communicate necessities to others in partnership – leading to delays, reluctance to share future information, a lack of knowledge on points of contact, and – perhaps most regretfully – a serious further offence (Frost and Lloyd, 2006). To reduce these difficulties, it is important to arrange regular communication with a governor (that is, a Family and Significant Others Lead) overseeing visits to ensure a positive working relationship to limit the communication breakdown.

Functional support

The practical role of the visit centre is to provide warmth, shelter and refreshments prior to visitation, as well as a place of preparation prior to entering the main visit hall. Arguably, the visitor centre was the most 'normalised' aspect of prison life – in terms of how warm and welcoming the service was, and the support provided to the family and prisoner, as a whole unit. The visitor centre was usually at the centre of the pastoral care provided during visitations (Loucks, 2002).

A factor that hinders the collaborative relationship between custodial and non-custodial staff is the fundamental differences in their priorities. Custodial staff were primarily focused on security, facilitating visits within strict rules and regulations, and by comparison, non-custodial staff were prioritising rehabilitation and providing support services. In my experience, while the relevant organisation would provide their functional purpose, they would also lack mutual understanding. It was common to see both custodial and non-custodial staff not understand the roles, responsibilities and expertise of one another. This lack of understanding often led to misconceptions, stereotypes and a lack of trust between the two groups, which would then impede our rehabilitative efforts. For example, it was common for families to be under suspicion of wrongdoing by prison officers – this suspicion would extend to us as non-custodial staff. Our functional support of providing fun activities for the children to do with their 'dad' (the prisoner) was often questioned as beyond what was necessary at the security search. Questions arose as to whether items were permitted in visits, whether members of staff had explicit permission, and our intentions as staff members on how we were using equipment (such as paper and coloured pens). All items and activities were given permission prior to visits and were routinely taken into the visiting area to entertain the younger children. These suspicions and the ensuing delays they caused hindered our ability to perform our function support at times. Because this behaviour would not go unnoticed by the families, it would also impact the prison officers' ability to maintain a good relationship with them.

Upon reflection, the challenges arose when the non-custodial role was viewed and treated as a separate entity within the prison environment. Families would often make the distinction between 'them', the uniformed prison officers, and 'us', the non-custodial staff. This would create a distrustful environment permeated with the negative assumptions families made about prison officers, who were regarded as constant barriers to their family time during visitation. However, the limitation of being openly seen and addressed as different is the relationship the third-party service has with prison staff. It was frequently a challenge to be perceived as an additional security hindrance by prison officers and quite often maintaining a hostile environment at times – or at least a distrustful environment between staff groups. Comparatively, the requirements of attending compulsory supervision meetings and adhering to community penalties under the supervision of probation also creates a barrier to family time. Probation officers can be viewed by families as being more of a hindrance in relation to their perceived role of adhering to 'red-tape', being 'nosy' in home visits, and being perceived as social workers – therefore, giving the wrong impression of their role and responsibilities (Coley and Devitt, 2020).

Stress-reducing support

The role of the visitor centre is an important part of making visitation less stressful and a place of comfort for prisoners' families – particularly for those with young children. Research consistently shows that prisoners who maintain positive relationships with their families are less likely to reoffend upon release. This support system can provide emotional stability, encouragement and a sense of purpose, all of which contribute to successful reintegration into society (Scott and Codd, 2010).

However, challenges can hinder the maintenance of family ties during a person's incarceration. These challenges include the financial costs of transportation and accommodation to the family and visiting prisons can be expensive, especially if the facility is located far from the family's residence; logistical issues in relation to coordinating visits around work, school or other commitments; understanding prison rules and regimes, security procedures and limitations on physical contact (Codd, 2008). In addition to this, the prison atmosphere during visits may be intimidating or uncomfortable for families, thus affecting the quality of the interaction. This may be exacerbated by prison staff who may have challenging attitudes towards visitors, as positive interactions with staff are crucial for fostering a supportive environment. It is beneficial for probation officers to maintain a positive relationship with service users' families as they can act as an extension to probation – assisting in the reinforcement of compliance, and encouraging a collaborative environment built on trust and transparent communication between practitioner, offender and family (Coley and Devitt, 2020).

Reflectively, as a response to the sometimes stressful interactions with prison staff, it was observed how families felt a certain level of relief and trust in the third-party service to support the family unit during visitation – rather than an entity focused on security and control. The literature shows that families are shown the 'humane' side of the prison system (Dixey and Woodall, 2012) – demonstrating consistency with the professional experiences of the author. Centres can be used as the link to help communications between families and the prison due to their non-uniformed 'laid back' attitude (Loucks, 2002). In contrast, the prison's perspective of family visits is usually associated with being a 'nuisance' and a risk to security (Broadhead, 2002) – especially given that prison visits are the most common way of smuggling drugs into the prison (Dixey and Woodall, 2012). The Woolf Report (1991) acknowledged the prison's aims to improve family links, although prisoners' families have reported hostility and negative attitudes from officers, potentially a result of the heightened security demands that cast suspicion upon the families themselves (Codd, 2008).

Upon reflection, I witnessed the continued struggle between maintaining a sense of normalcy, a welcoming supportive environment and ensuring prison security and reducing any risks to that security. It was common to find families more inclined to maintain a positive relationship with external agencies and to use my role to share their frustrations. Although I empathised with their frustrations to reduce stress and animosity, this did create a conflicting environment in my role. Skills in diplomacy and encouraging transparency were an effective approach in ensuring prison regulations and decisions are understood from the family's perspective, but also increased the likelihood of compliance of the rules with a better understanding of prison regulations.

Conclusion

The visitors' centre plays a crucial role in reducing visitation stress for prisoners' families by providing a comforting and normalised environment, as observed through positive feedback, highlighting its multifaceted support, and addressing the challenges of being perceived as a separate entity within the prison environment – my reflections emphasise the importance of fostering positive communication and understanding between families and prison staff. The reflections in this chapter highlight the importance of: (1) the visitor centre as more than a physical space, which serves as a vital mechanism for supporting families and prisons, which is aimed at mitigating the impact of imprisonment during the only 'normalised' family time they have; and (2) procedural challenges, communication gaps, and differing or competing priorities between agencies which can create limitations in how the respective agencies provide effective support.

Reflective prompts

- What is your role in conjunction with the core focus of offender management, and what are similarities and differences with other agencies that you work with?
- What are the 'pinch points' that may challenge the effective communication between agencies you may work with?
- Who are the relevant stakeholders for your offender management services? (Consider the offenders, families and other wider agencies.) What are the strengths and limitations with your relationships with other agencies? And what might underpin this?
- How can you ensure the multi-agency arrangement remains a strength to managing offenders in the context of your role?
- How can you enable transparency of your practice and decision-making to those relevant agencies and stakeholders?

References

Bales, W.D. and Mears, D.P. (2008) Inmate social ties and the transition to society, *Journal of Research in Crime and Delinquency*, 45(3): 287–321. doi: https://doi.org/10.1177/0022427808317574

Bersani, B.E. and Doherty, E.E. (2018) Desistance from offending in the twenty-first century, *Annual Review of Criminology*, 1(1): 311–334. doi: https://doi.org/10.1146/annurev-criminol-032317-092112

Broadhead, J. (2002) Visitors welcome – or are they?, *New Law Journal*, 152(5): 7014–7015.

Bryans, S., Martin, C. and Walker, R. (2002) *Prisons and the Voluntary Sector*, Waterside Press.

Canton, R. and Dominey, J. (2017) *Probation* (2nd edn), Routledge.

Codd, H. (2008) *In the Shadow of Prison: Families, Imprisonment, and Criminal Justice*, Willan Publishing.

Coley, D. and Devitt, K. (2020) The Family Involvement Project: Exploring the relationship between probation and service users' families. Available from: https://interventionsalliance.com/wp-content/uploads/sites/4/2021/07/Family-Involvement-Project-June-2020.pdf

Copsey, M. (2011) The Offender Engagement Programme: An overview from programme director, Martin Copsey. Available from: http://www.essexprobationtrust.org.uk/doc/The_Offender_Engagement_Programme_Overview_July_11.pdf

Coyle, A. (2002) *Managing Prisons in a Time of Change*, International Centre for Prison Studies.

Coyle, A. (2005) *Understanding Prisons: Key Issues in Policy and Practice*, Open University Press.

Criminal Justice Inspectorates (2023) Key principles of effective partnership work. Available from: https://www.justiceinspectorates.gov.uk/hmiprobation/wp-content/uploads/sites/5/2023/01/Principles-of-multi-agency-work.pdf

Criminal Justice Joint Inspection (2021) Neurodiversity in the criminal justice system: A review of evidence. Available from: https://www.justiceinspectorates.gov.uk/cjji/wp-content/uploads/sites/2/2021/07/Neurodiversity-evidence-review-web-2021.pdf

Cullen, F.T., Jonson, C.L. and Eck, J.E. (2012) The accountable prison, *Journal of Contemporary Criminal Justice*, 28(1): 77–95. doi: https://journals.sagepub.com/doi/abs/10.1177/1043986211432202

Dixey, R. and Woodall, J. (2012) The significance of 'the visit' in an English category-B prison: Views from prisoners, prisoners' families and prison staff, *Community, Work and Family*, 15(1): 29–47. doi: https://www.tandfonline.com/doi/abs/10.1080/13668803.2011.580125

Fortune, C.A., Ward, T. and Willis, G.M. (2012) The rehabilitation of offenders: Reducing risk and promoting better lives, *Psychiatry, Psychology and Law*, 19(5): 646–661. doi: https://doi.org/10.1080/13218719.2011.615809

Frost, N. and Lloyd, A. (2006) Implementing multi-disciplinary teamwork in the new child welfare policy environment, *Journal of Integrated Care*, 14(2): 11–17. doi: https://www.emerald.com/insight/content/doi/10.1108/14769018200600013/full/html

Giordano, P.C., Cernkovich, S.A. and Rudolph, J.L. (2002) Gender, crime, and desistance: Toward a theory of cognitive transformation, *American Journal of Sociology*, 107(4): 990–1064. doi: https://doi.org/10.1086/343191

Hancock, P.G. and Raeside, R. (2009) Modelling factors central to recidivism: An investigation of sentence management in the Scottish Prison Service, *The Prison Journal*, 89(1): 99–118. doi: https://doi.org/10.1177/0032885508330445

Hilder, S. and Kemshall, H. (2013) Multi-agency approaches to effective risk management in the community in England and Wales, in L. Craig, L. Dixon and T.A. Gannon (eds) *What Works in Offender Rehabilitation: An Evidence-Based Approach to Assessment and Treatment*, Wiley-Blackwell, pp 436–451.

Hirschi, T. (1969) *Causes of Delinquency*, Routledge.

HM Inspectorate of Probation (2023) The role of engagement for positive outcomes in probation, *Bulletin 2023/05*. Available from: https://www.justiceinspectorates.gov.uk/hmiprobation/wp-content/uploads/sites/5/2023/08/The-role-of-engagement-for-positive-outcomes.pdf

HM Prison and Probation Service (2019) HMPPS offender management in custody model. Available from: https://welcome-hub.hmppsintranet.org.uk/wp-content/uploads/2021/06/OMiC-Male-Closed-Estate-Operating-Model-blueprint-version-2.pdf

Home Office (2005) *Managing Offenders, Reducing Crime: The Role of the Voluntary and Community Sector in the National Offender Management Service*, Home Office.

Kazemian, L. (2019) *Positive Growth and Redemption in Prison: Finding Light Behind Bars and Beyond*, Routledge.

Kemshall, H. and Wood, J. (2007) Beyond public protection: An examination of community protection and public health approaches to high-risk offenders, *Criminology and Criminal Justice*, 7(3): 203–222. doi: https://psycnet.apa.org/doi/10.1177/1748895807078860

Klingele, C. (2019) Measuring crime: From rates of recidivism to markers of desistance, *The Journal of Criminal Law and Criminology*, 109(4): 769–817. doi: https://www.jstor.org/stable/48572943

Laub, J.H., Rowan, Z. and Sampson, R.J. (2018) The age-graded theory of informal social control, in D.P. Farrington, L. Kazemian and A.R. Piquero (eds) *The Oxford Handbook on Developmental and Life-Course Criminology*, Oxford University Press, pp 295–322.

Lewis, S. (2016) *Therapeutic Correctional Relationships: Theory, Research and Practice*, Routledge.

Lewis, S. (2019) Culture club assemble! The powerful role of multi-agent relationships in prison, in A. Pycroft and D Gough (eds) *Multi-Agency Working in Criminal Justice*, Bristol University Press, pp 187–206.

Loucks, N. (2002) *Just Visiting: A Review of the Role of Prison Visitors' Centres*, Prison Reform Trust and Action for Prisoners' Families.

Maguire, M., Grubin, D., Lösel, F. and Raynor, P. (2010) What works and the Correctional Services Accreditation Panel: Taking stock from an inside perspective, *Criminology and Criminal Justice*, 10(1): 37–58. doi: https://pure.southwales.ac.uk/en/publications/what-works-and-the-correctional-services-accreditation-panel-taki

Martin, D.J., Garske, J.P. and Davis, M.K. (2000) Relation of the therapeutic alliance with outcome and other variables: A meta analytic review, *Journal of Consulting and Clinical Psychology*, 68(3): 438–450. doi: https://psycnet.apa.org/doi/10.1037/0022-006X.68.3.438

Maruna, S. (2001) *Making Good: How Ex-Convicts Reform and Rebuild Their Lives*, American Psychological Association.

McNeill, F. (2006) A desistance paradigm for offender management, *Criminology and Criminal Justice*, 6(39): 39–62. doi: https://www.sccjr.ac.uk/wp-content/uploads/2009/01/A_Desistance_Paradigm_for_Offender_Management.pdf

Mills, A. (2005) 'Great expectations?': A review of the role of prisoners' families in England and Wales, *British Criminology Conference 2004*, 7: 1–24. doi: https://www.britsoccrim.org/volume7/001.pdf

Mills, A., Meek, R. and Gojkovic, D. (2011) Exploring the relationship between the voluntary sector and the state in criminal justice, *Voluntary Sector Review*, 2(2): 193–211. doi: https://doi.org/10.1332/204080511X583850

Mills, A., Meek, R. and Gojkovic, D. (2012) Partners, guests or competitors: Relationships between criminal justice and third sector staff in prisons, *Probation Journal*, 59(4): 391–405. doi: https://doi.org/10.1177/0264550512458475

Ministry of Justice and HM Prison and Probation Service (2019) *Strengthening Prisoners Family Ties Policy Framework*. Available from: https://www.gov.uk/government/publications/strengthening-prisoners-family-ties-policy-framework#:~:text=This%20Policy%20Framework%20sets%20out,family%2C%20significant%20others%20and%20friends

MoJ and NOMS (Ministry of Justice and National Offender Management Service) (2008) *Working with the Third Sector to Reduce Re-Offending: Securing Effective Partnerships 2008–2011*, Ministry of Justice.

National Offender Management Service (2015) *Rehabilitation Services Specification Custody*, National Offender Management Services. Available from: http://www.justice.gov.uk/downloads/offenders/psipso/psi20215/psi-04-2015-pi-01-2015-rehabilitation-services-custody.pdf.pdf

National Research Council (2014) *The Growth of Incarceration in the United States: Exploring Causes and Consequences*, The National Academics Press.

Neuberger, B. (2009) *Volunteering Across the Criminal Justice System*, The Cabinet Office. Available from: http://www.oneeastmidlands.org.uk/sites/default/files/library/volunteers%20in%20cjs.pdf

Ross, E.C., Polaschek, D. and Ward, T. (2008) The therapeutic alliance: A theoretical revision for offender rehabilitation, *Aggression and Violent Behaviour*, 13(6): 462–480. Available from: https://www.semanticscholar.org/paper/The-therapeutic-alliance%3A-A-theoretical-revision-Ross-Polaschek/6b12d345217aef9d9981d3e2331fd1e575a21284

Safran, J. and Muran, J. (2003) *Negotiating the Therapeutic Alliance: A Relational Treatment Guide*, Guildford Press.

Scott, D. and Codd, H. (2010) *Controversial Issues in Prison*, Open University Press.

Social Exclusion Unit (2002) *Reducing Reoffending by Ex-prisoners*, Social Exclusion Unit.

Sykes, G.M. (1958) *The Society of Captives: A Study of a Maximum-Security Prison*, Princeton University Press.

Vangen, S. and Huxham, C. (2003) Nurturing collaborative relations: Building trust in organisational collaboration, *Journal of Applied Behavioural Science*, 39(1): 5–31. doi: https://journals.sagepub.com/doi/10.1177/0021886303039001001

Woodall, J., Dixey, R., Green, J. and Newell, C. (2009) Healthier prisons: The role of a prison visitor's centre, *International Journal of Health Promotion and Education*, 47(1): 12–18. doi: https://www.tandfonline.com/doi/abs/10.1080/14635240.2009.10708152

The Woolf Report (1991) A summary of the main findings and recommendations of the inquiry into prison disturbances. Available from: https://prisonreformtrust.org.uk/wp-content/uploads/old_files/Documents/Woolf%20report.pdf

8

Creating space for reflection and connection: learning from the creative arts and the third sector

Jennifer Walmsley and Laura Haggar

Reflective practice is an integral part of probation work (Coley, 2016), with practitioners exploring a range of practical and ethical judgements (Goldhill, 2010). While emotional awareness forms an important part of the reflective process (Goh, 2019) within probation practice, emotional intelligence is required to establish therapeutic relationships between probation officers and people on probation as well as enabling an exploration of uncomfortable emotions and bias (Knight, 2014; Coley, 2016). Therefore, the creation of safe spaces for reflection and reflexivity may assist this process and support practitioner development.

However, it is recognised that probation workers face a range of workplace pressures and challenges that may impact the reflective process. For example, the Probation Service has had a time of considerable change through Transforming Rehabilitation (TR) reforms, organisational restructuring as His Majesty's Prison and Probation Service (HMPPS) and reunification (Tidmarsh, 2020; 2023; Carr, 2023). Organisational changes can affect issues associated with well-being (Treisman, 2018) and workload which can impact upon time and space for reflective practice (Clarke, 2013; Coley, 2016). Furthermore, within probation, organisational changes have impacted on practitioner 'burnout' as staff navigate their emotional responses to support the process of desistance

(Phillips et al, 2020). Probation workforce data (Ministry of Justice, 2024) demonstrates significant staffing gaps to be filled that increase pressures on staff, in addition to pressures of the role itself (Phillips et al, 2016; Tidmarsh, 2020). Therefore, while finding the space and time for reflection could be argued to be of even more importance in the current climate, this can prove difficult regardless of practitioners' recognition of its value.

With the current issues facing probation practitioners showing no sign of relenting, there is an opportunity to explore creative solutions within the workplace that support and empower staff. The National Criminal Justice Arts Alliance (NCJAA) (2024) identifies that arts and creativity in the criminal justice system can support improved well-being and highlight the growing body of evidence that supports the use of the arts within this setting (Lanskey et al, 2024). While much of the academic research pertaining to the arts in criminal justice focuses on service users (Arts Council England, 2018), there is research that provides some promising results around the scope for creativity to promote the professional development of criminal justice practitioners (Cox and Gelthorpe, 2008; Russell, 2022; Lanskey et al, 2024). However, creative interventions for criminal justice staff remain largely under-represented and so this chapter aims to start to bridge the gap, acknowledging the potential that the creative arts can bring to supporting reflective practice.

BearFace Theatre (BFT) is a community interest company that uses applied theatre methods to affect positive social change. Co-founded by Jennifer Walmsley and Kate Hadley, BFT has been designing and developing community-led arts-based activities in Hampshire and surrounding counties since 2012. BFT specialises in working with people affected by the Criminal Justice System (CJS) and aims to produce inclusive and high-quality performance, storytelling and bespoke applied theatre programmes, partnering with a range of statutory and non-statutory organisations. BearFace Theatre is not a performing arts or traditional theatre-based company; it is better described as 'creative action for social change' (Russell, 2022: 1).

In 2017 BFT began working across probation-led women's centres, delivering the 'Creating Change' programme. This programme uses an applied theatre, multi-arts, person-centred approach, aiming to encourage participants to build 'pro-social and strength-based narratives' (Russell, 2022: 1). It is an offence-free and forward-looking programme celebrating female empowerment, agency and self-worth. The work has been independently evaluated and researched since 2018, with positive results noted in relation to service-user experiences and principles of desistance (Russell, 2022). Through the delivery of this eight-session programme BFT have developed their working relationship with probation, creating an opportunity to empower practitioners, and create an innovative way for staff to connect and embrace reflection. This chapter explores these developments and considers the opportunities for creating space for connection and reflection to support the probation workforce, and aid practice with people on probation. Through a reflection on the learning from the use of creative methodologies such as applied theatre, this chapter will argue that reflective practice is essential practice and that it is important to dispel the discomfort that practitioners can face when viewing reflection as a 'luxury we can't afford' (Thompson and Thompson, 2023: 4).

Critical reflection in probation practice

Reflective practice has developed over the last four decades and the emphasis on equipping practitioners with the skills to explore their experiences has been a key feature of professional courses and continuing professional development (Fergusson et al, 2019; Goh, 2019). Kilminster et al (2009: 2) suggest that across a variety of contexts 'practitioners could develop their work by thinking critically about their actions'. Furthermore, in criminal justice professions, where professional judgement decisions are made in challenging situations (Phillips et al, 2016; 2020), reflective practice offers probation staff the ability to reflect on the rationale for their decision-making. In doing so they can consider future development and support subsequent decision-making in the moment via reflection-in-action (Schön, 1991), based on their knowledge of theory and practice (Lyons et al, 2019). Simply experiencing an event is not enough to enable the development of learning (Smart, 2017) so being able to reflect on the event enables the individual to have a sense of agency and promote change for their future development (Leigh, 2016). Reflection also provides practitioners with an outlet to problem-solve situations in a structured way (Malthouse et al, 2015) and avoid the pitfalls of rumination (Smart, 2017).

However, despite the benefits of reflection, there are a number of issues facing probation practitioners that are potential barriers to engagement. For example, making time for reflection can be difficult when there are significant workload and staffing pressures, with real risks of burnout occurring. Against a backdrop of a target-driven culture, high workloads and staff fear of scrutiny when things go wrong (Phillips et al, 2020), it can be easy to see how creating space for reflection can be difficult for probation practitioners.

A further consideration is the extent to which reflective practice can be seen as an insular process. Smart (2017) suggests that even when practitioners are engaged with the process of reflection when this is completed in isolation this can limit reflective outcomes to the extent of their own views and knowledge. Previous research has suggested that reflective seminar groups hold some potential for trainee officers (Goldhill, 2010) with similar findings for promoting reflective learning and identity development for law students (Darrow-Kleinhaus, 2012). This suggests that creating a space for reflective practice could be beneficial for probation practitioners. However, the importance of this being a 'safe' space to explore challenges cannot be understated.

Safety is a core value of trauma-informed practice; along with trust, choice, collaboration, and empowerment (Covington, 2014). Trauma-informed practice has seen increased attention when applied to people on probation (Covington, 2014; 2022); training Probation Officers (see Chapter 16) and within the broader justice system. The need to embed trauma-informed practice into probation to benefit both people on probation and practitioners is highlighted in the literature (Petrillo and Bradley, 2022; Senker et al, 2023). This reflects the experiences of trauma within client groups and staff members, as well as the recognition of vicarious, or secondary, trauma affecting staff and the broader organisation (Treisman, 2018; 2021a). The Culture Health and Wellbeing Alliance (CHWA) (nd) recognises that there needs to be an investment in a culture of care across organisations and that this requires a mutual effort from commissioners, funders, partners, participants and practitioners. Furthermore, there is an ever-expanding movement leaning towards a more reflective, relational and trauma-informed approach for practitioners and organisations alike who are working in trauma-saturated environments (Lewis, 2016; Taylor, 2019; Treisman, 2021a; Burman et al, 2024).

Promoting trauma-informed organisations can have a number of positive benefits for staff such as increasing empowerment, wellbeing and a sense of agency (Treisman, 2018; 2021a). The importance of creating spaces for reflective practice can be seen within research conducted by Burman et al (2024: 80) who highlight that 'being trauma-informed needs to extend to the care of staff', arguing that reflective practice gave staff the space to explore their emotions surrounding their experiences when in 'safe' and supportive environments.

While the work of BFT initially started with programmes for service users, the recognition of the need to support the professionals in the sectors they work in has become a BFT priority. In a bid to foster more ethically robust and stronger connections for effective working practices, BFT aims to build creative spaces for practitioners to come together to share their stories and collectively engage in open dialogue about what positive change looks like for them. The next section will explore the benefits of applied theatre and creative practice further, reflecting on the experiences of BFT co-founder Jennifer, as she has applied this learning to criminal justice work and probation.

Applied theatre and creative practice

As an applied theatre practitioner with over a decade of experience working with people affected by the criminal justice system, reflective practice is essential to the core ethics of my profession as well as my own mental health. Process-led drama work has been found to enable individuals to make sense of the world and help clarify and integrate learning (Baim et al 2002). Focusing on the intentions and processes of participatory art helps to assess the quality, and gather deeper understanding, of the work more holistically (Matarasso, 2019). The processing happens inside and outside the room, internally and externally, personally and professionally. This is our way of creatively reflecting on our practice, interwoven and embedded throughout the work to help support our continued learning and development as practitioners.

Having space to connect and reflect with others in our 'work-life community' is core to the BFT process, ensuring we keep communication open. This helps us as applied theatre facilitators to navigate the tensions felt within the bureaucracy of the larger organisations we work with. Using spontaneous creative approaches to gain new perspectives on systematic practices is deeply rooted in Moreno's 1930's psychodrama model. Moreno highlights our tendency for habitual thinking leading to autopilot behaviour (see Chapters 1 and 4) which can constrain our ability to act creatively and inhibits innovation (Sherbersky, 2014).

For example, using inspiration from the exercise 'Pulse Train' found in the Geese Theatre Handbook (Baim et al, 2002: 83) we can explore ideas surrounding controlling thoughts and impulsive behaviour while playing with concepts such as reaction vs response. This team activity invites competition and builds up anticipation and adrenaline; participants create an electric current by holding hands and sending a pulse down the line by squeezing their neighbour's hand. The reflection comes through the processing of the game where the practitioner may ask questions such as *'If the pulse is an internal thought or desire what might that thought or desire be for someone?', 'how do people control their impulses?'*. One female probationer related the metaphor of the pulse train to a chain of events representing her shoplifting which she had always deemed impulsive. This exercise led her to recognise that the act of taking the item was not the start of the thought process, rather, this started before she had even left the house. When applied to staff, this same exercise can be used to reflect on barriers to effective communication, for example, reactions to written communication or tone of voice. Through this reflection we were able to develop empathy for each other, taking a trauma-informed approach to exploring the responses of colleagues and interactions with other organisations.

In another exercise we used image theatre within small groups, to represent various keywords, thoughts and feelings. When working with staff groups 'frustration' led to much of the same images; people holding their heads, demonstrating pressure, and being pushed down by the work, the caseload, and the bureaucracy. In sharing with the other groups, an atmosphere of common unity within the space developed, creating a powerful sense of vulnerability, trust and community among us. The power of applied theatre and creative reflection in this way offers space to slow down and dissect these moments in time safely supporting solution-focused thinking.

As creative practitioners, reflective practice serves the important role of injecting fresh perspective into our work or, at the very least, opens up the possibility of responding to familiar situations in new ways (Chesner and Zografou, 2014). By integrating these principles to develop a more 'creative' reflective practice, group members can develop a more flexible, innovative, and responsive approach to problem-solving and personal development (Sherbersky, 2014).

Trauma and the creative arts

> Trauma is about trying to forget, hiding how scared, enraged or helpless you are. Theatre is about finding the truth…This requires pushing through blockages to discover your own truth, exploring and examining your own internal experience. (Van der Kolk, 2014: 335)

In 2021, BFT was awarded the *'Working with Trauma Silver Quality Mark'* from the charity One Small Thing. One Small Thing's aim is to redesign the CJS for women and their children, responding to the need for a better understanding around the effects of trauma (One Small Thing, nd). In maintaining a trauma-informed approach, we recognise that every group dynamic we work with is different despite the commonalities in the aims for delivery (Balfour, 2016) and we try to have as much compassion for ourselves as we do for the people we work with and for.

Having a small staff team affords us many benefits, enabling us to foster the right climate for growth (Lewis, 2016). However, staff retention and sickness is our highest risk and threat to the business if not made a priority. If every 'interaction is an intervention' (Treisman, 2018: 61) our organisation needs to be that 'safe' and supportive environment (Burman et al, 2024). Taking a trauma-informed approach for us means reflecting on the complex nature of the work and regularly checking in with each other in ways that feel right organisationally and individually, this is us 'model[ling] the model' (Treisman, 2018; 2021b: 71). The benefits of which are tangible in all our roles not just as facilitators, giving us the ability to stay activated and able to respond to the complexity of group dynamics with continued sensitivity and respect (Balfour, 2016).

Practical application

Through the implementation of 'Creating Change' across a probation region, BFT has direct experience of the benefits that diverse and innovative provision has for both probation practitioners as well as people on probation. The value of this for practitioners was a recurring theme within the independent evaluations of the programme: 'Staff state that this unique interaction provides an opportunity to gain a deeper understanding of their clients, and in turn enables them to offer better tailored support to service users on their journey towards desistance' (Russell, 2022: 19).

Russell (2020) states that BFT methods foster forward-looking and strength-based narratives among service users and participating staff. By employing applied theatre techniques, BFT creates transformational learning experiences (Russell, 2022; for more on this concept see Chapter 13) and provides opportunities for participants to explore concepts of self and identity (Boal, 2000). This approach positions learners as 'co-creators' of knowledge and places participants at the centre of the learning and creative process (Freire, 1993).

The origins of the work with probation and prisons were focused on addressing a need for an engaging, interactive and creative methodology to address the attitudes, thinking and behaviour of women on probation. However, through our connectedness and inclusion with probation practitioners, we have witnessed mirrored outcomes occurring when working with staff, as indicated in this quote from the evaluation of the programme: 'All staff interviewed explained that participating alongside SU's [service users] had broken down barriers and significantly improved their working relationships outside of the programme. They stated that the bottom up / co-produced methods employed by BFT allowed SU's to view them as "human"' (Russell, 2022: 19).

While the benefits that this creative space brought for both people on probation and staff members could be seen, the challenges to creating spaces for reflection and creativity in a more structured way remained. Paradoxically, the very working environment that requires embedding space to reflect can also undermine the staff's perception and ability to take the time and space to do this. As we have already noted, staff face a wealth of challenges such as high levels of stress, sickness and retention issues that challenge all aspects of the organisation. This also threatens the stability of the teams that support people on probation and can impact the work of partners in the third sector, highlighting the importance of connected and collaborative working (Dominey, 2019).

Working in HMPPS settings, BFT advocates for strong and meaningful collaborations to help develop and strengthen sustainable support networks bringing a richness of knowledge to the programmes. One method of achieving this is the importance we place on staff participation within the groups. Within ethical and professional boundaries, our work offers a range of benefits, including the opportunity to deepen insights for both staff and service users. It is within these moments of collaboration that a sense of equality and empathy is developed through co-production. This particular member of staff attended one of the staff sessions and was at first reluctant to participate: 'I've found it really hard, coz it is completely out of my comfort zone. I have had to make myself take part, because I am the person that sits back in the corner and watches everyone else. But as an experience, I would love to find more like it' (Participating staff member, Russell, 2022: 20). Mirroring behaviours we can observe with people on probation, here we witnessed a lack of confidence and a level of anxiety. Despite this initial barrier to participation, this member of staff went on to support the full programme and has continued to engage as part of a broader women's staff network:

> I wouldn't ask someone to do something that I wasn't willing to do myself. It's the same for work,

home, most things. It helps the women to see me as human, they think the support workers are sorted, but we are just like them, everyone with their own life issues. (Participating staff member, Russell, 2022: 20)

As an organisation, we aim to take a holistic approach attributing equal value and attention to the development of both staff and people on probation. Our positionality within HMPPS allows us the opportunity to champion the workforce and offer a bespoke approach that aims to support the emotional and personal development of staff and people on probation. In autumn 2022, as we emerged from the COVID-19 pandemic and reunification, we were due to start up a new 'Creating Change' group and found ourselves working with teams who had not met beyond email exchange or phone calls. In a bid to get everyone together in the same room face-to-face, we delivered workshops to the now blended staff team. These workshops proved to be successful and not only supported recruitment for the programme, but feedback from attendees reflected stronger working relationships between the referral partners, better communication, and gave us a chance to bond as people beyond our job titles.

Supporting staff well-being and reflection

The need to support female practitioners (Ellis-Devitt, 2020) has become a BFT priority. Emphasising the need for stronger connections and more effective working practices, we continue to build creative spaces for practitioners to come together, share their stories and collectively engage in open dialogue to explore what positive change looks like for them. This has taken a range of forms, through online sessions, face-to-face meetings and a large-scale event that drew together cross-sector agencies. We spent time hearing about each other's roles, exploring how to better work together and using applied theatre and other creative methods as a tool for creative well-being aiming to engage and inspire. There was a real warmth, buzz and enthusiasm in the rooms, despite shared feelings of overwhelm, stress and frustration

Figure 8.1: 'I need' poem developed by staff members

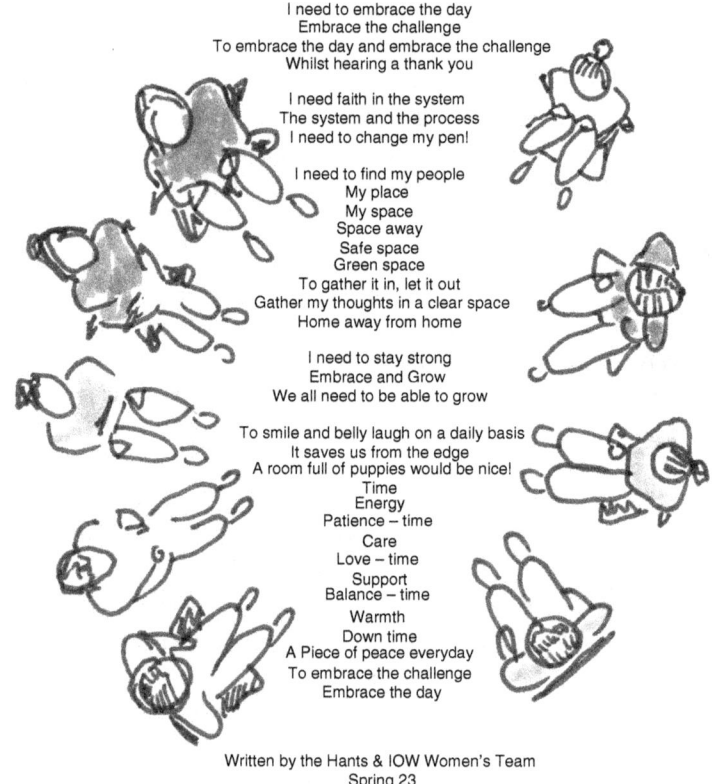

Source: Riddell (2022a)

with the system as a whole. Figure 8.1 provides an example of one such output.

In partnership with the probation women's strategic lead, since this initial meeting we continue to gather online or in person once a month. The group voted for a new group name, 'Create Reflect Unite Women', affectionately known as 'The CRUW'.

Collective purpose and hope for the group

- To bring women together who have the shared and common purpose of supporting people/women in the CJS.
- To develop a more effective and meaningful collaborative community culture.
- To establish and nurture relationships not just networks.
- To create a space for us to reflect on practice and be part of a trauma-informed approach rather than just delivering it to others!

In developing these sessions with practitioners, a number of themes have been identified that influence engagement and space for reflection: permission; the value of relational connection; trauma-informed practice; and creative reflection.

Permission

As noted by Thompson and Thomson (2023), reflection can be seen as something that is somewhat of a luxury for practitioners when faced with the pressures of the role. One of the key similarities I observe working in this sector is that more often than not we very rarely seem to afford ourselves the same compassion as we do for people on probation. An important aspect of CRUW is that this is supported by senior leaders within the probation area. This sets a precedent and also provides 'permission' to staff that taking this time is an important aspect of the role.

The value of relational connections for practitioners

The activities within the network sessions are reflective by nature and create a sense of equality in the room. Creative exercises enable us to collectively confront the realities felt individually and across the sector and these are shared in a way that feels safe, honest, vulnerable and relatable to everyone in the room. Creating reflective spaces opens up further conversation, exploring self-reflection and the reasons for engaging with the group; reinforcing identity and values associated with the role.

Trauma-informed practice

Working in this way has the ability to support a more trauma-informed system by collaboratively creating the space and sharing tools to explore the emotional challenges we face. Members of the group have stressed that these are often not easily communicated through one-to-one supervision and paper-based reporting. Furthermore, trauma-informed practice recognises the personal challenges that practitioners can face, as well as vicarious trauma that can be experienced within the role (Treisman, 2018). Through the establishment of these groups, the organisation can support the emotional well-being of practitioners across the organisation and the wider system.

Creative reflection

Through both the practical experience of delivering creative programmes and the underpinning literature, it can be seen that creativity can bring another dimension to the reflective process, aiding connection and sharing. As anecdotal feedback suggests, there is a real appetite from practitioners to take time to look after themselves, connect and reflect.

Conclusion

Reflective practice is integral to probation work and is a core part of probation training and continued professional development within the role. Reflection on decisions, ethical dilemmas and emotional responses enables reflexivity across all grades within the service. However, a range of barriers to creating space for reflection can be identified within the literature such as workloads and the impact of organisational changes.

The work of the creative arts and the third sector can offer important insights into how this space for reflection can be enabled at a local level, and the examples of the cross-sector work that BFT have developed provide opportunities to overcome barriers and connect with colleagues, enhancing community relationships between providers.

Creating space for reflection and connection

Figure 8.2: 'What I want to see' poem developed by staff members

What I want to see

Look close by
Look left
Look right
Reach out
Warmth for those battling life's curve balls

I want to see
Myself
Unpacked and home
Dogs on long walks
Sunshine, sea & sand
Kindness and warmth
Happiness
Happiness
Growth & happiness
To be strong
Selfless
Honesty
I want to feel the real
Compassion
Peace

I want peace

I want to see glittery landscapes
Tea in my favourite mug
Cold mornings
Sun, sun, sun
Sunshine & cats
The natural beauty of the world
I want to see only fish with heads on!

I want to see people standing up for one another
People standing up for Probation
I want to be given the freedom to see exactly what it can be
I want to see what we can be

Written by the Hants & IOW Women's Team
Spring 23

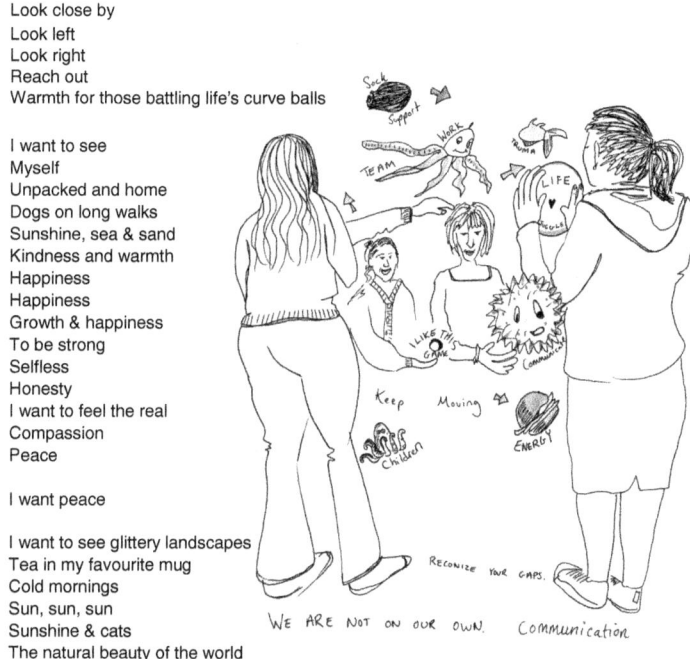

BEAR
FACE

Source: Riddell (2022b)

In addition to providing 'physical' space, whether online or face-to-face for practitioners, the use of applied theatre techniques also presents some useful learning. As can be seen through the examples provided within this chapter, these techniques enable critical thinking and perspective-taking in a non-confrontational and strengths-based way. Engaging in creative activities has demonstrated how practitioners can recalibrate themselves and reinforce the values and identity at the heart of the role.

Being trauma-informed has been at the core of BFT, both in working with service users and in the support of staff members. This runs through the organisation, with all staff actively encouraged to prioritise their emotional well-being and take time and space for themselves. This enables a reflective approach to the work and ensures that staff are modelling the behaviours that they encourage from others. As can be seen within the CRUW network, senior probation staff have been key to enabling and encouraging staff engagement and 'permission' to take time out.

While the CRUW network is still emerging, it has provided an innovative way for staff to engage in reflection, alongside nurturing emotional well-being. The group itself will continue to be developed, according to the needs of its members, promoting creative reflection and learning. The engagement of staff members across the sector demonstrates an appetite for connection, strengthening community ties and reflective space, developing a culture of care, even in difficult environments.

Reflective prompts

- What opportunities for creative reflective practice do you currently have in your office/local area?
- How might you utilise the networks around you to develop opportunities for collaborative working and connection?
- What would a safe space for reflection look like to you? And how might this be achieved in your local area?
- How could senior leadership support the implementation of collaborative and creative reflective spaces?

References

Arts Council England (2018) *Arts and Culture in Health and Wellbeing and in the Criminal Justice System: A Summary of the Evidence*. Available from: https://www.artscouncil.org.uk/arts-and-culture-health-and-wellbeing-and-criminal-justice-system-summary-evidence

Baim, C., Brooke, S. and Mountford, A. (2002) *The Geese Theatre Handbook*, Waterside Press.

Balfour, M. (2016) *The Art of Facilitation: 'Tain't What You Do (It's The Way That You Do It)'*, Griffith University.

Boal, A. (2000) *Theater of the Oppressed*, Pluto Press.

Burman, M., Crowley, A., Miguel, J., Ferreira, G., Gelsthorpe, L. and Glinski, J. (2024) Women working to support women: Psychosocial challenges, final report. Available from: https://www.sccjr.ac.uk/publication/women-working-to-support-women-psychosocial-challenges/

Carr, N. (2023) Should I stay or should I go? What to do about the probation staffing crisis, *Probation Journal*, 70(3): 221–223. doi: https://doi.org/10.1177/02645505231200125

Chesner, A. and Zografou, L. (2014) Philosophical and theoretical underpinnings, in A. Chesner and L. Zografou (eds) *Creative Supervision Across Modalities; Theory and Applications for Therapists, Counsellors and Other Helping Professionals*, Jessica Kingsley, pp 17–41.

Clarke, B. (2013) Practice values versus contract values: The importance of a culture of reflective practice, *British Journal of Community Justice*, 11(2–3): 109–114. Available from: https://www.mmuperu.co.uk/assets/uploads/bjcj_files/BJCJ_11.2-3_Clarke.pdf

Coley, D. (2016) Reflective practice: The cornerstone of what we do, Probation Institute. Available from: http://probation-institute.org/wp-content/uploads/2018/03/D-Coley-GSRA-March-2017.pdf

Covington, S. (2014) Creating gender-responsive and trauma-informed services for women in the justice system, *Magistrate*, 70(5): 2–3.

Covington, S. (2022) Creating a trauma-informed justice system for women, in S.L. Brown and L. Gelsthorpe (eds) *The Wiley Handbook on What Works with Girls and Women in Conflict with the Law: A Critical Review of Theory, Practice, and Policy*, John Wiley & Sons Ltd, pp 172–184.

Cox, A. and Gelsthorpe, L. (2008) Beats & bars: Music in prisons an evaluation, Institute of Criminology, *The Irene Trust*. Available from: https://irenetaylortrust.com/changing-lives/evaluations/BeatsandBars/

The Culture Health and Wellbeing Alliance (nd) Creativity and culture can support mental health if commissioners .... Available from: https://www.culturehealthandwellbeing.org.uk/creativity-and-culture-can-support-mental-health-if-commissioners

Darrow-Kleinhaus, S. (2012) Developing professional identity through reflective practice, *Touro Law Review*, 28, Touro Law Center Legal Studies Research Paper No. 14–19. Available from: https://ssrn.com/abstract=2347675

Dominey, J. (2019) Probation supervision as a network of relationships: Aiming to be thick, not thin, *Probation Journal*, 66(3): 283–302. doi:https://doi.org/10.1177/0264550519863481

Ellis-Devitt, K. (2020) Resilience, wellbeing and sustainability in women-led probation service delivery: Exploring the 'Women's Lead' role. Available from: https://interventionsalliance.com/exploring-the-womens-lead-role/

Fergusson, L., van der Laan, L. and Baker, S. (2019) Reflective practice and work-based research: A description of micro- and macro-reflective cycles, *Reflective Practice*, 20(2): 289–303. doi: https://doi.org/10.1080/14623943.2019.1591945

Freire, P. (1993) *Pedagogy of the Oppressed*, Penguin.

Goh, A. (2019) Rethinking reflective practice in professional lifelong learning using learning metaphors, *Studies in Continuing Education*, 41(1): 1–16. doi: https://doi.org/10.1080/0158037X.2018.1474867

Goldhill, R. (2010) Reflective practice and distance learning: Problems and potentials for probation training, *Reflective Practice*, 11(1): 57–70. https://doi.org/10.1080/14623940903500085

Kilminster, S., Zukas, M., Bradbury, H. and Frost, N. (2009) Introduction and overview, in H. Bradbury, N. Frost, S. Kilminster and M. Zukas (eds) *Beyond Reflective Practice: New Approaches to Professional Lifelong Learning*, Routledge, pp 1–10.

Knight, C. (2014) *Emotional Literacy in Criminal Justice: Professional Practice with Offenders*, Palgrave Macmillan.

Lanskey, C., Doxat-Pratt, S. and Gelsthorpe, L. (2024) An evaluation of the meaning and impact of arts programmes in criminal justice settings, *Inspiring Futures*. Available from: https://artsincriminaljustice.org.uk/our-work/research/inspiring-futures/

Leigh, J. (2016) An embodied perspective on judgements of written reflective practice for professional development in Higher Education, *Reflective Practice*, 17(1): 72–85. doi: https://doi.org/10.1080/14623943.2015.1123688

Lewis, S. (2016) *Therapeutic Correctional Relationships: Theory, Research and Practice*, Routledge.

Lyons, A., Mason, B., Nutt, K. and Keville, S. (2019) Inside it was orange squash concentrate: Trainees' experiences of reflective practice groups within clinical psychology training, *Reflective Practice*, 70(1): 70–84. doi: https://doi.org/10.1080/14623943.2018.1559804

Malthouse, R., Watts, M. and Roffey-Barentsen, J. (2015) Reflective questions, self-questioning and managing professionally situated practice, *Research in Education*, 94: 71–87. doi: https:/doi.org/10.7227/RIE.0024.

Matarasso, F. (2019) *A Restless Art: How Participation Won, and Why it Matters*, Calouste Gulbenkean Foundation.

Ministry of Justice (2024) *His Majesty's Prison and Probation Service Workforce Quarterly: March 2024*. Available from: https://www.gov.uk/government/statistics/hm-prison-and-probation-service-workforce-quarterly-march-2024/hm-prison-and-probation-service-workforce-quarterly-march-2024

National Criminal Justice Arts Alliance (2024) Arts and criminal justice. Available from: https://artsincriminaljustice.org.uk/arts-and-criminal-justice/

One Small Thing (nd) Working with trauma quality mark. Available from: https://onesmallthing.org.uk/quality-mark

Petrillo, M. and Bradley, A. (2022) Working with trauma in adult probation, *HMIP Academic Insights*. Available from: chrome-extension://efaidnbmnnnibpcajpcglclefindmkaj/https://www.justiceinspectorates.gov.uk/hmiprobation/wp-content/uploads/sites/5/2022/03/Working-with-trauma-in-adult-probation.pdf

Phillips, J., Westaby, C. and Fowler, A. (2016) 'It's relentless': The impact of working primarily with high-risk offenders, *Probation Journal*, 63(2): 182–192. doi: https://doi.org/10.1177/0264550516648400

Phillips, J., Westaby, C. and Fowler, A. (2020) Emotional labour in probation, *HMIP Academic Insights*. Available from: https://www.justiceinspectorates.gov.uk/hmiprobation/wp-content/uploads/sites/5/2020/04/Emotional-Labour-in-Probation.pdf

Riddell, H. (2022a) *I Need* [illustration] BearFace Theatre.

Riddell, H. (2022b) *What I Want to See* [illustration] BearFace Theatre.

Russell, A. (2020) *A BearFace Theatre CIC Programme for Hampshire & Isle of Wight Community Rehabilitation Company Evaluation Report 2019/20*. Available from: https://www.hampshireculture.org.uk/sites/default/files/inline-files/Creating%20Change%20Evaluation%20Report%202019%20-%202020_0.pdf

Russell, A. (2022) *Evaluation Report 2022 Creating Change: An Evaluation of the BearFace Theatre CIC Creating Change Programme Working with Female Service Users on Probation and Participating Staff in Cosham & Southampton*. Available from: https://www.google.com/url?q=https://static1.squarespace.com/static/664c868a9c0746509c376db8/t/6687baa80cb01c06ceff1c37/1720171177328/BearFace%2BCreating%2BChange%2B2022%2BEvaluation%2BReport%2B-compressed.pdf&sa=D&source=docs&ust=1730225048176039&usg=AOvVaw1z07RwjUCsb1epleMQAz8H

Schön, D.A. (1991) *The Reflective Practitioner: How Professionals Think in Action*, Routledge.

Senker, S., Eason, A., Pawson, C. and McCartan, K. (2023) Issues, challenges and opportunities for trauma-informed practice, *HMIP Academic Insights*. Available from: https://www.justiceinspectorates.gov.uk/hmiprobation/wp-content/uploads/sites/5/2023/11/Academic-Insights-Senker-et-al-FINAL.pdf

Sherbersky, H. (2014) Integrating creative approaches within family therapy supervision, in A. Chesner and L. Zografou (eds) *Creative Supervision Across Modalities: Theory and Applications for Therapists, Counsellors and Other Helping Professionals*, Jessica Kingsley, pp 89–109.

Smart, F. (2017) Poetic transcription with a twist: An approach to reflective practice through connection, collaboration and community, *Innovations in Education and Teaching International*, 54(2): 152–161. doi: http://dx.doi.org/10.1080/14703297.2016.1258323

Taylor, J. (2019) *The Reflective Journal for Practitioners Working in Abuse and Trauma*, Victim Focus.

Thompson, S. and Thompson, N. (2023) *The Critically Reflective Practitioner* (3rd edn), Bloomsbury.

Tidmarsh, M. (2020) The probation service in England and Wales: A decade of radical change or more of the same?, *European Journal of Probation*, 12(2): 129–146. doi: https://doi.org/10.1177/2066220320947243

Tidmarsh, M. (2023) Legacies of change: Probation staff experiences of the unification of services in England and Wales, *The British Journal of Criminology*, 64(2): 468–486. doi: https://doi.org/10.1093/bjc/azad042

Treisman, K. (2018) *Becoming a More Culturally, Adversity, and Trauma-informed, Infused, and Responsive Organisation*, Winston Churchill Memorial Trust.

Treisman, K. (2021a) PSDP–resources for managers of practice supervisors: A spotlight on organisational trauma: The system as 'client', Department for Education. Available from: https://practice-supervisors.rip.org.uk/assets/a-spotlight-on-organisational-trauma-the-system-as-client/

Treisman, K. (2021b) *A Treasure Box for Creating Trauma Informed Organizations*, vol 2, Jessica Kingsley.

Van der Kolk, B. (2014) *The Body Keeps the Score: Mind, Brain and Body in the Transformation of Trauma*, Penguin.

PART III

Reflections on contemporary issues of diversity in probation practice

9

Reflections of racially minoritised staff in the COVID-19 pandemic

Ashlea Swinford

The COVID-19 pandemic reshaped the landscape of many daily practices and in attempting to maintain some element of 'business as usual', the National Probation Service had to adapt swiftly to a delivery model in line with public health guidance. As practitioners transitioned to remote working, the heightened reliance on telephone supervision revealed an array of challenges (Phillips et al, 2021). This chapter seeks to reflect on my own experience as a practitioner in the wake of the global pandemic while considering the intersections between racial inequality, systemic bias and the transformative effects of the Black Lives Matter movement.

The year 2020 not only brought forth complexities of managing a public health crisis but also propelled conversations about structural inequalities, bias and discrimination. Against the backdrop of the Black Lives Matter movement and the tragic death of George Floyd in May 2020, the Probation Service, like many other sectors, became a microcosm reflecting broader societal disparities drawing attention to the disproportionate challenges faced by Black and minority ethnic individuals within the justice system. Then Prime Minister, Boris Johnson, set up a Commission on Racial Inequalities in response to the UK Black Lives Matter protests with a view to conducting a detailed examination of inequality across the country and set out an agenda for change (Walker, 2020). However, when the chair of the Commission concluded, 'we no longer see a Britain where the system is rigged against ethnic minorities' (Sewell et al, in UK Gov, 2021: 8), this led to widespread criticism, with many academics cited in the report claiming that they had been misrepresented (Moudin, 2021).

In the same month, in stark juxtaposition to the conclusions drawn by the Commision, the Race Equality in Probation report revealed alarming statistics underscoring the challenges faced by ethnic minority staff as it highlighted systemic failures to consider potential trauma and exposure to racism (HM Inspectorate of Probation [HMIP], 2021). This chapter will consider the impact of this period and changes in service delivery compounded by the pandemic. Through the lens of linguistic profiling, as conceptualised by Rice (2006), it seeks to provide a framework for reflecting on and understanding the intricacies of racial biases in remote probation practice, as central to the delivery model at the time and which continues to form part of current practice in many areas. Additionally, this chapter recognises the distinctions between linguistic and racial profiling, highlighting the subtle yet profound consequences of making snap judgements about individuals with diverse dialects.

By delving into these issues, this chapter aims not only to raise awareness but also to contribute to the formulation of safe working practices. With a particular emphasis on managing the emotional effects of structural inequality, bias and discrimination, the personal reflections shared in this chapter aspire to prompt debate, conversation and critical consideration of the future of probation practice in England and Wales. As a Black female probation officer in England during the pandemic, I will reflect on how this period influenced my interactions with probation clients, colleagues and the broader organisation, drawing on my personal experiences. There is recognition that the views and experiences shared are my own personal reflections and I do not seek to provide a narrative that speaks for anyone other than myself. It is hoped that those who have similar feelings feel some comfort in knowing that they are not alone and those who have not, take something away from the fact that everyone's pathways are different.

The Exceptional Delivery Model

The Probation Service's Exceptional Delivery Model (EDM) for England and Wales implemented on 24 March 2020, reduced face-to-face contact with people on probation as most staff were directed to work from home (Phillips et al, 2021). A review of the model published by the HMIP in November 2020 found that remote working was somewhat of a double-edged sword. While it brought with it new opportunities to engage, 'home working did not suit everyone' (HMIP, 2020: 4). In the report, reasons for this included 'juggling home schooling, caring for vulnerable relatives, managing complex personal relationships and delivering probation services' (HMIP, 2020: 4). The report goes on to note that 'some were thriving but others' emotional well-being was deteriorating' (HMIP, 2020: 8).

During the pandemic, a number of important skills and competencies remained integral to ensure the aims of the service were still being met, including risk assessments, case management, support for courts with regards sentencing and managing prison releases. Phillips et al (2020) recognised that among the published research on the impact of the pandemic, the relative strengths and weaknesses of remote communication were a recurring theme. Within these discussions, the importance of the staff–client relationship occurred frequently with studies such as Dominey et al's (2021) recognising that remote supervision made it difficult for people to create and nurture those relationships which are routinely seen as critical to good probation practice.

Establishing a therapeutic alliance has been a cornerstone of probation practice underpinning the efficacy of interactions between officers and those they are supervising (Ross et al, 2008). It encompasses a collaborative and trusting relationship that is formed which is considered essential to successful rehabilitation and improving overall criminal justice outcomes (Epperson et al, 2020). As articulated by Andrews and Bonta (2010), a positive therapeutic alliance aids in fostering an environment which is conducive to change, allowing for the open exchange of information and facilitating the development of tailored interventions based on the unique needs and circumstances of the individual.

Nahouli et al (2022) recognised that building a therapeutic alliance may be challenged by the dual role probation officers hold not only in needing to help meet the needs of the person that they are supervising but also bearing the responsibility of carrying out enforcement where it becomes necessary. These dynamics can be further complicated by the intersection of race and gender, adding layers of complexity to the expectations and interactions faced by staff. HM Prison and Probation Service workforce figures for September 2023 show that 75.7 per cent of probation staff identify as female (HMPPS, 2023). This has statistically been the case for nearly 30 years despite the fact that men make up the majority of people on probation (Hill, 2023) (see Chapter 11 for specific discussion in this area). As a female probation officer, it was therefore not surprising when the person sitting opposite me did not appear to immediately share the same characteristics as myself.

Given these disparities, probation officers often find themselves navigating a landscape fraught with preconceived notions and biases. With a disproportionate number of minority ethnic individuals overrepresented in various stages of the justice system, minoritised staff may face unique pressures, as they may be expected to bridge cultural gaps and provide an empathetic understanding that aligns with the experiences of those on probation who share their ethnic background (Wainwright et al, 2024). This added layer of expectation can intensify the already challenging task of balancing support and enforcement.

As of June 2023, 17.7 per cent of staff had declared their ethnicity as minority ethnic (HMPPS, 2023). Research conducted by the charity organisation, User Voice (2023), found that while the proportion of minority ethnic staff was reasonably representative of the racial composition of England and Wales, minority ethnic staff were under-represented in management grades. Evidently, while research in this area is limited, it is undoubtedly significant for an organisation to have a strong, detailed understanding of their workforce. Research tells us that fostering good employee relations and staff well-being is not only good for the individual staff member themselves but also for the organisation (McIntyre, 2021). One such area where this has shown particular importance is in retention (Employee Benefits, 2021). Carr (2023) recognised the staffing crisis that the Probation Service is facing along with many other public sectors. While there have been numerous recruitment campaigns and efforts to expand the training programme for new starters, the number of qualified probation officers has decreased over the past year leaving the issue of staff retention a significant concern (Carr, 2023).

The National Health Service has also experienced significant staffing issues with the Care Quality Commission highlighting that the pandemic had been a precipitating factor in staff's decisions to exit as well as less stressful conditions in other forms of employment (Care Quality Commission, 2022). The Police have faced similar challenges with high rates of resignation coming from Black and minority ethnic and female staff (Charman and Tyson, 2023). While the issue of staff retention is recognised, there is limited research exploring the reasons that staff have voluntarily resigned from probation (Haggar and McDermott, 2023) and even less is known about how those figures look when it comes to those from minority backgrounds. Operating at a level whereby staff are facing turbulence and dealing with high caseloads amidst staff shortages can further create an environment that is not conducive to promoting racial equality (Probation Institute, 2023).

The Black Lives Matter movement was globally amplified by findings that ethnic minority people had also been disproportionately affected by the pandemic (Kirby, 2020). The situation prompted 'The race equality in probation: the experiences of black, Asian and minority ethnic probation service users and staff inspection' (HMIP, 2021). The report was the first of its kind since 2004 and sought to further understand the working environment for minoritised groups. The inspection took place in the autumn of 2020 and highlighted a number of key findings in respect of minority ethnic staff, including concerns about how staff were being treated and their experiences of racial discrimination and bias.

Further reinforcing these concerns, Wainwright et al (2024) highlight the persistent lack of cultural understanding within the Probation Service, arguing that despite decades of anti-racist policies, meaningful change has been limited. Their research emphasises the systemic nature of these issues, situating contemporary probation within the broader structures of a post-colonial society.

While the report acknowledged that in some divisions (now regions), spaces were created for staff to discuss racial inequalities, it emphasised that such approaches were not universally implemented (HMIP, 2021). One key concern highlighted was the failure of managers to engage in discussions with staff members before assigning cases with a racial motivation, neglecting the potential impact on the supervisory working alliance.

Personal reflections

In the height of the pandemic, I qualified. After five years as a probation services officer, I had finally reached the goal of qualified status. What was to be a joyous moment of celebration and graduation was confined to the four corners of my home alongside a caseload shift almost overnight to managing 40+ people on probation with a range of complex, high-risk needs. The newly qualified officer period is routinely described as a state of protection, but as the October 2022 inspection of probation services in one West London Probation Delivery Unit highlighted: '[W]hen cases are allocated ... they were not always allocated to staff who were appropriately qualified and/or experienced. ... NQOs [newly qualified officers] being allocated extremely complex and challenging parole cases, less than six months after qualification', a matter that, from personal experience, was not isolated to this Probation Delivery Unit (HMIP, 2022: 9).

Shortly after my qualification, I found myself supervising a high-risk individual who had just received a short-term custodial sentence for a racially motivated offence. An offence which added to an unenviable list of over 50 prior convictions. With additional needs tied to mental health, they were released into 24-hour supported accommodation and, as part of the EDM model, my responsibility extended to providing additional supervision through telephone sessions. A transition to face-to-face meetings would take place once there had been a lift of nationwide restrictions.

The complex dynamics at the supported accommodation, including incidents involving the public, showcased the delicate balance required in managing risks. What unfolded, however, was a revelation during telephone supervision where a therapeutic alliance seemed established, leading to more frequent interactions. Routinely, staff at the supported accommodation would also contact me to assist them in de-escalating situations as they identified me as the only person the individual would listen to. On the one hand, I felt somewhat pleased to have built an alliance in this way, in the hope that in due course, this would support my efforts to encourage rehabilitation. On the other, the remote nature of our sessions had concealed my identity as a Black officer. While maintaining the therapeutic alliance meant I was able to support risk management and be a welcomed ally for the accommodation staff, I felt a huge conflict in this and apprehensive about the return of face-to-face sessions which would inevitably reveal my identity. I considered the fact that as an involuntary client, this individual should be prepared to work with whomever they had been allocated, respecting the professional and terms of their order (Trotter, 2014). Nevertheless, I could not help but feel vulnerable, grappling with the prospect of facing potential bias upon the revelation of my identity, which threatened my own well-being in the process. My workload capacity left little space for extensive introspection or addressing these concerns, compounding the challenges I faced in navigating this delicate situation. I also harboured a sense of responsibility towards my fellow colleagues, recognising that they too were burdened with increasing caseloads. We often found ourselves pondering the question, 'If I don't take this case, then who will?' Unfortunately, escalating staff shortages only echoed the resounding answer: 'no one'.

Within a matter of minutes into our first face-to-face session, the level of engagement plummeted culminating in a torrent of racial abuse. This case profoundly impacted me, it exemplified the repercussions of inadequate allocation strategies underlining the intricate challenges of navigating racial motivations, mental health complexities, and propensities for being exposed to victimisation in probation work. The racial abuse hurled during the session underscored the emotional toll embedded in the complexities of probation work as well as the consequences of poor case allocation and case management support.

Exploring the impact of racism within the medical profession highlights parallels with the experiences of probation officers. The refusals of care based on the ethnicity of the caregiver resonate with the challenges faced by probation practitioners in an environment where protections against harassment and abuse are crucial, mandated by the Equality Act 2010. However, raising such matters poses challenges for employees, echoing the broader hesitancy observed in various professional settings to report instances of discrimination or harassment (Rhead et al, 2020). Fear of retaliation, concerns about professional repercussions, and a lack of confidence in the effectiveness of reporting mechanisms may further contribute to a culture of silence and under-reporting (Cortina and Magley, 2003). The stigma associated with whistleblowing and the potential impact on career progression further compound these challenges, creating a complex web of barriers to speaking out against discriminatory practices (Miceli and Near, 1985). Therefore, addressing the challenges inherent in reporting racial prejudices within the Probation Service demands a multifaceted approach, encompassing changes in organisational culture, enhanced whistleblower protection, and proactive measures to encourage open dialogue and reporting without fear of reprisal. The pandemic added another layer to these challenges. The shift to remote environments may have impacted the accessibility of managers, potentially hindering the ease with which employees could seek support or report incidents promptly. This change in working dynamics emphasises the need for robust systems that ensure clear communication channels and support structures, especially in situations involving sensitive matters like racial prejudices.

Linguistic profiling and remote working

Further complicating matters are forms of racism, such as linguistic profiling. Instances of being told 'You don't sound Black' reveal deep-seated stereotypes (Kurinec and Weaver, 2021). Studies (Zaami and Madibbo, 2021) have shown that factors like an individual's name and speech patterns may influence outcomes in professional settings, especially as services shift towards remote practices. These challenges deepen the complexities of building therapeutic alliances and establishing professional relationships, necessitating a nuanced understanding of the impact of remote engagement. However, they can also have an impact on wider professional relationships. In considering this, I reflect upon a time I was told by a professional on the telephone whom I had never met, 'Well, you know how Black boys are', with reference to a person I was supervising.

Linguistic profiling and the impact on probation staff in the UK is a largely under-researched area. While the EDM model meant this changed way of working could have exposed staff to a greater risk of this during the pandemic, communication routinely involves contact with others via telephone and may further expose staff to the prospects of this irrespective of the unique set of circumstances presented by COVID-19. The concern with linguistic profiling is the subsequent pressure to sound a particular way and curb accents or dialects to be perceived in a particular manner (Rice, 2006).

In 2021, Equality Matters published an article that stated 'people of colour have always felt pressure to hide their personal identities in professional environments. Now virtual work has complicated code-switching even more' (Ekemezie, 2021). The article explores the consciousness of mannerisms and accents that individuals may adopt in order to be perceived in a particular way. The term 'code-switching' is discussed as a term given to the way in which an individual may change the way they speak, the words they use, their dialect or mannerisms in order to adapt to a certain environment or situation, with this routinely being the case in environments such as work in order to refrain from emphasising or perpetuating negative stereotypes. While not exclusive to marginalised people, the article recognises the effect that systemic racism has on marginalised individuals to seek to 'fit in', before recognising that this kind of behaviour can lead to 'emotional exhaustion and burnout' (Ekemezie, 2021).

On the one hand, changing our language and presentation can demonstrate that we are in tune with a specific environment. Presenting in a professional work meeting would not require the same tone and mannerisms as meeting up with a group of friends, for example. Code-switching is therefore undoubtedly something we all do in our daily lives and with little thought on it. However, research has identified that those from marginalised backgrounds have to do this more often than those who belong to a dominant social group (Baggs, 2018).

As employees sought to adapt to remote working environments during the pandemic, different modes of communication became more pronounced. This swift transition to virtual platforms, where professionals had to navigate a remote platform with its own set of conventions and etiquette, involves not only adapting one's verbal communication but the art of virtual engagement and visual and written cues to maintain clear and efficient engagement. While the home environment may well have been a place where self-expression need not be compromised, the change in communication may have made code-switching more challenging, leading individuals to feel more exposed. Understanding the implications of code-switching and linguistic profiling is essential to dismantling stereotypes and biases that may influence decision-making processes. Individuals should be assessed based on their professional competencies and merits rather than prejudiced assumptions derived from speech patterns or linguistic attributes. By having an awareness of code-switching and mitigating the impact of linguistic profiling, the Probation Service can create an inclusive environment that values diverse communication styles and ensures fair treatment for all individuals, contributing to a more equitable and just criminal justice system.

The experiences discussed underscore the urgent need for comprehensive research exploring the nuanced intersections of race, mental health and victimisation in probation work. The reflections provided offer a poignant portrayal of how the role of probation officers, including their vulnerability to victimisation, can have extensive repercussions. They also shed light on how systemic and societal biases can compound the difficulties confronted by probation officers. Building on this, Wainwright et al (2024) apply Critical Race Theory to argue that racism within probation is not just a matter of individual bias but is embedded in the very structures of the criminal justice system, necessitating a shift in approach from diversity training to structural reform.

Addressing these issues requires a multifaceted approach, encompassing not only policy adjustments but also systemic changes within the criminal justice system. As the Probation Service grapples with these complexities, it becomes imperative to foster an environment where all staff, irrespective of their racial backgrounds, feel supported and valued, contributing effectively to the overarching goals of rehabilitation and justice.

Recognising the need for probation officers to navigate between professional norms and potential biases should be considered as part of ongoing support in the workplace. Linguistic biases, along with promoting open dialogues about code-switching, can enhance the effectiveness of supervision and foster an environment where probation practitioners feel supported in discussing their experiences to improve their position in the workplace among their colleagues and other professionals. This approach not only contributes to staff well-being but also aids in building trust and rapport with people on probation.

Conclusion

The societal aftermath of COVID-19 continues to unfold, and the lessons learned during the pandemic are shaping the future of probation practice. The reunification of the service and the introduction of a new workforce strategy signal a critical juncture for addressing the persistent issues of racial inequality and systemic bias that have long affected minoritised staff. The shift towards hybrid working models, combining remote and in-person supervision, presents both opportunities and challenges that warrant careful consideration.

Reflecting on the findings of the 2021 race equality in probation report and subsequent updates, it is clear that while some progress has been made, significant disparities remain. In 2023, the reinspection found that there was still some dissatisfaction among staff (HMIP, 2023). The latest updates underscore ongoing concerns about the representation and treatment of minority ethnic staff, particularly in leadership roles. 'The reasons why minority probation staff ... are less satisfied than white staff need exploring with them' (HMIP, 2023: 4). The report goes on to highlight that staff continue to provide accounts that they are experiencing 'poor management, discrimination, concerns ignored, and lack of encouragement to progress' (HMIP, 2023: 4).

Some recommendations have been highlighted as being hindered in their progress as a result of the backlog from the pandemic, including many new senior officers not receiving key training in people management, which includes lessons in diversity and inclusion. The knock-on effect is that many staff continue to experience poor management of key issues (HMIP, 2023).

Another area to examine is the increased use of hybrid working, now a staple in many probation areas. Looking ahead, studies should reflect on the long-term effects of COVID-19 and focus on how the EDM model influenced the development of therapeutic alliances, the management of high-risk offenders and the well-being of probation officers. In September 2023, the Chief Inspector of Probation at that time, Justin Russell, identified that remote working was a key factor in poor performance and critical assessments of people on probation. Research on the impact of remote working during the pandemic highlights the complexities of maintaining effective supervision and therapeutic alliances through telephone and virtual contact. The work of Dominey et al (2021) and others has shown that remote supervision can hinder relationship building, a cornerstone of successful probation practice. The emotional labour associated with navigating racial biases and linguistic profiling in a remote context adds another layer of difficulty for minoritised staff. Understanding how these dynamics play out in a hybrid model is essential for developing equitable and effective probation practices and safe work spaces.

The concept of 'safe allocation' and robust support from managers are crucial components of this new hybrid era. Ensuring that cases are assigned with careful consideration of the probation officer's experience and potential vulnerabilities is vital. Moving forward, it is imperative that managers engage in open dialogues with their teams, provide tailored support and foster an environment where staff feel valued and protected. In 2023, the East of England Probation Service became 'the first government body to sign a new charter aimed at combating racism in the public sector' (Unison, 2023). This includes seeking to improve the experiences of Black and minority ethnic staff through championing a racially diverse workforce, implementing anti-racist initiatives and ensuring that staff are engaging in equality training. By signing the Unison's Anti-Racist Charter, they have also held themselves accountable and subject to reviews of their progress in the future, reinforcing their commitment to staff.

By learning from the challenges faced during the pandemic and leveraging new workforce strategies, the Probation Service has the opportunity to create a more just and supportive environment for both staff and those under supervision. This future-focused approach will not only enhance the quality of probation practice but also contribute to broader efforts to achieve racial equality within the justice system.

Reflective prompts

- In what ways can the Probation Service address racial inequalities and support minority staff to create a more inclusive and equitable work environment including the fair and safe allocation of cases?
- With the rise of hybrid working, what role does linguistic profiling play in probation practice, and how can officers mitigate its impact to ensure fair and unbiased interactions with those on probation?
- While the COVID-19 pandemic has catalysed the adoption of hybrid working, what further exploration is needed to understand its lasting implications in probation practice?

References

Andrews, D.A. and Bonta, J. (2010) Rehabilitating criminal justice policy and practice, *Psychology, Public Policy, and Law*, 16(1): 39–55. doi: https://doi.org/10.1037/a0018362

Baggs, M. (2018) Code-switching: How BAME and LGBT people 'blend in', *BBC News Newsbeat*, 26 October. Available from: https://www.bbc.co.uk/news/newsbeat-45978770

Care Quality Commission (2022) *State of Care Report 2021–2022*. Available from: https://www.cqc.org.uk/publication/state-care-202122/workforce

Carr, N. (2023) Probation services in the spotlight, *Probation Journal*, 70(1): 3–5. https://doi.org/10.1177/02645505231163766

Charman, S. and Tyson, J. (2023) Over and out: The damaged and conflicting identities of officers voluntarily resigning from the Police Service, *Policing and Society*, 33(7): 767–783. doi:https://doi.org/10.1080/10439463.2023.2200249

Cortina, L.M. and Magley, V.J. (2003) Raising voice, risking retaliation: Events following interpersonal mistreatment in the workplace, *Journal of Occupational Health Psychology*, 8(4): 247–265. doi: https://doi.org/10.1037/1076-8998.8.4.247

Dominey, J., Coley, D., Devitt, K.E. and Lawrence, J. (2021) Putting a face to a name: Telephone contact as part of a blended approach to probation supervision, *Probation Journal*, 68(1): 394–406. doi: https://doi.org/10.1177/02645505211050870

Ekemezie, C. (2021) Why it's hard for people of colour to be themselves at work, *Equality Matters*, 21 January. Available from: https://www.bbc.com/worklife/article/20210119-why-its-hard-for-people-of-colour-to-be-themselves-at-work

Employee Benefits (2021) The importance of workplace wellbeing on staff retention. Available from: https://employeebenefits.co.uk/the-importance-of-workplace-wellbeing-on-staff-retention

Epperson, M.W., Sawh, L. and Sarantakos, S.P. (2020) Building a therapeutic relationship between probation officers and probationers with serious mental illnesses, *CNS Spectrums*, 25(5): 723–733. doi: https://doi.org/10.1017/s1092852919001871

Haggar, L. and McDermott, M. (2023) The point of no return? Exploring why people leave the Probation Service, *Probation Quarterly*, 28: 45–50. doi: https://doi.org/10.54006/kfgz6850

Hill, A. (2023) More male staff could help with offenders, says England and Wales Chief, *The Guardian*, 4 April. Available from: https://www.theguardian.com/society/2023/apr/04/men-help-offenders-england-wales-probation-kim-thornden-edwards

HMIP (HM Inspectorate of Probation) (2021) Race equality in probation: The experiences of black, Asian and minority ethnic probation service users and staff. Available from: https://www.justiceinspectorates.gov.uk/hmiprobation/inspections/race-equality-in-probation/

HMIP (2022) An inspection of probation services in Hammersmith, Fulham, Chelsea, Kensington & Westminster PDU. Available from: https://hmiprobation.justiceinspectorates.gov.uk/document/an-inspection-of-probation-services-in-hammersmith-fulham-kensington-chelsea-westminster-pdu/

HMIP (2023) Race equality in probation follow-up: A work in progress. Available from: https://www.gov.uk/government/publications/race-equality-in-probation-follow-up-a-work-in-progress

HMPPS (HM Prison and Probation Service) (2023) HM Prison and Probation Service workforce quarterly: June 2023. Available from: https://www.gov.uk/government/collections/national-offender-management-service-workforce-statistics

Kirby, T. (2020) Evidence mounts on the disproportionate effect of COVID-19 on ethnic minorities, *The Lancet Respiratory Medicine*, 8(6): 547–548. doi: https://doi.org/10.1016/S2213-2600(20)30228-9

Kurinec, C.A. and Weaver, C.A. (2021) 'Sounding black': Speech stereotypicality activates racial stereotypes and expectations about appearance, *Frontiers in Psychology*, 12. doi: https://doi.org/10.3389/fpsyg.2021.785283

McIntyre, K. (2021) Why wellbeing in the workplace is so important, *People Management*, 3 November. Available from: https://www.peoplemanagement.co.uk/article/1744109/why-wellbeing-workplace-important

Miceli, M. and Near, J. (1985) Characteristics of organizational climate and perceived wrongdoing associated with whistle-blowing decisions, *Personnel Psychology*, 38: 525–544. doi: https://doi.org/10.1111/j.1744-6570.1985.tb00558.x.

Moudin, A. (2021) Experts cited in No. 10's race report claim they were not properly consulted, *The Guardian*, 1 April. Available from: https://www.theguardian.com/world/2021/apr/01/experts-cited-in-no-10s-race-report-claim-they-were-not-properly-consulted

Nahouli, Z., Mackenzie, J.-M., Aresti, A. and Dando, C. (2022) Rapport building with offenders in probation supervision: The views of English probation practitioners, *Probation Journal*, 70(2): 104–123. doi: https://doi.org/10.1177/02645505221137448

Phillips, J., Albertson, K., Collinson, B. and Fowler, A. (2020) Delivering desistance-focused probation in community hubs: Five key ingredients, *Probation Journal*, 67(3): 264–282. doi: https://doi.org/10.1177/0264550520939176

Phillips, J., Westaby, C., Ainslie, S. and Fowler, A. (2021) 'I don't like this job in my front room': Practising probation in the COVID-19 pandemic, *Probation Journal*, 68(4): 426–443. doi: https://doi.org/10.1177/02645505211050867

Probation Institute (2023) Position paper on race equality, August. Available from: https://static1.squarespace.com/static/5ec3ce97a 1716758c54691b7/t/64e3127976da863ebb4c4efd/1692603002 637/Race+Equality.pdf

Rhead, R., Chui, Z., Bakolis, I., Hazard, B., Harwood, H., MacCrimmon, S., et al (2020) The impact of workplace discrimination and harassment among NHS staff working in London Trusts: Results from the TIDES study, *British Journal of Psychiatry*, 7(1): 1–8. doi: https://doi.org/10.1192/bjo.2020.137

Rice, P. (2006) Linguistic profiling: The sound of your voice may determine if you get that apartment or not, *Washington Post*, 2 February. Available from: https://source.wustl.edu/2006/02/linguistic-profiling-the-sound-of-your-voice-may-determine-if-you-get-that-apartment-or-not/

Ross, E.C., Polascheck, D.L.L. and Ward, T. (2008) The therapeutic alliance: A theoretical revision for offender rehabilitation, *Aggression and Violent Behavior*, 13(6): 462–480. doi: https://doi.org/10.1016/j.avb.2008.07.003

Trotter, C. (2014) *Working with Involuntary Clients: A Guide to Practice* (3rd edn), Routledge. doi: https://doi.org/10.4324/9781315880587

UK Gov (2021) *The Report of the Commission on Race and Ethnic Disparities*. Available from: https://www.gov.uk/government/publications/the-report-of-the-commission-on-race-and-ethnic-disparities

Unison (2023) East of England Probation Service makes commitment to stamp out racism. Available from: https://eastern.unison.org.uk/news/2023/08/east-of-england-probation-service-makes-commitment-to-stamp-out-racism/

User Voice (2023) *The Voice of People on Probation: Race Equality Review Inspection*. Available from: https://www.uservoice.org/wp-content/uploads/2023/05/User-Voice-Race-Equality-Review-Report.pdf

Wainwright, J., Burke, L. and Collett, S. (2024) 'A lack of cultural understanding and sometimes interest': Towards half a century of antiracist policy, practice and strategy within probation, *Probation Journal*, 71(2): 1–23. doi: https://doi.org/10.1177/02645505231213977

Walker, P. (2020) Boris Johnson criticised over 'victimisation' comment as he set up racism inquiry, *The Guardian*, 14 June. Available from: https://www.theguardian.com/world/2020/jun/14/johnson-criticised-over-victimisation-comment-as-he-sets-up-racism-inquiry

Zaami, M. and Madibbo, A. (2021) 'You don't sound black': African immigrant youth experiences of discrimination in the labor market in Calgary, *International Journal of Intercultural Relations*, 83: 128–138. doi: https://doi.org/10.1016/j.ijintrel.2021.06.003

10

Reflections on probation: co-creating the probation experience with Black male service users

Nicole Nyamwiza

There is currently limited empirical evidence exploring effective methods for reducing reoffending among Black, Asian and minority ethnic individuals that are in contact with the Probation Service. The lack of research in this area is concerning, especially considering that one in eight of the 240,000 people managed by the Probation Services are from ethnic minority backgrounds (Ministry of Justice, 2022). That said, the over-representation of Black and minority ethnic groups at every stage of the UK's criminal justice system has been acknowledged (Walker, 2020), therefore, there is a need for further analysis in this area. Ball et al (2022) support this position, arguing that the lack of focus on addressing racial discrimination and improving the prospects of desistance for ethnic minorities on probation is a practical and ethical failure.

As noted by Williams and Durrance (2017), the failures mentioned earlier also affect the public. This is because these failures identified a lack of public awareness of racial discrimination in the criminal justice system and the scarcity of probation interventions designed for people from ethnic minority backgrounds that are on probation. These failures need further scrutiny due to the disconnect between the number of ethnic minority people in the UK and the number of people in our criminal justice system. The over-representation of non-white individuals can be seen throughout all elements of the justice system; from stop and search and arrest rates, to numbers incarcerated (Lammy, 2017; Prison Reform Trust, 2023). With that said, while there is an over-representation of several ethnic groups, this chapter aims to focus on the experience of Black people on probation, specifically Black men, and explore what 'co-creation' can look and feel like for them. As noted by Baines et al (2022), co-creation within public services is best described as the process where service users contribute to implementing and shaping the services that they access, and that affect them. As a result, current research notes that co-creation has become an imperative focus and process within public policy. This chapter will explore how practitioners can develop a co-created approach to support over-represented groups in the Probation Service and act as a navigation tool.

Racial disparity in the criminal justice system

Although Black people are disproportionately affected by criminal justice legislation, there is a focus on Black men because they are primarily over-represented compared to Black women and have been central to the connection between 'deviance and Blackness'. The relationship between deviance and 'Blackness' can be fully understood by exploring the concept of 'Blackness' and its development. Research indicates that the term Blackness was created to describe Black skin and an internal characteristic of the Black group (Hrabvosky, 2013). However, it is widely recognised in literature that there is a wide range of prejudices in society that automatically assume a lower status for Black skin compared to other racial groups (Banaji et al, 2021).

Nevertheless, only a few studies have focused on exploring exactly why Black skin is considered inferior. This is important because we must consider why human beings are humiliated based on their external appearance and skin complexion. There is evidence to suggest that the negative connotation of Black skin and Black people stretch as far back as 1441, when Black skin was regarded as 'damned' and one of the reasons for enslavement (Hrabovsky, 2013: 66).

Considering the experiences of Black men is necessary as studies have identified that successive generations of Black people in the UK have felt over-policed as suspects of crime since the 1950s (Palmer, 2013). The over-policing and sentencing of Black individuals inadvertently cause them to be over-represented within the Probation Service. Data on the number of Black individuals supervised by probation is difficult to obtain, however, His Majesty's Inspectorate of Probation (2023) indicate that 19 per cent of the probation caseload is non-white and from observations in internal inspections, the over-representation is clear. Furthermore, it is already noted by a plethora of studies that there is a distrust of law enforcement officials among Black communities, and this is justified considering the 'turbulent' relationship between ethnic minority groups and law enforcement agencies (Macdonald and Stokes, 2006; Sharp and Atherton, 2007; Whitson, 2012; Shiner et al, 2018; Warde, 2023).

Similarly, it is essential to focus on our criminal justice system, as the over-representation of Black people in it, and the negative connotations attached to it, can lead to an influx of wider issues. For example, engagement with the justice system can lead to difficulties in their education, housing and future employability prospects. This can further impact their general stability and overall well-being and, most importantly, it can impact their perception of self (Nyamwiza, 2022).

Unfortunately, the feelings noted here are reinforced within other areas in society, for example, the criminal justice system, with research noting that Black and ethnic minority people are disproportionately sanctioned (Perea, 2020). Further exploration into this is imperative as such experiences can have profound effects on these individuals' lives and often result in double standards of definition and control, which medicalises criminal behaviour within white ethnic groups and criminalises Blackness. With that said, this chapter does not seek to deny that some individuals within Black communities engage in criminality; instead, this chapter aims to explore their narratives and deconstruct the relationship between deviance and Blackness.

Overall, the concepts explored here demonstrate that there is a clear connection between the notion of deviance, Blackness and criminal behaviours. Positively, this has been considered within research to improve probation practice. Shingler and Pope (2018) completed a rapid evidence assessment that sought to explore the effectiveness of rehabilitation and probation interventions for Black, Asian and other minority ethnic people and identified a need for more evidence to fully understand how practitioners can improve outcomes for people from ethnic minority backgrounds. However, they sought to explore promising approaches to provide the best outcomes for individuals from these groups. For example, ensuring that rehabilitation approaches were culturally sensitive and consistent with service users' cultural norms.

As a probation practitioner, it would be helpful for you to explore your positionality and consider how these interlock with your practice with Black men on probation. While we are in positions to support and care for the well-being and rehabilitation of these individuals, it can be challenging to navigate through this as an agent of law enforcement. This juxtaposes practitioners with the Probation Service, which aims to enable individuals to achieve desistance from crime, with a focus on risk management. However, it is known that the process of achieving desistance can be arduous, especially for those from disadvantaged backgrounds, which is, unfortunately, the reality for many Black men who encounter the criminal justice system.

As a Black woman, I often consider how my proximity to Black men may cause me to believe that I am 'well equipped' to support them or help them navigate complex matters. However, in reality my understanding is limited due to a lack of lived experience of the criminal justice system. While considering and acknowledging this can be daunting, it helps to explore it and approach the issue.

This can be achieved by embedding cultural competency in your practice. Research by Muzychenko (2008) suggests that cultural competence can be identified as the appropriateness and effectiveness of one's behaviour in an alien cultural environment. Further research by Wilson et al (2013: 900) notes that cultural competence is 'the acquisition and maintenance of culture-specific skills' for convenient reasons. Therefore, cultural competence enables practitioners to understand better the unique cultural, social and historical factors that may shape the experiences of Black males within the criminal justice system.

Black men's experience on probation and co-creation

Before exploring what co-creation may look like in practice, it is important to consider the Black experience of probation. It is essential to note that the research discussed throughout this chapter will not be able to conceptualise the experience of all Black service users, but it will provide some general contextual insights that may serve practitioners well. The discussion of probation outcomes and race is not a new phenomenon, as Steinmetz and Henderson (2015) highlight, previous studies have found that the race of an individual on probation is likely to impact their success or rehabilitation prospects.

The findings are concerning because ethnic minority groups are over-represented in the probation system, yet they are more likely to have unsuccessful outcomes. This assertion is supported by recent findings from the Prison Reform Trust (2023), which identified that prison staff underestimated the cultural requirements of Black and ethnic minority groups, as well as Gypsy, Roma and traveller groups. A third of Black prisoners said their ethnicity impacted their rehabilitation and resettlement planning, but this was not taken into consideration by staff members. While this is within a prison context, it may likely be similar in the community.

Similarly, Black men are more likely to 'fail' probation in comparison to their white male counterparts because of rearrest or technical violations (Onifade et al, 2011). This is also likely to be influenced by the fact that Black men are more likely to be considered high-risk in risk assessment than others. These experiences and stigma are likely to impact an individual's experience negatively. The experience of Black people on probation was previously examined by HM Inspectorate of Probation in 2021 and 2023. The findings noted that African/Caribbean people were more likely to receive poorer service outcomes than white people. Further findings indicated that Black people were less likely to receive a comprehensive, unbiased pre-sentence report. This is highly problematic as pre-sentence reports are vital for sentencing and providing the judicial system with contextual information on a person.

Furthermore, Black people on probation were identified as being less likely to benefit from multi-agency engagement and rehabilitative services. However, they were more likely to be subject to enforcement action (Hilder, 2010; Morgan, 2013; Ball et al, 2022; Sirdifield et al, 2024). These findings demonstrate that the Black experience on probation appears to be quite limiting for many service users and ineffective for their rehabilitation. The negative experiences of Black service users also impacted ethnic minority probation staff, who felt isolated and poorly managed, which can suggest insufficient service to Black service users and a disadvantage to Black staff (Morgan, 2013).

My own experience as a probation officer reminds me of the difficulties of managing a majority Black caseload and hearing them recall their negative experiences and feelings of 'injustice'. Current research in this area highlights that 'procedural justice' is needed. As Nelson and Appel (2021) noted, procedural justice can be identified as unbiased, caring, respectful and participative treatment by decision-makers. The theoretical basis of procedural justice is that when people perceive they have been treated according to fair and just processes, they are more likely to engage and comply positively with such authority. As a result, individuals are more likely to have higher levels of engagement and compliance, which may improve their chances of rehabilitation. This is an essential point, as probation practice is centred on rehabilitation. The findings on Black people's experience on probation indicate that the relationship and understanding between a service user and practitioner is integral.

A study by the HM Chief Inspector of Prisons (2022) found that Black men in prison described race discrimination as a persistent factor in their prison experience. For example, it is highlighted that Black prisoners felt that their requests were denied due to their skin colour, or that they experienced racial microaggressions. However, it is noted that white staff in prisons felt that there was truly little racism that occurred or even none. While staff did not mean to undermine how the prisoners reported feeling, it is essential to note that our own experiences or lack of experience with racism and prejudice may limit our understanding of others. This may serve as a barrier to engagement as it may be difficult for staff to recognise that they work within an institutionally racist environment. To overcome this, practitioners can seek to engage in reflective practices to ensure they have an outlet to process their decision-making while at work.

It is essential to consider that the issues examined here can be explored through 'whole systems thinking', which can allow you as a practitioner to understand your Black service users as individuals and consider how other factors related to them influence their experience on probation. This concept can be intricately linked to the whole systems approach, which seeks to provide a better connected criminal justice experience (Pycroft and Bartollas, 2014).

The concept of whole systems thinking can start with the idea of co-created criminal justice provision. According to Loeffler and Bovaird (2019), there has been a recent increase in focus on the role of co-production in public services and among policy makers. Co-creation involves collaborating with stakeholders to help shape the design or delivery of a service or product (Brandsen and Honigh, 2018). This is particularly crucial for our criminal justice provisions, as research indicates that engagement between Black communities and the criminal justice system can be intricate (Lammy, 2017). A key issue related to this is the perceived lack of understanding of service user needs or the limited involvement of service users in developing the resources and interventions used to 'manage' them. This concern was identified decades ago in the Scarman Report (1981, in Scarman and Home Office, 1982), which argued that British criminal justice services were institutionally racist, leading to a lack of trust between law enforcement and Black individuals.

This lack of trust correlates with the findings of the HM Inspectorate of Probation report (Carr, 2022), which highlighted that probation services must show more significant consideration and certainty in their work with Black and minority groups. Therefore, co-creation can be seen as an imperative aspect of achieving this, as Black people are over-represented at every stage of the criminal justice system. Black people are also unfortunately subject to stigmatisation in every stage of their socialisation process, which may make them internalise the public perception of them. This may also impact their ability to engage with practitioners, as they may fear pre-emptive criminalisation within their supervision sessions or risk assessments (Fitzgibbon, 2007).

There has been a surplus of research on co-creation in youth services, as it has been identified that service users are more likely to 'buy-in' or engage with a service they may have influenced. Academic researchers have found the use of 'co-creating' research through participatory action research particularly useful (Pain et al, 2019). Using participatory action research, the community members affected by the research subject are enlisted as co-researchers and are given a chance to develop and address questions. Similarly, this approach should be sought to be used within criminal justice systems in which Black people are overwhelmingly over-represented. However, they have no insight or involvement in creating rehabilitations pathways that suit their needs.

Barriers to engagement

As explored in the previous section, Black service users have often felt marginalised by the criminal justice system, which is likely to limit their compliance and engagement. Several barriers to engagement often impact individuals from ethnic minority groups experience of the criminal justice system. Findings by Shingler and Pope (2018) identified that current intervention programmes provided by the Probation Service may not be entirely relevant to the experiences of ethnic minority groups, and notably Black people. This may be due to material not aligning with the cultural experiences of these individuals. There was also an exploration of whether there being more staff from ethnic minority backgrounds would help overcome these barriers. While this may provide effective or more favourable outcomes, it is essential to note that interventions co-designed directly with the Black men on probation are more likely to have a personalised service user-led influence and approach, which may help negate some barriers.

Furthermore, it is essential to note that a majority, if not all, of the people on probation are not willing participants in the sense that they have not voluntarily engaged with the service, which may impact their ability to engage with co-creation in practice meaningfully (Trotter, 2022). This assertion is illustrated further by Osborne (2017), who argues that co-creation works well within the private, for-profit sector as businesses engage with customers who have 'bought in' to a product; however, people who are 'coerced' are less likely to do so. Similarly, Baines et al (2022: 454) highlight that 'customer retention' is essential in co-designed services; however, repeat service users are seen as a failure and obstacle to desistance within the Probation Service.

Another critical factor to consider is resistance from practitioners, as co-creation requires you to change how you work as a professional. There has been much research on power dynamics within criminal justice practice and why the authoritarian approach is needed in risk management (Kemshall, 2000; Petrillo, 2007; Tidmarsh, 2021). Therefore, it may be difficult for a practitioner to begin 'bargaining' or sharing power with someone they are required to risk manage. Inevitably, this can create challenges in situations that involve enforcement or addressing breaches, as service users may resist or find it difficult to navigate the boundary between genuine co-production and compliance. This is further identified in research by Lewis (2016), who notes that there are various incidents that occur in the practitioner–servicer user relationship that can cause ruptures/roadblocks in the professional relationship. However, practitioners can take steps to overcome these using therapeutic methods. These incidents can also promote learning opportunities for both the practitioner and service user.

The roadblocks identified earlier could be overcome by incorporating a strengths-based approach, which is traditionally rooted in social work practice. As noted by McCashen (2005), a strengths-based approach is a mechanism that focuses on an individual's self-determination and strength. It ties closely to the Good Lives Model (Purvis et al, 2011) and promotes holistic practice.

Co-creation in practice

The concepts explored so far can lead us to consider what 'co-creation' looks like in probation practice. As noted in earlier sections, co-creation is deeply rooted in collaborating with other key stakeholders to guide the design process of a particular project or matter. Co-creation can occur in numerous ways throughout criminal justice system practice, such as intervention design;

as demonstrated by Armani et al (2018), probation and prison services in Ireland found that music has helped reduce prisoners' anxiety and stress. They further note that this intervention enabled prisoners to take control of their future by developing skills, providing employment and supporting them on release. Research has noted that creative engagement methods work well in various working environments and relationships. Armani et al (2018) found that drama-based programmes and artistic approaches work well with young people. However, little insight has been provided into what is effective for adult and Black offenders, demonstrating a rationale for further exploration.

There are several current interventions in probation practice, such as the practitioner toolkits, which are full of helpful tools, methods and interventions to guide supervision sessions. Evaluation findings by Baines et al (2022) indicate that the 'My Direction' programme was an excellent attempt to personalise the process of desistance through co-creation and strengths-based working. In doing so, they identified that the standardised 'one size fits all approach' is not working within probation practice. Co-creation negates the need for standardisation, as it focuses on the individual service user's needs and views and can align with them intrinsically.

Fox et al (2013) further note that the criminal justice sector can adopt similar methods to social care when navigating the challenge of reforming our approaches and developing innovative person-centred rehabilitation. However, more needs to be mentioned in the context of intersectionality, social stratification and service user engagement. Some areas that will support practitioners in delivering this may include ensuring that we work collectively with Black communities and involve their leadership, align interventions with service user interests, ensure that content is accessible to all, and have an awareness of cultural differences.

This can help promote cohesiveness, essential when implementing 'whole systems thinking'. Research by Ardoin et al (2022) notes that when done effectively, civic engagement can help improve the overall outcomes of a project and can shift away from 'lip service'. From my own research, Black community leaders often feel that they are encouraged to engage in negative dialogue surrounding their communities, that is, youth violence and 'Black on Black crime', but rarely included in progressive dialogue that may promote positive outcomes for their community. This draws closely to previous arguments of tokenism and the impact that this can have on the credibility and legitimacy of findings.

This also draws back to the points raised earlier surrounding cultural competence. Similarly, research surrounding co-creation in youth justice practices identified that building trust and developing supportive relationships were essential for creative participatory practices (Creaney et al, 2023). While this is important within probation practice, it is also essential to consider the dynamics and circumstances in which this relationship/rapport is developed. Co-creation can manifest in several ways for Black service users. For example, honouring and encouraging the experiences of lived experience mentors can be a powerful and holistic tool for Black service users. This can be supported by Buck et al (2021), who identified that working with individuals with lived experiences can help add legitimacy and credibility to work. However, it is to be approached with caution as while there are benefits, it is essential to ensure that lived experiences are not exploited.

With that said, having service user forums led by people with authentic, similar life experiences may support us in developing rapport and rehabilitation plans. Service users providing insight into what approaches work for them may also be helpful; for example, tone and language are often barriers that must be readily explored. A strong focus on building a genuine rapport with service users can help practitioners develop a prosocial approach. This has been evidenced through research by Loeffler and Bovaird (2019), who found that co-production helped improve crime reduction and public safety concerns.

It is essential to acknowledge that there are many areas of our practice that service users cannot influence, such as enforcement and sentencing. However, we can empower them to be proactive and engaged in some areas, and we should champion and utilise these small opportunities for significant changes to our probation service. This ideal is not a new phenomenon and has been demonstrated by research which identified that the process of co-production offers intrinsic benefits for individuals involved (Carr,

2018). Despite the positive uses of co-creation identified in this chapter, the ideology has faced critique for its implementation in practice. Bevir et al (2019) identify that the use of co-creation may be considered 'tokenism' and, on some levels, exploitative. Therefore, practitioners and the Probation Service need to ensure that equity is maintained throughout the process.

As a Black woman who has lived in London for most of my life, I understand why young Black men resist engaging with the criminal justice system. Based on my own experiences and my understanding of the experiences of Black people, I believe that a 'co-created' approach will help improve relations between Black service users, staff, and their rehabilitation journey. I recognise that it can be difficult to encourage people to see the value in participating in something they initially did not want to do. Allowing them to take the lead and make decisions on matters that will impact them the most will empower them. As a practitioner, it was often challenging to support people in a system that I felt was flawed and over which I had little influence. I also acknowledge that despite my proximity to Blackness, I do not have the same tragic life experiences or understanding that many of the service users may have. Allowing them to share their experiences with others who have gone through similar situations will not only help them change their lives but also impact the lives of others. I realised that assuming my racial proximity to them would always give me a 'deeper understanding' was a disservice to them and myself. Instead, we must let them shape and influence their experiences and outcomes. Fortunately, there are already interventions in place that prioritise individual differences and a service user-focused approach. However, we need to focus on individuals who are over-represented in our system.

Conclusion

This chapter has explored co-creation in practice and considered its potential effectiveness for Black service users. There is limited research in this area, so it is difficult to quantify its effectiveness in terms of probation outcomes, recidivism and desistance. However, it is essential to note that there is evidence of the co-creation process assisting with improving the relationship between practitioners and service users, which is invaluable. As it is this relationship that will help the service user navigate through their journey of change. The concepts discussed throughout this chapter have demonstrated that co-creation can promote social justice, self-efficacy, accountability and legitimacy. These can support the individual throughout their rehabilitation, which is at the heart of your engagement with them as a probation practitioner.

Reflective prompts

- What does co-creation look like to you?
- Why is it vital for us to centre our practice around the experiences of service users?
- How can you improve your understanding and practice with Black men on probation?
- What factors may cause you to resist change in your practice?
- How can you enhance your cultural competence skills?

References

Ardoin, N.M., Bowers, A.W. and Gaillard, E. (2022) A systematic mixed studies review of civic engagement outcomes in environmental education, *Environmental Education Research*, 29(1): 1–26. doi:https://doi.org/10.1080/13504622.2022.2135688

Armani, J., Mager, B. and De Leon, N. (2018) Service design in criminal justice: A co-production to reduce reoffending, *Irish Probation Journal*, 15: 137–148.

Baines, S., Fox, C., Harrison, J., Smith, A. and Marsh, C. (2022) Co-creating rehabilitation: Findings from a pilot and implications for wider public service reform, *Probation Journal*, 69(4): 452–471. doi: https://doi.org/10.1177/02645505211065683

Ball, K., Singh, A. and Worsfold, T. (2022) Race equality in probation services in England and Wales: A procedural justice. Available from: https://mmuperu.co.uk/bjcj/articles/race-equality-in-probation-services-in-england-and-wales-a-procedural-justice-perspective/

Banaji, M.R., Fiske, S.T. and Massey, D.S. (2021) Systemic racism: individuals and interactions, institutions and society, *Cognitive Research: Principle and Implications*, 6(82): 1–21. doi: https://doi.org/10.1186/s41235-021-00349-3

Bevir, M., Needham, C. and Waring, J. (2019) Inside co-production: Ruling, resistance, and practice, *Social Policy and Administration*, 53(2): 197–202. doi: https://doi.org/10.1111/spol.12483

Brandsen, T. and Honigh, M. (2018) Definitions of co-production and co-creation, in T. Brandsen, B. Verschuere and T. Steen (eds) *Co-Production and Co-Creation: Engaging Citizens in Public Services* (1st edn), Routledge, pp 9–17.

Buck, G., Tomczak, P. and Quinn, K. (2021) This is how it feels: Activating lived experience in the penal voluntary sector, *The British Journal of Criminology*, 62(4): 822–839. doi: https://doi.org/10.1093/bjc/azab102

Carr, N. (2022) Race equality and probation: A view from the frontline, *Probation Journal*, 69(2): 135–137. doi: https://doi.org/10.1177/02645505221097517

Carr, S. (2018) Who owns co-production?, in P. Beresford and S. Carr (eds) *Social Policy First Hand*, Policy Press, pp 74–83.

Creaney, S., Burns, S. and Day, A.M. (2023) Theory and practice of co-production and co-creation in youth justice, *Safer Communities*, 22(3): 149–155. doi: https://doi.org/10.1108/SC-07-2023-054

Fitzgibbon, D.W. (2007) Institutional racism, pre-emptive criminalisation and risk analysis. *The Howard Journal of Criminal Justice*, 46(2): 128–144. doi: https://doi.org/10.1111/j.1468-2311.2007.00461.x

Fox, A., Fox, C. and Marsh, C. (2013) Could personalisation reduce re-offending? Reflections on potential lessons from British social care reform for the British criminal justice system, *Journal of Social Policy*, 42(4): 721–741. doi: https://doi.org/10.1017/S0047279413000512

Hilder, S. (2010) Multi-agency working with black and minority ethnic offenders, in A. Pycroft and D. Gough (eds) *Multi-agency Working in Criminal Justice: Control and Care in Contemporary Correctional Practice*, Policy Press, pp 65–80.

HM Chief Inspector of Prisons (2022) The experiences of adult black male prisoners and black prison staff. Available from: https://www.justiceinspectorates.gov.uk/hmiprisons/wp-content/uploads/sites/4/2022/12/The-experiences-of-adult-black-male-prisoners-and-black-prison-staff-web-2022.pdf

HM Inspectorate of Probation (2021) Race equality in probation: The experiences of black, Asian and minority ethnic probation service users and staff. Available from: https://www.justiceinspectorates.gov.uk/hmiprobation/inspections/race-equality-in-probation/

HM Inspectorate of Probation (2023) Race equality in probation follow-up: A work in progress. Available from: https://www.justiceinspectorates.gov.uk/hmiprobation/inspections/race-equality-in-probation-follow-up/

Hrabovský, M. (2013) The concept of 'Blackness' in theories of race, *Asian & African Studies*, 22(1): 65–88.

Kemshall, H. (2000) Researching risk in the probation service, *Social Policy and Administration*, 34(4): 465–477. doi: https://doi.org/10.1111/1467-9515.00204

Lammy, D. (2017) *The Lammy Review: An Independent Review into the Treatment of, and Outcomes for, Black, Asian and Minority Ethnic Individuals in the Criminal Justice System*. Available from: https://www.gov.uk/government/organisations/lammy-review

Lewis, S. (2016) *Therapeutic Correctional Relationships: Theory, Research and Practice*, Routledge.

Loeffler, E. and Bovaird, T. (2019) Assessing the impact of co-production on pathways to outcomes in public services: The case of policing and criminal justice, *International Public Management Journal*, 23(2): 205–223. doi: https://doi.org/10.1080/10967494.2019.1668895

Macdonald, J. and Stokes, R.J. (2006) Race, social capital, and trust in the police, *Urban Affairs Review*, 41(3): 358–375. doi: https://doi.org/10.1177/1078087405281707

McCashen, W. (2005) *The Strengths Approach*, St Luke's Innovative Resources.

Ministry of Justice (2022) *Offender Management Statistics Quarterly: July to September 2021*. Available from: https://www.gov.uk/government/statistics/offender-management-statistics-quarterly-july-to-september-2021/offender-management-statistics-quarterly-july-to-september-2021#:~:text=Between%20July%20and%20September%202021%2C%20there%20was%20a%20smaller%20decrease,indeterminate%20sentences%2C%20of%2025%25

Morgan, R. (2013) Race, probation, and inspections, in S. Lewis, P. Raynor, D. Smith and A. Wardak (eds) *Race and Probation*, Willan, pp 41–57.

Muzyychenko, O. (2008) Cross-cultural entrepreneurial competence in identifying international business opportunities, *European Management Journal*, 26(6): 366–377. doi: https://doi.org/10.1016/j.emj.2008.09.002

Nelson, N. and Appel, O. (2021) Perceived procedural justice enhances correctional officers' organizational citizenship behavior: Correlational and causal evidence from Israel, *Criminal Justice and Behavior*, 49(2): 164–180. doi: https://doi.org/10.1177/00938548211043557

Nyamwiza, N. (2022) Black people are often associated with deviance – but I never understood the true impact until I was racially profiled, *The Conversation*, 12 April. Available from: https://theconversation.com/black-people-are-often-associated-with-deviance-but-i-never-understood-the-true-impact-until-i-was-racially-profiled-179259

Onifade, E., Petersen, J., Bynum, T.S. and Davidson, W.S. (2011) Multilevel recidivism prediction: Incorporating neighborhood socioeconomic ecology in juvenile justice risk assessment, *Criminal Justice and Behavior*, 38(8): 840–853. doi: https://doi.org/10.1177/0093854811407026

Osborne, S.P. (2017) From public service-dominant logic to public service-dominant logic to public service logic: Are public service organizations capable of co-production and value co-creation?, *Public Management Review*, 20(2): 225–231. doi: https://doi.org/10.10.80/14719037.2017.1350461

Pain, R., Whitman, G. and Milledge, D. (2019) *Participatory Action Research Toolkit: An Introduction to using PAR as an Approach to Learning, Research, and Action.* Practice Guide. Durham University. Available from: https://www.youngfoundation.org/institute-for-community-studies/repository/participatory-action-research-toolkit-an-introduction-to-using-par-as-an-approach-to-learning-research-and-action/

Palmer, S. (2013) Black perspectives on race, crime and justice, in C. Phillips and C. Webster (eds) *New Directions in Race, Ethnicity and Crime*, Routledge, pp 97–117.

Perea, J.F. (2020) Immigration policy as a defense of white nationhood, *Georgetown Journal of Law and Modern Critical Race Perspectives*, 12: 1–13. Available from: https://www.law.georgetown.edu/mcrp-journal/wp-content/uploads/sites/22/2020/07/GT-GCRP200001.pdf

Petrillo, M. (2007) Power struggle: Gender issues for female probation officers in the supervision of high-risk offenders, *Probation Journal*, 54(4): 394–406. doi: https://doi.org/10.1177/0264550507083538

Prison Reform Trust (2023) *Prison: The Facts*, Bromley Briefings Summer 2023. Available from: https://prisonreformtrust.org.uk/project/prison-the-facts/

Purvis, M., Ward, T. and Willis, G. (2011) The good lives model in practice: Offence pathways and case management, *European Journal of Probation*, 3(2): 4–28. doi: https://doi.org/10.1177/206622031100300202

Pycroft, A. and Bartollas, C. (2014) Introduction, in A. Pycroft and C. Bartollas (eds) *Applying Complexity Theory: Whole System Approaches to Criminal Justice and Social Work*, Policy Press, pp 15–38.

Scarman, L.G.S.B. and Home Office (1982) *The Scarman Report: The Brixton Disorders 10–12 April 1981: Report of an Inquiry by the Right Honourable the Lord Scarman, Presented to Parliament by the Secretary of State for the Home Department*, Penguin.

Sharp, D. and Atherton, S. (2007) To serve and protect? The experiences of policing in the community of young people from black and other ethnic minority groups, *The British Journal of Criminology*, 47(5): 746–763. doi: https://doi.org/10.1093/bjc/azm024

Shiner, M., Carre, Z., Delsol, R. and Eastwood, N. (2018) The colour of injustice: 'Race', drugs and law enforcement in England and Wales. Available from: https://www.release.org.uk/publications/ColourOfInjustice

Shingler, J. and Pope, L. (2018) The effectiveness of rehabilitative services for Black, Asian and minority ethnic people: A rapid evidence assessment, *Ministry of Justice Analytical Series*, HM Prison and Probation Service.

Sirdifield, C., Parkhouse, T., Mullen, P. and Nadia (2024) The characteristics of high-quality health and social care for people on probation: Professional and lived experience perspectives, *Probation Journal*. doi: https://doi.org/10.1177/02645505231222961

Steinmetz, K.F. and Henderson, H. (2015) On the precipice of intersectionality: The influence of race, gender, and offense severity interactions on probation outcomes, *Criminal Justice Review*, 40(3): 361–377. doi: https://doi.org/10.1177/2153368715619656

Tidmarsh, M. (2021) *Professionalism in Probation: Making Sense of Marketisation*, Routledge.

Trotter, C. (2022) *Working with Involuntary Clients: A Guide to Practice*, Routledge.

Walker, S. (2020) Systemic racism: Big, Black, mad and dangerous in the criminal justice system, in R. Majors, K. Carberry and T.S. Ransaw (eds) *The International Handbook of Black Community Mental Health*, Emerald Publishing Limited, pp 41–60.

Warde, B. (2023) *Colorblind: Indigenous and Black Disproportionality Across Criminal Justice Systems*, Springer International Publishing.

Whitson, M. (2012) *Law Enforcement in the Fog of Mistrust Solving the Problem of Black Mistrust of Law Enforcement*, PhD Thesis, Gonzaga University.

Williams, P. and Durrance, P. (2017) Resisting effective approaches for BAME offenders in England and Wales: The triumph of inertia, in P. Ugwudike, P. Raynor and J. Annison (eds) *Evidence-based Skills in Criminal Justice*, Policy Press, pp 373–396.

Wilson, J., Ward, C. and Fischer, R. (2013) Beyond culture learning theory: What can personality tell us about cultural competence?, *Journal of Cross-Cultural Psychology*, 44(6): 900–927. doi: https://doi.org/10.1177/0022022113492889

11

Reflections of female probation practitioners: navigating the challenges of working with male offenders

Michelle McDermott, Laura Haggar and Jennifer Grant

In March 2024, 75.7 per cent of staff in the Probation Service were female (MoJ, 2024a). In contrast, at the same time, the probation caseload was almost 91 per cent male (MoJ, 2024b). Recent media coverage has portrayed this gender divide as a concern, influenced by the current Chief Probation Officer's suggestion that male practitioners may be better at challenging male-perpetrated violence against women and girls (Hill, 2023; Shaw, 2024). The evidence base suggests that both men and women have skills and attributes which benefit working with men on probation (Ireland and Berg, 2008; Kirkwood et al, 2023). Therefore, rather than focus on the perceived differences in the skill set between female and male practitioners, this chapter will present that any concern about the gender divide should instead be directed at managing and supporting the impact of working with men on probation for female practitioners.

While female officers reflect the majority of the workforce, there is limited attention in the literature to the impact this has on their relationships with people on probation, or the challenges female practitioners face. Kirkwood et al (2023: 2527) go so far as to say that probation 'work "with" men is positioned as a neutral practice where gender is absent or ignored'. As such, for the many women employed by the Probation Service, concern perhaps should be focused on the occupational hazard (Ireland and Berg, 2008) posed by regular threats and intimidation perpetrated by men on probation. The normalisation of abuse towards female practitioners reflects the wider context of our patriarchal society, which is often ignored in probation research. Yet, violence against women and gender inequality have an impact on probation practice (McCormack and Lantry, 2022). Hegemonic masculinity affects how men interact with the women they are supervised by, within the context of the therapeutic alliance. By virtue of striving for therapeutic relationships with men who have socially influenced expectations and assumptions about responding to women (Cramer et al, 2024), there can be ruptures in supervisory relationships. This is because ruptures are generally caused when there is a lack of agreement about who holds authority (Miller and Rollnick, 2002), with women not traditionally expected to be in this position. Importantly, the impact of trying to 'fix' supervisory relationships characterised by abuse can be at the expense of the female practitioners' well-being (Morran, 2008).

This chapter does not seek to negate the skills and innate attributes of male practitioners, rather it intends to bring to the fore reflection on female skills and experiences. In doing so it will explore what it means to work within a setting where women hold the power traditionally attributed to men. Three ex-probation officers, with a combined 38 years in the Probation Service, will document their shared experiences to address the academic gaps regarding female experiences in the probation workforce (Zettler, 2019). Particular events encountered by the authors while working with men subject to probation have made us acutely aware of the gendered nature of our roles. While individual to each of us, we can categorise our experience through the lenses of misogyny, risk to personal safety and vulnerability. This chapter will provide an opportunity for reflection on the barriers, opportunities and safe working practices for female practitioners in the Probation Service and explore the implications for reflective practice. In addressing these gaps, we are mindful that all of the authors are reflecting from a white, cis-gender, heterosexual perspective. The terms female and women are not labels that accurately represent the entirety of the relevant workforce, nor do our experiences reflect every woman's. This compendium has attempted to address the female experience intersectionally, and readers can also find perspectives from Black and lesbian female authors in Chapters 9, 10 and 12.

The 'paradoxical feminisation' of the Probation Service

The feminisation of the Probation Service is a relatively recent occurrence (see Annison, 2007; 2013). Female probation officers have only outnumbered their male counterparts since 1993 (Annison, 2007). Since this time, practitioner roles have seen decreasing levels of pay and rising levels of responsibility, set within an increasingly managerialist criminal justice system (Annison, 2013). Currently, the Probation Service's typical entrant is a recent graduate from a female-dominated social science higher education course (Tidmarsh, 2023). Given most entrants are joining externally via the training programme (HMPPS, 2024), an assumption has been made that women continue to dominate the workforce because the trainee positions' salary and benefits tend to attract young graduates. While this may be a contributing factor, the apparent feminisation of the Probation Service is more complex than this.

Despite its dissociation from social work training, the Probation Service remains a caring profession (Dominey and Canton, 2022). Thus, it can be presumed that some women are drawn to practitioner posts because of traditional female roles. Women are expected to play a nurturing role within family and community contexts, and there is undoubtedly a nurturing aspect to rehabilitative practice (Mawby and Worrall, 2013). Yet, probation practitioners do not spend a large amount of their working day undertaking tasks that align with this. Instead, the Probation Service has a key responsibility to reduce reoffending (HMPPS, 2021).

To reduce reoffending, the role of rehabilitation is focused on protecting the public (Petrillo, 2019). Thus, regular practitioner tasks involve enforcement and risk management-related activities, including report writing and testing for substance misuse (DeMichele and Payne, 2018). Therein lies the 'paradoxical feminisation' of the role (Worrall, 2008: 330), wherein practitioners are expected to manage dangerous populations of offenders instead of befriending them (Mawby and Worrall,

2013). As the introduction has highlighted, these tasks can lead to ruptures in the therapeutic alliance (Miller and Rollnick, 2002), which are regularly exacerbated by the impact of masculinity and the occupational hazard of threatening behaviour. This results in emotional labour being performed by female practitioners, wherein emotions must be managed to meet organisational objectives (Hochschild, 1983). Managing these emotions masks the impact of difficult interactions on female practitioners, at the expense of their well-being and relationships both in and outside of the workplace (Petrillo, 2007).

Male power and the therapeutic alliance

While there is the emphasis on public protection as a key aim of the Probation Service (HMPPS, 2021), the collaborative relationship between a client and practitioner, otherwise known as the therapeutic alliance, has garnered attention in the correctional space given its positive links to promoting rehabilitation and reducing recidivism. Characterised by mutual trust and respect, with an emphasis on shared goals, the therapeutic alliance can enhance engagement and adherence with interventions (Rex, 1999). The evidence base for the therapeutic alliance originates from the field of psychiatry/counselling, where, for the most part, clients are willing participants. Trotter (2023) highlights the challenging position practitioners are in when attempting to implement the principles of the therapeutic alliance with mandated clients, where the practitioner role is not solely to think about what is best for the client, but the needs of victims, the public and the requirements of the organisation. These challenges are of course present for all practitioners and not unique to female probation workers, but, as will be discussed, the practitioners' gender can lead to unexplored barriers to the therapeutic alliance.

The dominant 'hegemonic' masculinity in Western societies has been argued to result in exaggerated heterosexuality, often translated into misogynistic and patriarchal attitudes (Fielding, 1994, as cited in Cowburn, 1998). Hegemonic masculinity has been observed as strongly present in male prisons in England and Wales (Cowburn, 1998), which a significant number of men supervised by probation will have experienced. This affects how men perceive and interact with the women they are supervised by. A recent study of probation practitioners found that masculinity can pervade the supervisory relationship, resulting in sexist views being displayed (Nahouli et al, 2023). Cramer et al's (2024) study highlighted differences in how male participants interacted with the male and female facilitators on domestic abuse programmes run by the Probation Service, finding that female practitioners were more regularly dismissed and silenced by participants, who afforded more discursive power to the male facilitators. This has been framed as re-establishing male power (Connell and Messerschmidt, 2005).

As highlighted, the current pathways to probation qualification have resulted in a high number of young, female graduates (Hamilton, 2018). The most recent workforce bulletin shows that 81.5 per cent of those who started as trainee probation officers in 2023/2024 were female, and half of these were under 30 years of age (HMPPS, 2024). Age has been highlighted as an additional difficulty in the supervisory relationship, with Nahouli et al (2023) suggesting that older probation practitioners felt they had an advantage in building rapport. Cramer et al (2024) further support this, having found younger female facilitators were most regularly dismissed by men on probation.

While qualifying as probation officers through differing routes, all three authors shared this demographic of recent recruits, having joined the service in their early 20s as university graduates. To demonstrate male power, Author 2 shares the written reflections she submitted for her academic qualification during training. Case B was a white British, middle-aged, heterosexual man who was assessed as posing a high risk of serious harm to his ex-partner and children. He was on licence for breaching a non-molestation order due to moving near the victims. It is quickly apparent the author felt unsafe working with him:

> My reflections on my work with Case B highlight the emotional impact of working with high-risk offenders who control the supervisory relationship (Petrillo, 2007). Although Case B did not do anything specifically to threaten me, his presence made me feel on edge and intimidated. In one session Case B told me that he felt fine towards the victim, and then

> stated that this was despite him spending three years in prison because of her ... the way he made me feel meant that I did not continue this discussion for as long as I usually would as I did not want to continue being in a room alone with him.

By this stage in the training, this author had been intimidated by several men. It is possible that to protect their emotional well-being, without realising, a process of re-drawing boundaries with the men she worked with was reinforcing traditional male power (Connell and Messerschmidt, 2005). This is concerning, given the author had yet to qualify as a probation practitioner, and demonstrates the compounding difficulties of age and gender within the supervisory relationship. The implicit intimidation in this example is not always how male power is demonstrated. As a woman in their early 20s, it is quite possible that feeling vulnerable also affected their decision-making:

> I felt intimidated and never directly questioned him about the obsessive qualities I witnessed when he spoke about a previous ex-partner. ... Being intimidated by Case B led me to apply a practical focus in our sessions, which had positive results in regards to employment. However, this meant that I discounted risk management work, which is seen as paramount with high-risk offenders.

Repeated occurrences of patriarchal challenge have an emotional and professional impact on female practitioners. This reflection highlights this beginning early in this author's probation career. Research has highlighted that some female practitioners modify how they set boundaries and behave in their practice with men on probation (McCulloch et al, 2021), perhaps in an attempt to debilitate these effects. This can occur when threats are implied, but also when they are clear and explicit.

Threats and intimidation

Ruptures in the therapeutic alliance often occur when decisions are made that the person on probation disagrees with (Lewis,

2016). Petrillo's (2007) study emphasised that female practitioners must contend with resistance to the power their role holds. Ruptures therefore regularly involve risk assessments and licence condition decisions.

Violence and threats of violence have been described as an 'occupational hazard' for front-line staff in the police and prisons (Ireland and Berg, 2008). This culture of acceptance can also be seen in social work, with Waterhouse noting 'threats and intimidation are par for the course' (2023: para 6). While the values that shape and underpin these professions are distinct, they each centre around interactions with people who are at their most vulnerable and in situations that give rise to heightened emotions. Perhaps unsurprisingly, then, threats of violence have also been normalised by front-line probation practitioners (Denney and O'Beirne, 2003). Where verbal abuse and intimidation become the norm, practitioners can often underestimate credible threats, particularly when they are in response to practitioner decision-making. As was the case with Author 1, who at the time was working in a public protection team several years post qualification:

> Simon was serving a custodial sentence for a series of violent offences of such severity it led to the victim, his then partner, being blinded in one eye. As his automatic release date moved closer, his contact with me intensified, with his intent to secure an alternative residence to an Approved Premises. Simon's risk of serious harm deemed initial residence at an Approved Premises to be necessary, and when met with this assessment, his tone became increasingly annoyed and agitated with his last contact resulting in me being subjected to a tirade of abuse, which included a slew of derogatory and degrading terms targeting my gender. As practitioners it is important to recognise the frustration in the people who we supervise and appreciate the anger sometimes directed towards us is actually aimed at the system who we represent (Trotter, 2023). Despite this knowledge, this did feel personal, the derogatory comments were not intermittently sprinkled with a series of

negative statements about the Probation Service that I had come to experience with other people who I supervised. Perhaps knowing that he was in custody and I was not being subjected to such abuse face-to-face allowed some detachment from the situation, and this detachment remained when Simon's abuse escalated to threats. This time he spoke calmly, reminded me that he knew people who had access to guns and could find out where I lived. At this point I informed him that the conversation was likely monitored and I was terminating the call.

The events that unfolded reflect how Author 1 had already normalised this behaviour, seeking to alert prison staff to temporarily restrict contact but with a view to continue with the supervisory relationship once 'Simon' had the opportunity to reflect on his own behaviour. Instead, police action resulted in safeguarding for the author, including the need to take different routes home over a prolonged period of time, and Simon eventually being convicted, receiving a further term of imprisonment and a restraining order. What this author had deemed a 'normal' albeit distressing response from someone in a high-stress situation, was, to the police, a credible threat. This experience highlights the conflict between the desire to help people on their desistance journey to the detriment of personal safety. Emphasis is rightly given in the literature about the relational aspect of the work (Senior et al, 2016) and the need to work through roadblocks and ruptures in the relationship (Lewis, 2014), however, there can be a tendency for practitioners to be blinkered in their attempts to reconcile supervisory relationships for fear of failure, and in this author's experience, take defensive action to protect themselves in the moment, thus failing to acknowledge the emotional impact of the experience (Ferguson, 2018), or indeed potential danger.

Space for guided reflection in such circumstances is therefore critical to both personal safety and for practitioners to find ways forward, either in their relationship with the perpetrator of the aggression or with other people on probation. Furthermore, reflective supervision can allow individuals to process the emotional impact of such an event (Westaby et al, 2021), while simultaneously helping to foster resilience among practitioners (see Chapter 5).

Misogyny, romanticisation and vulnerability

The evidence base has not explicitly sought to capture the views of men subject to probation on the issue of gender as a factor within their supervisory relationship. However, research from the prison environment can be utilised, given this criminal justice agency has also seen a significant increase of women in its workforce (Liebling and Price, 2001; Phoenix, 2023). While not directly transferable to the probation setting, Crewe's (2006) study of 520 inmates at HMP Wellingborough does highlight some points of relevance. The pervasive nature of sexualised behaviour, comments and fantasies towards female prison officers demonstrate male prisoners' tensions in accepting female authority. Although heightened and sexualised in the prison environment, this mirrors issues raised in our reflections, for example, all authors have been subjected to comments about our appearance, particularly concerning dress, which results in female practitioners being mindful of what they are wearing (Nahouli et al, 2023).

Other tactics employed to demonstrate male power can involve flirting (Petrillo, 2007), as Author 1 recollects persistent unsolicited attention escalating to letters and cards sent by a male convicted of domestic and sexual offending who mistook the relational aspects of the therapeutic relationship of care and empathy for that of a romantic one. How well a practitioner can navigate such situations depends on a range of factors, not least the support from leadership (Lewis, 2014). For example, when raising this with her line manager, the author was made to feel partly responsible for creating an environment in which this behaviour could occur, which highlights why practitioners in similar situations may choose not to disclose such events (Littlechild, 1997). Despite an outward appearance of 'power' held by criminal justice practitioners, similarities with how women are perceived in such situations can be seen within the wider evidence base of victim blaming (Taylor, 2020), with the woman's 'power' limited. Thus presenting another layer of complexity of female practitioners feeling able to disclose behaviours without fear of being blamed or viewed as an 'incompetent' practitioner. This inevitably can have a significant impact on practitioners' emotional well-being, spilling into areas of their lives outside of the workplace. Several studies, for example, have highlighted the effects on personal relationships and heightened anxiety generally, due to the vulnerabilities exposed through repeated instances of intimidation and manipulation within their practice (Petrillo, 2007; Morran, 2008).

The feelings of vulnerability and the emotional labour that this takes within supervisory relationships are illustrated by Author 3's experience:

> X was a high-risk domestic abuse perpetrator, who I had taken over the supervision of from a male practitioner. For a number of reasons this was not a straightforward case, and being a high-risk MAPPA [Multi Agency Public Protection Panel Arrangements] case, with a number of safeguarding concerns, the preparation for X's release from prison was complex. As I took over the case at the more active resettlement phase of his sentence and had to apply risk assessment and restrictions, it was clear that X perceived me as problematic as compared to his previous officer. This may also have been affected by biases held by X, for example, Cramer et al's (2024) study found that female facilitators were perceived by domestic abuse programme participants as being confrontational towards them as men, sometimes due to their assumed bias towards the female victim. X very quickly became well known in the office as he and his family contacted the office several times a day to complain and challenge me about the restrictions in place. I worked hard to try to form a therapeutic alliance with X, recognising that while he made me uncomfortable, this was an important aspect of the process and risk management of the case. Superficially, X engaged with one to one sessions but his comments in sessions suggested that he was trying to 'bait' me. Lewis (2016: 130) found that 'baiting' was a tactic used by some practitioners as a means of gaining power within a correctional

relationship. In this instance this was reflected in X appearing to want to elicit a response from me and gain control of the narrative within our sessions. For example, in his description of his romantic relationships, and ease at gaining women's attention, knowing that these were areas of concern for me. He would attempt to push boundaries with me in terms of questioning my own relationship (I wear a wedding ring) and our interactions felt like a constant power struggle. By this point in my career I felt more comfortable challenging this behaviour but it can become exhausting to go into battle each week but this can be a regular occurrence when you have a caseload made up of largely domestic abuse perpetrators.

As can be seen in the previous reflections in this chapter, this could also lead to desensitisation and a shift in what officers feel that they should be able to 'take' within the role. The cumulative impact of this can be seen within the research (Petrillo, 2007; Phillips et al, 2018), with a risk of burnout for staff increased through their application of emotions within the relationship. As Phillips et al highlight, this risk is somewhat mitigated when practitioners engage in 'deep' rather than 'surface' acting forms of emotional labour, 'either directly or indirectly through the alignment of inner feelings with emotional labour expectations. This can be achieved through either invoking those emotions through experience or through a trained imagination' (2020: 5).

While this notion of 'deep acting' does not specifically address issues of gender, it does provide some further insight into the value of space for guided reflection when faced with challenging cases. Furthermore, the focus of that reflection is important, with the emphasis upon the practitioner to work through ruptures and be mindful of their actions and responses situated within the literature (Lewis, 2016), while the role of gender and the complexity of this as a dynamic remains largely underexplored. Therefore, recognition of this would be valuable from the position of supervision with probation staff.

The gender dynamic can be illustrated further in the family roles held by practitioners, adding a potential layer of vulnerability and blurring of boundaries between work and home, particularly when considering that a component of establishing a therapeutic alliance can also include the use of practitioner disclosure (Trotter, 2023). The evidence base for what self-disclosure consists of and its benefits in the correctional space is limited (Phillips et al, 2018). Therefore, it is unsurprising that it does not consider how the sharing of personal information can heighten a female practitioner's vulnerability in the supervisory relationship, as Author 3 reflects further:

> Given X's offending, and behaviour towards me, I did not feel safe to share my role as a mother with a young child, however, when I was unable to attend a meeting due to childcare issues, this information was shared by another member of staff with X. At our next meeting X presented this to me; I can still remember how this revelation to me hung in the air, the power in that statement, and my own feelings of vulnerability. A couple of weeks later, I collected my daughter from nursery and saw X on the way home. While I don't think he saw me, and so there were no 'rational' concerns in this regard, it provided another blur of the work/home life for someone whose case required a large amount of emotional labour, especially as I was in the early stages of pregnancy.

This example highlights how what can be considered 'public' information by one member of staff can be deeply personal to another. While viewed as part of the course to developing trust within the therapeutic alliance, disclosures can only be made when practitioners feel safe to do so and, as this reflection demonstrates, decisions around safe disclosure can be impacted by gender.

Opportunities and forward reflections

This chapter aimed to highlight the experiences of female probation practitioners and offer insights into how officers navigate emotionally intensive work where their gender is a critical component of the supervisory relationships. The authors acknowledge that the salient reflections relate to negative interactions with men convicted of domestic abuse and sexual offending, mirroring similar practitioner experiences captured by Petrillo (2007) and Kirkwood et al (2023). Gender is therefore perhaps a more prominent feature within the supervisory relationship where such behaviour and the underlying misogynistic attitudes and beliefs are present.

This is not to say that all men convicted of these offences will seek to threaten or intimidate female practitioners, on the contrary, there are important opportunities for practitioners to develop meaningful and constructive relationships supporting positive outcomes for people on probation and their victims. For example, Crewe (2006) found that female prison staff provided the opportunity for some men to behave chivalrously; to feel vulnerable; and to engage in conversations they would find more difficult with male officers. Similar has been found in the Probation Service. Women can use their gender to counteract the impact of patriarchal struggle within the supervisory relationship when they legitimately use power attached to their role (Petrillo, 2007). Episodes of male anger, hostility and sexualisation of the supervisory relationship can therefore be used to strengthen the therapeutic alliance, providing a space free of judgement to explore what may be beneath the surface, for example vulnerability and fear (Sweet, 2012).

A fundamental requirement to work safely through such episodes is a culture of reflective practice. Much like the people we supervise, practitioners also need a space free of judgement to consider whether their responses and actions are appropriate based on the encounter or whether it has triggered unconscious biases, or brought personal experiences to the fore. Similarly, reflective supervision can enable practitioners to deal with the intensity of emotions, and in certain circumstances give permission, without a label of failure, to withdraw from the supervisory relationship.

While the authors share many similar experiences to the ones reflected upon in this chapter, we too acknowledge the number of positive experiences we have had in supervising men. It was a privilege to support them in having healthy relationships and relationships with the women and girls in their lives.

Reflective prompts

- To what extent do you think gender has impacted on your practice?
- When you have identified gender as a difficulty within a supervisory relationship, have you been able to consider this in broader terms than the person on probation's offence type?
- How well do you think the organisation understands the impact of male power on the supervisory relationships? In what ways can you offer support to those you work with?
- How have you managed incidents of romanticisation within the therapeutic alliance? What role has reflection played in this?
- Self-disclosure can be a way of developing mutual trust within a therapeutic relationship. What personal information would you be willing to share with people you supervise while feeling safe?

References

Annison, J. (2007) A gendered review of change within the probation service, *Howard Journal of Criminal Justice*, 46(2): 145–161. https://doi.org/10.1111/j.1468-2311.2007.00462.x

Annison, J. (2013) Change and the probation service in England and Wales: A gendered lens, *European Journal of Probation*, 5(1): 44–64. https://doi.org/10.1177/206622031300500104

Connell, R.W. and Messerschmidt, J.W. (2005) Hegemonic masculinity: Rethinking the concept, *Gender and Society*, 19(6): 829–859. https://doi.org/10.1177/0891243205278639

Cowburn, M. (1998) A man's world: Gender issues in working with male sex offenders in prison, *The Howard Journal*, 37(3): 234–251. https://doi.org/10.1111/1468-2311.00095

Cramer, H., Eisenstadt, N., Päivinen, H., Iwi, K., Newman, C. and Morgan, K. (2024) 'I am not taking sides as a female at all': Co-facilitation and gendered positioning in a domestic abuse perpetrator program, *International Journal of Offender Therapy and Comparative Criminology*. https://doi.org/10.1177/0306624X241254699

Crewe, B. (2006) Male prisoners' orientations towards female officers in an English prison, *Punishment and Society*, 8(4): 395–421. https://doi.org/10.1177/1462474506067565

DeMichele, M. and Payne, B. (2018) Taking officer time seriously: A study of the daily activities of probation officers, *Probation Journal*, 65(1): 39–60. https://doi.org/10.1177/0264550517748358

Denney, D. and O'Beirne, M. (2003) Violence to probation staff: Patterns and managerial responses, *Social Policy and Administration*, 31(1): 49–64. https://doi.org/10.1111/1467-9515.00323

Dominey, J. and Canton, R. (2022) Probation and the ethics of care, *Probation Journal*, 69(4): 417–433. https://doi.org/10.1177/02645505221105401

Ferguson, H. (2018) How social workers reflect in action and when and why they don't: The possibilities and limits to reflective practice in social work, *Social Work Education*, 37(4): 415–427. https://doi.org/10.1080/02615479.2017.1413083

Hamilton, P. (2018) Gender matters in the PQiP, *Probation Quarterly*, 9: 38–41.

Hill, A. (2023) More male staff could help with offenders, says England and Wales probation chief, *The Guardian*, 4 April. Available from: https://www.theguardian.com/society/2023/apr/04/men-help-offenders-england-wales-probation-kim-thornden-edwards

HMPPS (HM Prison and Probation Service) (2021) The target operating model for probation services in England and Wales, Probation Reform Programme. Available from: https://assets.publishing.service.gov.uk/government/uploads/system/uploads/attachment_data/file/1061047/MOJ7350_HMPPS_Probation_Reform_Programme_TOM_Accessible_English_LR.pdf

HMPPS (2024) HM Prison and Probation Service workforce quarterly: March 2024. Annex prison and probation officer recruitment March 2024, HMPPS. Available from: https://www.gov.uk/government/statistics/hm-prison-and-probation-service-workforce-quarterly-march-2024

Hochschild, A.R. (1983) *The Managed Heart: Commercialization of Human Feeling*, University of California Press.

Ireland, C. and Berg, B. (2008) Women in parole: Respect and rapport, *International Journal of Offender Therapy and Comparative Criminology*, 52(4): 474–491. https://doi.org/10.1177/0306624X07307782

Kirkwood, S., Mullins, E., McCulloch, T. and Cree, V.E. (2023) Ideological dilemmas in social work: Justice social workers in Scotland talk about gender in practice, *British Journal of Social Work*, 53(5): 2521–2538. https://doi.org/10.1093/bjsw/bcac221

Lewis, S. (2014) Learning from success and failure: Deconstructing the working relationship within probation practice and exploring its impact on probationers, using a collaborative approach, *Probation Journal*, 61(2): 161–175. https://doi.org/10.1177/0264550514523816

Lewis, S. (2016) *Therapeutic Correctional Relationships: Theory, Research and Practice*, Routledge.

Liebling, A. and Price, D. (2001) *The Prison Officer*, Waterside Press.

Littlechild, B. (1997) 'I needed to be told that I hadn't failed': Experiences of violence against probation staff and of agency support, *The British Journal of Social Work*, 27(2): 219–240. http://www.jstor.org/stable/23714636

Mawby, R.C. and Worrall, A. (2013) *Doing Probation Work: Identity in a Criminal Justice Occupation*, Routledge.

McCormack, L. and Lantry, N. (2022) Patriarchy, transgenerational trauma, and passion for change: Vicarious exposure to domestic violence in facilitators of men's behavior change programs, *Traumatology*. https://psycnet.apa.org/doi/10.1037/trm0000428

McCulloch, T., Cree, V.E., Kirkwood, S. and Mullins, E. (2021) 'Within my work environment I don't see gender as an issue': Reflections on gender from a study of criminal justice social workers in Scotland, *Probation Journal*, 68(1): 8–27. https://doi.org/10.1177/0264550520939153

Miller, W.R. and Rollnick, S. (2002) *Motivational Interviewing: Preparing People for Change* (2nd edn), Guilford Press.

MoJ (Ministry of Justice) (2024a) *HM Prison and Probation Service Workforce Statistics*. Available from: https://www.gov.uk/government/collections/national-offender-management-service-workforce-statistics

MoJ (2024b) *Offender Management Statistics Quarterly: January to March 2024*. Available from: https://www.gov.uk/government/statistics/offender-management-statistics-quarterly-january-to-march-2024

Morran, D. (2008) Firing up and burning out: The personal and professional impact of working in domestic violence offender programmes, *Probation Journal*, 55(2): 139–152. https://doi.org/10.1177/0264550508090272

Nahouli, Z., Mackenzie, J.-M., Aresti, A. and Dando, C. (2023) Rapport building with offenders in probation supervision: The views of English probation practitioners, *Probation Journal*, 70(2): 104–123. https://doi.org/10.1177/02645505221137448

Petrillo, M. (2007) Power struggle: Gender issues for female probation officers in the supervision of high risk offenders, *Probation Journal*, 54(4): 394–406. https://doi.org/10.1177/0264550507083538

Petrillo, M. (2019) Female probation and parole officers, in F.P. Bernat, K. Frailing, L. Gelsthorpe, S. Kethineni and L. Pasko (eds) *The Encyclopedia of Women and Crime*, John Wiley and Sons.

Phillips, J., Fowler, A. and Westaby, C. (2018) Self-disclosure in criminal justice: What form does it take and what does it achieve?, *International Journal of Offender Therapy and Comparative Criminology*, 62(12): 3890–3909. https://doi.org/10.1177/0306624X17751528

Phillips, J., Westaby, C. and Fowler, A. (2020) Emotional labour in probation, *HMIP Academic Insights* 2020/03. Available from: /https://www.justiceinspectorates.gov.uk/hmiprobation/wp-content/uploads/sites/5/2020/04/Emotional-Labour-in-Probation.pdf

Phoenix, J. (2023) The creation of mixed-sex prisons by stealth, Centre for Crime and Justice Studies. Available from: https://www.crimeandjustice.org.uk/resources/creation-mixed-sex-prisons-stealth

Rex, S. (1999) Desistance from offending: Experiences of probation, *The Howard Journal of Criminal Justice*, 38: 366–383. doi: https://doi.org/10.1111/1468-2311.00141

Senior, P., Ward, D., Burke, L., Knight, C., Teague, M., Chapman, T., et al (2016) The essence of probation, *British Journal of Community Justice*, 14(1): 9–27. Available from: https://mmuperu.co.uk/bjcj/articles/the-essence-of-probation/

Shaw, D. (2024) Thousands of prisoners are about to be released early. Is probation ready?, *The Spectator*, 9 September. Available from: https://www.spectator.co.uk/article/thousands-of-prisoners-are-about-to-be-released-early-is-probation-ready/

Sweet, H.B. (ed) (2012) *Gender in the Therapy Hour: Voices of Female Clinicians Working with Men*, Routledge/Taylor & Francis Group.

Taylor, J. (2020) *Why Women Are Blamed For Everything: Exploring the Victim Blaming of Women Subjected to Violence and Trauma*, Constable.

Tidmarsh, M. (2023) Gender in a 'caring' profession: The demographic and cultural dynamics of the feminisation of the probation service in England and Wales, *Probation Journal*: 1–21. https://doi.org/10.1177/02645505231221240

Trotter, C. (2023) *Working with Involuntary Clients: A Guide to Practice* (4th edn), Taylor & Francis.

Waterhouse, S. (2023) As social workers, threats and intimidation are par for the course, *Professional Social Work Magazine*, 15 August. Available from: https://basw.co.uk/about-social-work/psw-magazine/articles/social-workers-threats-and-intimidation-are-par-course

Westaby, C., Phillips, J., Fowler, A. and Ainslie, S. (2021) An evaluation of the implementation of reflective practice supervision standards in the national probation service, Helena Kennedy Centre for International Justice. doi: 10.7190/shu.HKCIJ.07.21

Worrall, A. (2008) Gender and probation in the Second World War, *Criminology and Criminal Justice*, 8(3): 317–332. https://doi.org/10.1177/1748895808092432

Zettler, H.R. (2019) Female probation officers, in F.P. Bernat, K. Frailing, L. Gelsthorpe, S. Kethineni and L. Pasko (eds) *The Encyclopedia of Women and Crime*, John Wiley and Sons.

12

Unspoken journeys: reflections of lesbian probation practitioners

Kath Wilson, Daniella Nudd, Hollie Neal and Victoria Jones

This chapter will consider current issues in relation to lesbian women as both probation practitioners and service users of the Probation Service. Evidence will be explored suggesting lesbian women are disproportionately represented among those sentenced by courts across Britain. Reasons for this over-representation, in both prisons and as those supervised by the Probation Service, will be discussed along with the disadvantages that some of these women face. This chapter will then examine models and tools employed by the service to assess risk of reoffending which may lead to an over-assessment of risk for lesbians and therefore impact upon their sentencing. Desistance as an approach to supervision will be discussed, along with its limitations when applied to lesbians.

In terms of positionality, we are four white women who have had different journeys of 'coming out' between 1980 and 2010. For the purposes of consistency, the authors have agreed to adopt the term 'lesbian' for this chapter, despite not all personally aligning with this label. We will discuss sensitivities surrounding terminology later in the chapter. We will also reflect on our experiences as probation practitioners; we all worked as probation officers before becoming lecturers at De Montfort University. Issues of identity for lesbian workers within the criminal justice system (CJS) will be considered, including some of the dilemmas and opportunities this experience provided. Feelings of 'shame' continue to affect lesbian women; we will explore how stigma can impact self-worth. This chapter will reflect upon when the authors have experienced negativity and how they managed these dilemmas over a period of change. Within this discussion, the authors talk about invisible identities and how this can impact upon well-being as probation practitioners.

Lack of research, particularly in the UK

Any discussion of lesbians and the CJS should be prefaced with the fact that there is limited research and writing on this matter (Woods, 2015). Chesney-Lind and Eliason (2006) argue that academics, including criminologists, have been at best 'quiet' and at worst contributed to theory and research that has pathologised marginalised groups, particularly lesbians.

Ideas about what constitutes a 'good woman' remain ever present in the CJS (Rutter and Barr, 2021). Chesney-Lind and Eliason (2006) argue that violence, for example, is associated and perceived as more 'natural' for men; women who are violent are seen in terms of being 'masculinised'. This framework of 'masculinity' implies simplistic notions of 'good' and 'bad' women. Good women are passive and feminine, which crucially allows for the demonisation of some women, particularly from marginalised groups, including lesbians, who are less likely, they argue, to display those 'traditional' characteristics.

Robson (1998) points to some basic methodological considerations: how do we identify a lesbian from newspaper reports or trial transcripts, as if a woman thinks that non-disclosure may lead to a more favourable outcome, she may hide or deny this aspect of her identity (Benoit et al, 2005). Hidden populations can be difficult to reach and capture in research and monitoring exercises. Robson (1998: 39) concludes that 'we have generally failed to address the multitude of issues provoked when a lesbian becomes a criminal defendant', and while written in 1998, there has been limited change.

Over-representation

Existing research indicates that lesbians are disproportionately represented before the courts in the United States (Farr, 2000;

Meyer et al, 2017), Australia (Simpson et al, 2019) and the UK (Fernandes et al, 2020). In terms of incarceration, the number of those identifying as lesbian in the United States is 33 per cent, with a further 9.8 per cent describing themselves as 'sexual minorities' (Meyer et al, 2017). In Australia this figure is 37 per cent (Simpson et al, 2019). HM Prison and Probation Service (HMPPS) (2023) estimates that one in 20 (4 per cent) men and one in four (23 per cent) women in prison identify as gay/lesbian or bisexual. The Bromley briefings (Halliday, 2023) reported that 31 per cent of women in prison report as either lesbian or bisexual. These figures are higher than in the general population which is around 3 per cent for women.

In September 2020, 7 per cent of the people being supervised by the Probation Service identified as lesbian or bisexual, equating to 1,324 people, with an additional 95 describing themselves as 'other' (Ministry of Justice, 2021). Explanations for higher rates of contact with the CJS include homelessness (Albert Kennedy Trust, 2014), often caused by family rejection or violence (Irvine, 2010). LGBTQIA+ youth are more likely to experience higher rates of bullying and victimisation at school, leading to truancy and expulsion (Snapp et al, 2015), school being a resilient factor in the lives of young people who refrain from offending. Young lesbian women reported that homelessness often puts them into vulnerable positions including rough sleeping, substance use and self-medication to ameliorate physical and mental pressures (Knight and Wilson, 2016). Thus, increasing the likelihood of contact with policing agencies. Graziano and Wagner (2011) found that lesbians and bisexual young women in the juvenile justice system are much more likely to have experienced trauma than any other group.

Research from Australia indicates some disproportionality is related to the way lesbians are viewed by those in authority and the way their behaviour is interpreted by law enforcement (Asquith et al, 2017). This can mean that in public spaces, behaviours including public intimacy can lead to negative consequences when the police use discretionary public order powers. In particular, young lesbians and women of colour appear to be 'read' by police in negative ways. Their ways of self-expression, including sexuality, are seen as defiant and aggressive (Dwyer, 2011).

Criminalising behaviour that may be overlooked if performed by other groups and which, if policed aggressively, can spark an escalation of interaction between this marginalised group and authorities. Critically, the research from both America and Australia indicates that there are intersectional issues, as women of colour constitute significant numbers of lesbians who are arrested and/or imprisoned.

Research and experiences of lesbians in prisons

One of the few areas where there is lesbian visibility is their representation in prison and other dramas involving crime (Chesney-Lind and Eliason, 2006). The pairing of 'lesbian' and 'criminal' has become a stereotype most often 'played out' in prison dramas such as *Bad Girls* and *Orange is the New Black*. Depictions of lesbians as jealous, violent and aggressive 'masculine women' over-populate these dramas and must have a real material impact on how they are viewed and treated in the CJS (Millbank, 2004).

In their research, Carr et al (2020) found that a more nuanced approach was needed when discussing lesbian relationships in prisons. The idea that 'jail gays' existed was accepted by inmates and officers. They found a demarcation with 'being' gay, which contained the narrative of 'coming out' and personal struggle, and those who were 'situational'. Officers were likely to express the view that 'jail gays' were heterosexual: 'They're not gay, they're only with girls when they're in prison' (Carr et al, 2020: 555). Some women in same-sex relationships, who had previously identified as heterosexual, however, were themselves unsure if they were 'jail gays' now. One woman, previously heterosexual, had commenced a same-sex relationship a few months into a long sentence. She described the relationship, over three years later, as the most authentic relationship she has experienced: 'So, it's my first sober relationship I've ever been in in my entire life. All the other ones have been drink and drug related … so I know this one is definitely deep down for real … it's like I'm a completely different woman after meeting her' (Carr et al, 2020: 556). For probation officers working with women on release from custody, if such stories are sidestepped or ignored, an opportunity to encourage a move towards desistance could be lost.

Reflecting on approaches to issues of diversity

It is therefore likely that lesbian women feature on the caseload of those being supervised by probation practitioners. The Probation Service as an organisation has promoted diversity and attempts to challenge discrimination as part of its policy and practice. In early 2000, Diversity and Equality consistently appeared on the probation training agenda. The introduction of *The Heart of the Dance: A Diversity Strategy* (National Probation Service, 2003), while criticised for superficially addressing some protected characteristics, such as sexuality (Hilder, 2007), intended to underpin a commitment to anti-discriminatory practice.

For newcomers to the service, diversity was perceived as central to probation values and culture. This early career naivety and optimism went on to align with the views of Canton (2011) who challenged any positive impact of the strategy on the 'Occupational Culture' of this time. One author highlights how classroom-based diversity training was mandatory, often facilitated by external providers who sought to 'elegantly challenge' practitioner views and develop reflective insight into the nuances of language and difference. This backdrop provided context for the New Choreography (2001), which incorporated the inclusion of sexual orientation and disability into the diversity narrative, seeking to encourage confidence that openness about sexuality as a protected characteristic would be met with the support and inclusion, evident in some office settings. Indeed, Ellsworth et al (nd) suggest that colleagues have much more influence in creating an inclusive environment than any well-intentioned structure and supportive mechanisms such as staff networks.

In 2003, the autonomy of Local Probation Services was lost, replaced by National Probation Directorate oversight, followed by the National Offender Management Service in 2008. Local training arrangements were replaced by national structures and a move to online independent learning. Personal growth in anti-discriminatory practice was observed through policy rhetoric rather than self-reflection and challenge through training. The authors found that the safe space in which previous important discussions were held gradually eroded, along with practitioner confidence to be their authentic self. Reflections on how these changes may have correlated with the lesbian practitioner's experience of inclusivity will be discussed later in this chapter.

Current intervention practices and how they relate to lesbians

If some issues that lesbians face are different, then we need to consider the tools and approaches currently used to assess risk and manage interventions to maximise the chances of rehabilitation. An initial barrier to recording the number of lesbians who might be on caseloads is the process in which this information is gathered. The question of sexuality, for example, is asked at initial contact with the Probation Service and on reception into prison. This is often completed at the same time as numerous induction forms, at a time where rapport has not been established between practitioner and service user. Individuals may feel uncomfortable to disclose their sexuality at this point.

Desistance

A useful example of current rehabilitative efforts and how they relate to lesbians is the use of desistance approaches. Desistance is a key approach, based on research which indicates that people will mature, that their life courses will develop and that they will transition to non-offenders (Laub and Sampson, 2003). As part of this transition, people will develop more prosocial attitudes and behaviours while developing their social capital such as employment, marriage, family ties and formation (Carlsson, 2013). It is envisaged that in drawing on this social capital, they will be more able to reduce and desist from offending (Maruna, 2001). As part of the desistance journey, individuals might look at their own identity, how they began to offend and how their identity has changed to one of non-offender.

Research around the LGBTQIA+ community has consistently recognised that normative life trajectories (Freeman, 2010) are not necessarily transferable onto LGBTQIA+ people (Berggren et al, 2020). Desistance narratives around, for example, 'making good' and being one's true self, are important ingredients to the journey of desistance. The criticism is that a life schedule of events that occur in a certain order and at a particular time is not particularly relevant or helpful when considering lesbians. Indeed, in some sections of the lesbian community, the idea of embracing institutions including marriage, seen as harmful to women, is challenged (Barker, 2013).

The desistance approach also looks at the development of social capital. This might include success at education, family support, obtaining permanent employment, accommodation, and social stability (Snapp et al, 2015). These areas, as discussed earlier, are where LGBTQIA+ people experience difficulties. The assessment tools and case management processes used by HMPPS may therefore need to be used in a more nuanced way. Lesbians who may not conform to maturity and lifetime trajectories, including expectations of getting married, having children, or having them later in life, can be disadvantaged in risk assessments and management using desistance approaches.

The Risk, Need, Responsivity model

A second model that has come to dominate probation practice is the Risk, Need, Responsivity (RNR) approach (Bonta, 2023). This seeks to focus resources on those more at risk of reoffending by assessing and managing risks, focusing on criminogenic needs and ensuring interventions respond to individual needs. The RNR model has been critiqued for gender bias by using male samples and applying these to the needs of women (Messina and Esparza, 2022). Roig-Palmer and Lutze (2021: 3) argue that it should be applied with sensitivity to LGBTQIA+ people as, in practice, assessments tend to default to 'heteronormative gendered systems of oppression'. Roig-Palmer and Lutze (2021), in their study of young LGBTQIA+ adults, sought to identify prevention strategies given their over-representation in young adult offending institutions. They reported that participants had invested substantial amounts of emotional labour in consistently navigating hostile spaces and toxic relationships to avoid potential offending situations; much of this labour is invisible to those interacting with them.

They further found that LGBTQIA+ youths were more likely to be assessed as low risk in terms of offending but high in terms of need. There is the possibility of an overestimation of risk when behaviour, explained as survival strategies, can be interpreted as aggressive and viewed incorrectly as criminogenic. Overall, LGBTQIA+ people are assessed at the lower end of risk of reoffending. As the focus of this model tends to be on risk of reoffending and serious harm, LGBTQIA+ young adults, who may have distinct needs relating to marginalisation, complicated by social stigma, and the associated emotional and physical trauma, do not have their distinct needs met as they are not considered at a high enough level of risk to merit resources.

The term responsivity refers to designing interventions based on the most effective way to engage individuals. For lesbians this would require the use of strategies aligned with their learning needs and identities. This can be problematic if the population is hidden but even if not, relevant staff training related to lesbian individuals is needed. Roig-Palmer and Lutze (2021) consider whether a warm, respectful and collaborative working alliance can be achieved in the absence of appropriate modelling, reinforcement and problem-solving. They emphasise that any interventions delivered to lesbian and gender non-conforming girls should provide social care and be trauma informed to address their risks and unique needs.

Research into LGBTQIA+ resilience indicates that narratives of 'coming out', and difficulties or barriers encountered, can inform the development of resilience. Simply allowing people to develop their own narrative around 'coming out' or their identity can be a supportive intervention on its own (Peel et al, 2023). Peel et al (2023) identify benefits of a shift from a 'deficits' model (RNR) in mental health, to a more resilience-based approach – a shift that is recognisable for probation practitioners.

In addition, if we consider Leverentz's (2006) argument that when men are involved in the lives of women subject to the CJS, some men are primarily in the role of promoting the criminal behaviour and causing victimisation, it is therefore possible that a lesbian relationship, in some circumstances, might prove to be a protective factor in desistance. Rutter (2019) points to the importance of relationships in promoting desistance, that qualities of trust, being respected and not being judged are critical in desistance supportive relationships. For probation practitioners, therefore, the determination of the supportive meaningful relationship is paramount, rather than the gender of the person involved.

We wish to encourage probation practitioners to engage in discussions around discrimination and experiences of being lesbian. While we might assume that these conversations take place, we know, for example, from the 2023 HMIP inspection related to race equality that 'in the cases inspected there was still little evidence that probation staff had spoken with minority ethnic people on probation about their ethnicity, culture, religion, and experiences of discrimination, or planned interventions that were responsive to these diversity factors' (HMIP, 2023: 3). It is possible therefore that practitioners are failing to discuss identity and relationships.

Reflections on being a lesbian probation practitioner

This territory can be confusing to navigate as practitioners, including terms we use and how we use them. While we have adopted the term 'lesbian' for this chapter, only one of us uses this term regularly to identify ourselves. The term lesbian comes from the Greek Island of Lesbos where the ancient poet Sappho lived and where fragments of her work were found to contain romantic poetry to another woman. Some use 'gay' or 'gay woman' while others prefer not to label themselves. This reflects changes in both society and the LGBTQIA+ community over the past 40 years, the period we have practised in. While in the 1980s there were few terms to identify women who were emotionally and sexually attracted to women, there are now more terms to use. When our discussions developed it emerged that we had all heard the term 'lesbian' used as an insult and some wanted to steer clear of this label, at a time in their lives when they were coming to terms with their sexuality. Further, lesbians who came out in the 2000s have seen the term as limiting, while they see their sexual identity as an important aspect of their identity, they do not necessarily want it to be seen as the defining aspect.

While we have of course all experienced life differently, feelings of stigma and shame have impacted on us all and it remains a tangible part of our experience. Goffman suggested that:

> [A] stigmatized person is trained first of all in others' views of persons like himself ... the standards he has incorporated from the wider society equip him to be intimately alive to what others see as his failing, inevitably causing him, if only for moments to agree that he does indeed fall short of what he really ought to be. (Goffman, 1963, cited in Goffman, 1990: 160)

We have all encountered people who have viewed our lesbianism as a failing and, at the same time, we all have degrees of internalised homophobia. Berzon (1979) explains that children are exposed to anti-gay jokes, they are aware of stereotypes about butch, ugly lesbians and effeminate men. While this was written in the 1970s, research indicates that shame remains a factor in the lives of lesbians.

In the workplace we have experienced shame to come out, and sometimes, shame in not coming out. We have, for example, been in staff rooms when asked about 'husbands' and not responded that our partner is a woman, while colleagues who were aware of this fact were present. We do not necessarily want to 'come out' all of the time and particularly when the issue is raised without notice. We acknowledge therefore that we have not always acted as role models to those new to the organisation, who seemed less confident. Nor have we consistently come out to service users to whom we might have provided an environment to discuss their feelings of minority stress and stigma, to model strength, resilience and that life as a lesbian can be positive. Crawley's (2004) research around the public and private lives of prison officers identifies front and backstage display of self, where identity is constantly managed and negotiated, and we can relate to this. These experiences have stayed with us, struggles of being 'out' and not being 'out' as probation practitioners as well as expectations of others as to whether we should be 'out', reactions to being pregnant, issues with service users or other occurrences. It can leave one feeling uncertain, as Goffman (1990) explains, making us recall events that left us feeling inadequate to situations, questioning our own responses.

Gomes and Felix (2019) identified several reasons why lesbians do not disclose their sexuality in the workplace. They concluded that when 'outing' themselves threatens the sense of individual distinctiveness and personal belonging, lesbians may stay silent about their sexuality at work. They highlighted that non-disclosure of sexual identity can be damaging for emotional well-being and mental health. So, while there have been many positive changes in terms of, for example, 'rights' for lesbians, in the CJS sector, Ellsworth (2021) suggests that employees from LGBTQIA+ communities still feel uncomfortable to talk openly about themselves.

One author who started probation practice during the *Heart of the Dance* era was initially comfortable to disclose her sexuality, but recognised a marked change in levels of comfort as changes in organisational approaches to diversity and inclusion were apparent. This author experienced homophobia for the first time when working in a multi-disciplinary team. A masculine police presence was prevalent and jokes about sexuality and related microaggressions were framed as police culture. Sklansky (2007) suggests that police culture often appears as an 'unquestioned orthodoxy', having now become so routinely accepted. The author was disappointed that senior leaders were also accepting of this rhetoric and not supportive in response to a complaint.

Many 'jokes' in this multi-disciplinary environment were linked to both sexuality and gender, offending in two areas in the context of intersectionality. Any challenges from colleagues were delivered with a light-hearted sentiment that indicated this was perhaps just the wrong time and place for such humour. The author is ashamed to admit having remained silent or loosely engaging in self-deprecating humour, as a misinformed attempt to qualify for in-group status (Tajfel and Turner, 1979), and a desire to blend in. Subsequently, the author retreated in the workplace and withdrew from social events, wanting to be defined only by professional output.

One author found that ten years after recruitment, a sense of responsibility encouraged self-disclosure of sexuality, to promote difference and combat heteronormativity to support a safe and welcoming environment for lesbian hostel residents recently released from custody. It is not a coincidence that disclosures in the latter years were very much triggered by self-determination, rather than a perceived sense of protection from organisational values.

Conclusion

Lesbians constitute a disproportionate number of people in prison and on probation, and while research was initially drawn from America, this trajectory is becoming apparent in Britain. The reasons for this over-representation seem multifaceted. Young lesbians are more likely to be bullied at school, to leave home earlier and become homeless. The consequences of homophobia, homelessness and the way they are policed means they are more likely to be arrested using discretionary powers. In addition, homelessness and lack of social capital can lead to problematic use of alcohol and substances, leading to possible mental health issues, all of which can lead to an increased likelihood of contact with police and justice agencies.

A growing body of research around interventions employed with women helps us consider how probation practitioners might work with lesbians. The application of both desistance and RNR approaches need to be considered and some of their limitations acknowledged when working with the distinct needs of lesbians.

It might appear intrusive to enquire about a person's sexuality, nevertheless as probation practitioners we are skilled at asking questions about difficult subjects. For some lesbians, their sexuality might be part of their desistance narrative, how they overcame family breakdown, homelessness or substance use. Allowing service users to articulate their narrative around 'coming out' or aspects of their experience is recognised as part of a desistance journey and can be a valuable part of the supervisory process. The probation practitioner role encompasses skills of positive relationship building and mentoring, and Rutter and Barr (2021) advocate that a fundamental part of practice should allow for feelings of shame and stigmatisation to be explored, and that without this process, desistance from both crime and harm is unlikely to occur.

Discussing sexuality and asking people to self-define instead of completing a tick-box exercise are ways of encouraging people to disclose their sexuality at an early stage in the supervisory relationship. This approach benefits the working relationship moving forwards in an open and productive manner, enabling the provision of resources to support lesbian service users going forward.

Reflective prompts

- Which factors do you think are most significant in explaining why lesbians are disproportionately represented in the criminal justice system?
- You may find yourself confused as to the best approach in terms of language when working with lesbians. What terms do you use and can you reflect on what has influenced your choice?
- How do you think information regarding sexuality could be gathered in a more responsive way to enable practitioners to build a rapport at induction?

References

Albert Kennedy Trust (2014) LGBTQ+ youth homelessness. Available from: https://blog.ukdataservice.ac.uk/lgbtq-homelessness/

Asquith, N., Dwyer, A. and Simpson, P. (2017) A queer criminal career, *Current Issues in Criminal Justice*, 29(2): 167–180.

Barker, A. (2013) *Not the Marrying Kind: A Feminist Critique of Same-sex Marriage*, Palgrave Macmillan.

Benoit, C., Janssen, M. and Phillips, R. (2005) Community-academic research on hard-to-reach populations: Benefits and challenges, *Qualitative Health Research*, 15(2): 263–282. https://doi.org/10.1177/1049732304267752.

Berggren, K., Gottzén, L. and Bornäs, H. (2020) Queering desistance: Chrononormativity, afterwardsness and young men's sexual intimate partner violence, *Criminology and Criminal Justice*, 20(5): 604–616. https://doi.org/10.1177/1748895820937328

Berzon, B. (1979) Developing a positive gay identity, in B. Berzon and R. Leighton (eds) *Positively Gay*, Celestial Arts, pp 1–14.

Bonta, J. (2023) The risk-need-responsivity model: 1990 to the present, *HM Inspectorate of Probation Academic Insights* 2023/06. Available from: https://www.publicsafety.gc.ca/cnt/rsrcs/pblctns/rsk-nd-rspnsvty/index-en.aspx

Canton, R. (2011) *Probation: Working With Offenders*, Willan.

Carlsson, C. (2013) Masculinities, persistence, and desistance, *Criminology*, 51(3): 661–693. https://doi.org/10.1111/1745-9125.12016

Carr, N., Serisier, T. and McAlister, S. (2020) Sexual deviance in prison: Queering identity and intimacy in prison research, *Criminology & Criminal Justice*, 20(5): 551–563. https://doi.org/10.1177/1748895820937401

Chesney-Lind, M. and Eliason, M. (2006) From invisible to incorrigible: The demonization of marginalized women and girls, *Crime, Media, Culture*, 2(1): 29–47. https://doi.org/10.1177/1741659006061709

Crawley, E.M. (2004) *Doing Prison Work: The Public and Private Lives of Prison Officers*, Willan.

Dwyer, A. (2011) Policing lesbian, gay, bisexual and transgender young people: A gap in the research literature, *Current Issues in Criminal Justice*, 22(3): 415–433. http://dx.doi.org/10.1080/10345329.2011.12035896

Ellsworth, D., Hancock, B. and Schaninger, B. (nd) LGBTQ+ inclusion in the workplace: How to take action to support LGBTQ+ employees, McKinsey Global Publishing. Available from: https://www.mckinsey.com/capabilities/people-and-organizational-performance/our-insights/lgbtq-plus-inclusion-in-the-workplace

Ellsworth, P.C. (2021) Truth and advocacy: Reducing bias in policy-related research, *Perspectives on Psychological Science*, 16(6): 1226–1241. https://doi.org/10.1177/1745691620959832

Farr, K.A. (2000) Defeminizing and dehumanizing female murderers, *Women and Criminal Justice*, 11(1): 49–66. https://doi.org/10.1300/J012v11n01_03

Fernandes, F.L., Kaufmann, B. and Kaufmann, K. (2020) *LGBT+ People in Prisons: Experiences in England and Scotland*, University of Dundee. Available from: https://doi.org/10.20933/100001165

Freeman, E. (2010) *Time Binds: Queer Temporalities, Queer Histories*, Duke University Press. https://doi.org/10.1215/9780822393184

Goffman, E. (1990) *Stigma: Notes on the Management of Spoiled Identity*, Penguin Books.

Gomes, R. and Felix, B. (2019) In the closet: A grounded theory of the silence of gays and lesbians in the workplace, *Cadernos EBAPE. BR*, 17(2): 375–388. https://doi.org/10.1590/1679-395174796

Graziano, J.N. and Wagner, E.F. (2011) Trauma among lesbians and bisexual girls in the juvenile justice system, *Traumatology*, 17(2): 45–55. https://doi.org/10.1177/1534765610391817

Halliday, M. (2023) *Bromley Briefings Prison Factfile*, Prison Reform Trust. Available from: https://prisonreformtrust.org.uk/publication/bromley-briefings-prison-factfile-january-2023/

Hilder, S. (2007) Anti-discriminatory practice, in R. Canton and D. Hancock (eds) *Dictionary of Probation and Offender Management* (1st edn), Willan, pp 9–11.

HMIP (HM Inspectorate of Probation) (2023) Race equality in probation follow-up: A work in progress. Available from: chrome-extension://efaidnbmnnnibpcajpcglclefindmkaj/https://www.justiceinspectorates.gov.uk/hmiprobation/wp-content/uploads/sites/5/2023/09/Race-equality-in-probation-follow-up-thematic-inspection-v1.0.pdf

HMPPS Offender Equalities Annual Report (2023) https://www.gov.uk/government/statistics/hmpps-offender-equalities-annual-report-2022-to-2023

Irvine, A. (2010) We've had three of them: Addressing the invisibility of lesbian, gay, bisexual, and gender nonconforming youths in the juvenile justice system, *Columbia Journal of Gender and Law*, 19(3). https://doi.org/10.7916/cjgl.v19i3.2603

Knight, C. and Wilson, K. (2016) *Lesbian, Gay, Bisexual and Transgender People and the Criminal Justice System*, Macmillan.

Laub, J.H. and Sampson, R.J. (2003) *Shared Beginnings, Divergent Lives: Delinquent Boys to Age 70*, Harvard University Press.

Leverentz, A.M. (2006) The love of a good man? Romantic relationships as a source of support or hindrance for female ex-offenders, *Journal of Research in Crime and Delinquency*, 43(4): 459–488. https://doi.org/10.1177/0022427806293323

Maruna, S. (2001) *Making Good: How Ex-convicts Reform and Rebuild Their Lives*, American Psychological Association.

Messina, N.P. and Esparza, P. (2022) Poking the bear: The inapplicability of the RNR principles for justice-involved women, *Journal of Substance Abuse Treatment*, 140. https://doi.org/10.1016/j.jsat.2022.108798

Meyer, I., Flores, A. and Stemple, L. (2017) Incarceration rates and traits of sexual minorities in the United States: National inmate survey, 2011–2012, *American Journal of Public Health*, 107(2): 267–273. https://doi.org/10.2105/AJPH.2016.303576

Millbank, J. (2004) It's about this: Lesbians, prison, desire, *Social and Legal Studies*, 13(2): 155–190. https://doi.org/10.1177/0964663904042550

Ministry of Justice (2021) Response to a freedom of information request from the author, 12 May.

National Probation Service (2003) *The Heart of the Dance: A Diversity Strategy for the National Probation Service for England and Wales 2002–2006*, Home Office.

Peel, E., Rivers, I., Tyler, A., Nodin, N. and Perez-Acevedo, C. (2023) Exploring LGBT resilience and moving beyond a deficit-model: Findings from a qualitative study in England, *Psychology and Sexuality*, 14(1): 114–126. https://doi.org/10.1080/19419899.2022.2063754

Robson, R. (1998) *Sappho Goes to Law School*, Columbia University Press.

Roig-Palmer, K. and Lutze, F.E. (2021) Confronting oppression: Reframing need and advancing responsivity for LGBTQ+ youth and young adults, *Women and Criminal Justice*, 32(1): 1–27. https://doi.org/10.1080/08974454.2021.1962482

Rutter, N. (2019) *The Golden Thread: Service User Narratives on Desistance, the Role of Relationships and Opportunities for Co-produced Rehabilitation*, Doctoral Thesis, Manchester Metropolitan University.

Rutter, N. and Barr, U. (2021) Being a 'good woman': Stigma, relationships and desistance, *Probation Journal*, 68(2): 166–185. https://doi.org/10.1177/02645505211010336

Simpson, P.L., Hardiman, D. and Butler, T. (2019) Understanding the over-representation of lesbian or bisexual women in the Australian prisoner population, *Current Issues in Criminal Justice*, 31(3): 365–377. https://doi.org/10.1080/10345329.2019.1668339

Sklansky, D.A. (2007) Seeing blue: Police reform, occupational culture, and cognitive burnn, in M. O'Neill, M. Marks and A. Singh (eds) *Police Occupational Culture: New Debates and Directions*, Elsevier, pp 19–46.

Snapp, S., Hoenig, J., Fields, A. and Russell, S. (2015) Messy, butch, and queer, *Journal of Adolescent Research*, 30: 57–82. https://doi.org/10.1177/0743558414557625

Tajfel, H. and Turner, J. (1979) An integrative theory of intergroup conflict, in W.G. Austin and S. Worchel (eds) *The Social Psychology of Intergroup Relations*.

Woods, J.B. (2015) The birth of modern criminology and gendered constructions of homosexual criminal identity, *Journal of Homosexuality*, 62(2): 131–166. https://doi.org/10.1080/00918369.2014.969053

PART IV

Teaching, learning and professional development

13

'SCOPE' for reflection: a framework of transformative outcomes for probation officer training

Ben Keysell

This chapter explores the potential value of reflective practice in promoting a framework of 'transformative' learning outcomes for the Professional Qualification in Probation (PQiP). Transformative education can be summarised as 'an innovative pedagogical approach that empowers learners to critically examine their contexts, beliefs, values, knowledge and attitudes with the goal of developing spaces for self-reflection, appreciation of diversity and critical thinking … transforming knowledge, attitudes and skills' (UNESCO, 2017: 4). Key models are explored in terms of application to PQiP, alongside discussion of the fluid nature of probation culture, implications for training and how a more transformative focus may enhance practice. Findings are considered from an evaluation of a pilot transformative framework, focusing on achievement of outcomes and pedagogical methods most conducive to success. Reflections are also made on my own experiences of integrating elements of transformative learning into design and delivery of PQiP teaching. Conclusions support the use of reflective practice to enable transformative outcomes and complement the more 'instrumental' aims of qualification. In particular, promoting critical reflection on how learners' own values, experiences and perspectives influence their personal practice is encouraged throughout all aspects of teaching and assessment. A revised framework of transformative outcomes is proposed using the acronym 'SCOPE': *Self-awareness, Critical consciousness, Organisational values, Professional identity and resilience* and *Ethical humility*. Links to continuous professional development are considered and it is acknowledged that true assessment of transformation may require a holistic, longitudinal approach. The chapter therefore ends with some reflective prompts to consider how this could be promoted.

Review of literature

Dirkx (1998) highlights that the definition of transformative learning and how it may be fostered are open to varying perspectives, however he outlines four fundamental models. These are explored in what follows, alongside two related concepts of 'organisational values' and 'ethical humility', to inform the basis of a reflective framework for probation training.

Critical consciousness (Freire, 1970)

Freire (1970) was sceptical of what he termed 'banking education', with students expected to uncritically accept facts or opinions as presented by teachers. He believed that education should empower learners to overcome social inequality by developing 'critical consciousness', that is, evaluating and questioning the socio-political context of their experiences via a reflective method of 'praxis', whereby students are 'distanced from their world of everyday action in order to see it in a different, more critical, light with a view to transforming it' (Freire, 1970, quoted in Mayo, 1993: 12). In the context of PQiP it is important for learners to remain sensitive to evolving socio-political agendas and how they may influence organisational practices. Probation training was separated from its previous social work roots in the 1990s and has continued to evolve since this time (Burrell and Petrillo, 2022). This took place alongside increasingly punitive and managerialist cultures within the organisation (Lancaster, 2003) and several authors expressed concern about how training may shape the values of staff entering the profession, potentially undermining the fundamental supportive, person-centred ideals of practice (Treadwell, 2006; Skinner and Goldhill, 2013). Themes of challenging marginalisation also have parallels with the overarching organisational ethos of rehabilitation. McNeill (2012) highlights how the stigma of criminal conviction can exacerbate a cycle of social exclusion, necessitating four distinct forms of rehabilitation, summarised as:

1. Personal: promoting individual change or improvement, for example in attitudes or thinking.
2. Legal/judicial: restoring individuals to the citizenship they had prior to conviction.
3. Moral: mediating harm done to victims or communities.
4. Social: encouraging a sense of reintegration and belonging to prosocial networks.

Burrell and Petrillo (2022) propose that frameworks for probation training should focus explicitly on promoting all of these forms. In relation to social and moral rehabilitation in particular, they emphasise the need to position practice 'as part of a broader project to challenge structural inequality', suggesting that 'this aspect of learning and development is not nurtured, which can make the learning feel obsolete' (2022: 181). Active reflection on 'critical consciousness' then is included as a transformative outcome for PQiP learners, in order to foster a more holistic approach to rehabilitation.

Perspective transformation (Mezirow, 1991)

Mezirow's central theme is that adult learners will have developed a set of core beliefs and values over the course of their lives, which can shape their perception of education. He outlines these 'frames of reference' as a two-step process, beginning with 'habits of mind' (broad patterns of thinking, feeling or behaving). These often become quite fixed in early life by influence of peers, upbringing and culture, leading to 'points of view' (attitudes, judgements or feelings towards specific people or situations). While points of view can be dynamic and flexible, they remain largely determined by more enduring habits of mind, which can be prone to limitation, distortion or bias. A key aspect of

Mezirow's pedagogy is presenting 'disorienting dilemmas', that is, situations which encourage learners to reflect on, challenge and, where necessary, reconstruct their core beliefs and/or recognise the validity of alternative perspectives. Again, this has relevance to PQiP learners, who may re-enter academia with ingrained points of view. These can potentially manifest in practice as 'unconscious bias' towards cases on the basis of offence type, personal characteristics, and so on (Mullineux et al, 2019). Therefore, it is important to encourage reflection on how frames of reference may shape personal interactions. Burrell and Petrillo (2022) further emphasise how a failure to confront and address negative emotions towards individuals convicted of serious violent or sexual offences can lead to overly judgemental or punitive approaches. They highlight the importance of 'reflective engagement with ethical and moral dilemmas' (2022: 184), to support the aim of moral rehabilitation. Mezirow's model then (together with Boyd's 1991 concept of 'individuation') informs the proposed transformative dimension of 'self-awareness'.

Identity transformation (Daloz, 1986)

Daloz viewed adult learning as an opportunity for personal development or growth, whereby learners move from one 'identity' to another (for example, 'parent/worker' to 'student/learner'). While generally liberating, this shift can be daunting or stressful. Daloz (1986) proposed that key roles for educators should be to design learning activities in a manner that encourages specific reflection on changes in identity and ensuring that appropriate sources of support are in place to help make sense of this. Learners undertaking the PQiP will initially enter the service as Probation Service officers, where levels of responsibility are lower than those of qualified probation officers (under previous arrangements they were employed as 'trainee' probation officers, again with lower and typically less serious caseloads). Interviews with newly qualified staff have highlighted how the shift in professional identity on graduation can be a source of some anxiety (Gregory, 2007; Forbes, 2010). Burrell and Petrillo (2022) expressed additional concern about the liminal space which PQiP candidates currently occupy and how this may lead to confused or ambiguous identities, that is, whether they view themselves primarily as students/learners or fully integrated employees of the service. A number of authors have also demonstrated how the Transforming Rehabilitation agenda impacted negatively on qualifying staff's perceptions of their own professionalism and legitimacy (Deering and Felizer, 2017; Cooper, 2021). Parmar and Nudd (2021) highlight how the impact of change is likely to be ongoing post-unification and that staff may continue to experience issues of vulnerability and anxiety. Therefore, 'professional identity and resilience' is proposed here as a specific dimension for transformative reflection.

Individuation (Boyd, 1991)

Boyd viewed the aims of adult learning as providing opportunities for introspection, making participants more conscious of their 'unknown selves'. While this can be difficult to measure in a structured framework (Dirkx, 1998), developing awareness of internal schemas could be beneficial for probation staff in terms of the complexity of issues they will encounter in practice (for consideration of this using the creative arts, see Chapter 8). Phillips et al (2022: 2) highlight the important quality of 'professional curiosity', defined as 'the capacity and communication skill to explore and understand what is happening ... rather than making assumptions or taking things at face value'. They discuss how managerialist agendas have led to practitioners interpreting this primarily as a tool for assessing risk, however it can also be crucial to more therapeutic decisions and supportive problem-solving. One means they suggest for enabling staff to appreciate the breadth and depth of professional curiosity is for it to be explicitly promoted in training, encouraging reflection on how learners' own 'structural, relational and emotional' issues may interact with those of people on probation. Burrell and Petrillo (2022) highlight the importance of reflexivity and practitioners understanding their individual qualities in relation to promoting personal rehabilitation. They identify these characteristics as key to a wider 'culture of learning', enabling more desistance-focused approaches to practice. Along with Mezirow's (1991) model of perspective transformation, Boyd's theories inform the dimension of 'self-awareness' in the proposed framework.

Transformation and organisational values

The current academic framework for probation training (HMPPS, 2022) is based around key themes referred to as the 'three pillars', namely *professional ethics, values and practice*; *rehabilitation and change agency*; and *risk management and assessment*. These provide the basis for the core modules and their intended learning outcomes. Many of these are phrased as instrumental, practice-based objectives such as ability to prepare reports, sustain inter-agency relationships, and so on. Some, however, imply a more transformative focus, for example 'reflect on practice and continuously develop and demonstrate the professional ethics and values of the Community Justice sector'. This focus on the wider values of the organisation is important to ensure that practice takes account of official professional frameworks and protocols. However, there is potential for feelings of conflict or challenges to legitimacy when changing organisational expectations may be inconsistent with learners' individual values or sense of professionalism. To mitigate these tensions, the dimension of 'organisational values' emphasises the need to uphold the underpinning values of the Probation Service, while also reflecting on and maintaining sensitivity to the fluid nature of practice. Alongside this, the dimension of 'professional identity' encourages learners to maintain a sense of resilience when there may be dissonance between the dimensions of *personal*, *professional* and *organisational* values (Skinner and Goldhill, 2013).

Transformation and 'ethical humility'

Reamer (2023: 5) defines 'ethical humility' as 'a quality where practitioners are less than absolutely certain about their moral instincts and judgements'. More specific characteristics underpinning this include realism and honesty about one's own skills or abilities, recognising and learning from previous mistakes, remaining open to new or conflicting ideas and retaining a sense of self-perspective. Reamer goes on to outline the importance of probation staff maintaining awareness of the complex ethical implications of decisions and the challenges this can bring. Judgements often have to be made under pressure and in situations where there may be competing demands, for example maintaining standard agency protocols while also considering the best interests of individual cases. A failure to maintain this sense of fallibility can lead to moral disengagement or 'satisficing' (aiming for a 'satisfactory or adequate result, rather than the ideal or optimal solution' [Reamer, 2023: 5]). 'Ethical humility' is therefore included as a specific dimension within the proposed framework to mitigate these risks.

Wider criticism of the concept of transformative education has focused on challenges in defining and measuring achievable progress (Nerstrom, 2014). However, its principles have been actively integrated into curricula and learning activities in other professional fields such as nursing (Tsimar and Downing, 2020), graduate medical training (Vipler et al, 2021) and also in frameworks for prisoner education (Clark, 2016). While they do not explicitly use the term, Tangen and Briah (2018: 143) make a tentative case for a transformative approach in probation, commenting that in recent years training 'has focused too much on developing standardised skills and enforcement, at the expense of the kind of academically rigorous thinking required to resolve the ethical and moral dilemmas experienced by probationers and probation officers alike'.

Carr (2020: 7) also suggested that the academic component should have a wider focus than simply imparting theoretical knowledge, advocating the promotion of qualities such as 'mastery and innovation ... a degree of responsibility and autonomy involving the ability to manage complex professional activities'.

It is acknowledged that PQiP learners are under considerable time pressures (Burrell and Petrillo, 2022) and may prioritise 'instrumental' aims of achieving professional qualification and learning practical skills. The framework proposed is primarily intended for academic providers to embed transformation into existing PQiP activities so that teaching can be designed to encourage more explicit reflection on relevant areas. While it is important that this does not make the extrinsic aims of qualification more onerous, these elements should not be seen as mutually exclusive. Cranton (2016: 79) suggests that often 'instrumental learning ... spirals into transformative learning ... in turn, transformative learning can lead people to the further need to instrumental learning'. Probation as an organisation has been criticised for providing few opportunities for continuous professional development beyond the professional qualification itself (Bowen, 2021). This may potentially pose barriers to maintaining positive practice, if learners feel dissonance between perceptions of the role presented in training and the reality of their experiences when qualified (Burrell, 2022). The relationship between transformation and continuous professional development is then important to consider and could be viewed as cyclical. Promoting a critically reflective approach throughout training may increase appetite for further learning and development. Equally, though, true transformation may be a longer-term process, dependent on ongoing reflection and maintenance of applying theory in practice.

A common thread through transformative models is the importance of active reflection, with respective emphasis on socio-political contexts, frames of reference, sense of identity and previously 'unknown' aspects of the self. An initial transformative framework for PQiP was created as part of my own research dissertation (Keysell, 2022), completed while unification of probation, awarding of contracts for academic providers and development of the new training curriculum were taking place. Research also focused on how current teaching of PQiP may support transformation and which methods may be most effective in this respect. Following the COVID-19 pandemic in mid-2020, academic teaching on PQiP at the University of Portsmouth has been delivered exclusively online. This includes live seminars via platforms such as Google Meets or Microsoft Teams, and asynchronous content/activities using the Virtual Learning Environment 'Moodle'. Buchanan and Senior (2003) highlighted the potentially isolating impact of distance learning in probation, however they also believed it could place more emphasis on self-directed study over instrumental teaching, promoting potential benefits in terms of critical and reflective thinking. While online technologies were relatively new at the time, they made a case for these as distinct from traditional 'correspondence' based distance learning and more conducive to student-centred education. Fowler et al (2023) explored the experiences of PQiP learners during the pandemic and found mixed views in relation to exclusively online study. Some respondents echoed previous concerns about isolation and lack of interaction with peers, however others were positive about the convenience and flexibility of being able to access and revisit resources in their own time. Meyers (2008) and Hiller (2018) have looked explicitly at the link between online teaching and transformative learning in their respective disciplines of criminal justice studies and law. Both discuss the value of using a range of technologies to support learning as well as how the 'anonymity' of online forums for reflective discussion may empower learners to be more self-critical and contribute their own perspectives.

Research findings and personal reflections

The transformative dimensions proposed in the original pilot framework were referred to as 'critical awareness and reflection', 'professional identity and resilience', 'organisational values', 'recognising personal perspectives and values' and 'complex and interpersonal problem-solving'. Measures of successful outcomes were primarily restricted to self-report from a graduating cohort. However, using a mixed methods approach, including quantitative questionnaires and focus groups with both learners and staff, some encouraging findings were made in all dimensions. Staff and students felt that the proposed transformative outcomes were relevant to the role of a qualified probation officer and that there was value in explicitly promoting these in teaching. While this was a small-scale study, student responses (n=6) generally indicated that learners felt they had achieved some level of transformation over the course of the programme. Specific focus is made here on the dimension 'professional identity and resilience'. While over 70 per cent of respondents stated positive outcomes, only 50 per cent expressed confidence they would be able to maintain these in the longer term. Those who reported less confidence raised concerns about the continuing uncertainty of how the service itself may evolve. This potentially reinforces the importance of ongoing learning and reflection to enable maintenance of transformation, however there were again positive findings in relation to this, with all respondents saying that they had an increased commitment to continuous professional development on completion of the programme.

In terms of the teaching activities and methods most beneficial to transformation, two were consistently identified by respondents in both quantitative and qualitative feedback, namely completing assignments with a specific reflective focus and one-to-one tutorials with teaching staff. Learners in the focus group were particularly positive about how the former had been implemented at Portsmouth. Assignments for each module typically included one 'reflective essay' where learners were required to critically reflect on examples of their practice with specific cases in terms of how theoretical concepts and learning from the module were applied. One participant in the focus group commented: 'Reflection has been personally the greatest bit for me. What I'm going to be using going forward is reflecting on the cases I have and linking to the theory' (Participant 1). This finding is consistent with the principles suggested by Meyers (2008) and Hiller (2018) about how transformation can be maximised by setting tasks with 'real-world' applications and promoting reflection on action-oriented solutions. While learners on this cohort had not been explicitly taught models of transformative learning, several gave examples of potential 'disorienting dilemmas' (Mezirow, 1997). For example, some recognised how reflecting on applications of theory with specific cases had demonstrated that concepts they had previously seen as purely academic did have genuine value in practice. Others talked about how reflection had enabled changes of perspective, for example overcoming biases to work more objectively with cases such as sexual offenders.

The issue of tutor support links to Daloz's (1986) concept of educators taking a mentoring role to promote transformation of identity. Cranton (2016) also emphasises the importance of assisting learners in negotiating any difficulties they may experience on the transformative 'journey'. Participants spoke positively about the reflective approach teaching staff had taken, encouraging them to think of examples from their own practice to enable them to make sense of concepts and recognise how their knowledge had developed. For example: 'I definitely like the one to ones with a tutor, where you were able to like really just approach and say where your mind was ... it's good to have that chance to tunnel down as to what the actual point is' (Participant 3).

However, while respondents recognised their own responsibility to contact tutors when needed, several commented that online teaching had presented barriers in terms of staff 'visibility' and felt this was not always conducive to a proactive approach. The final item on the questionnaire asked participants whether they felt exclusively online delivery was most appropriate for the programme or if their preference would have been for either a completely face to face or a 'blended' approach (as defined by Bonk and Graham, 2012). In responses, 83 per cent opted for blended and 17 per cent for online only, indicating that all recognised some value to existing methods. However, Meyers (2008) emphasises that the foundation of enabling the levels of reflection and critical discussion necessary for transformation is for learners to feel that online learning environments are welcoming, inclusive and encouraging. Hiller (2018) also highlights the importance of students feeling supported by both educators and peers to mitigate anxieties about distance learning. This was therefore identified as an area for consideration in future course design. Based on my research findings and a subsequent review of up-to-date literature, the following suggestions are made for embedding transformative frameworks into course delivery.

Teaching transformative content

Transformative outcomes by nature cannot formally be 'taught' in the same way as facts or theory (Grabove, 1997). However, Cranton (2016) discusses how educators can empower students to achieve transformation by encouraging critical self-reflection on their ongoing learning and development. This can be supported by actively teaching underpinning concepts and models of transformative theory itself to provide a foundation for critically reflective practice, as well as a 'benchmark' for personal transformation. In my own teaching, I have included specific lesson content on how reflective practice can develop a sense of professional identity and awareness of how values may inform practice. Explicit input is given on key transformative models, encouraging learners to reflect on experiences within their practice that could be seen as 'disorienting dilemmas' or any previously unknown aspects of themselves identified through learning. Other lessons across Level 6 modules also cover the changing socio-political context of the Probation Service and the impact of specific milestones such as Transforming Rehabilitation on organisational culture. Again, critical reflection is encouraged on issues such as potential marginalisation, with emphasis on how personal, professional and organisational values may interact, as well as maintaining legitimacy and resilience when there may be conflict.

Creating safe spaces for critical reflection

Both Meyers (2008) and Hiller (2018) highlight the importance of a safe and welcoming online environment to enable transformative reflection. Inductions to both the overall PQiP programme and specific modules can therefore provide a crucial foundation and create a sense of confidence in engaging with critical discussion. Within the Level 6 induction, sessions are included where learners meet with their own personal tutors to discuss support available and raise any immediate questions or concerns. This can help to mitigate identified issues of perceived visibility. All modules now include a welcome video from the coordinator. These can emphasise the reflective and critical focus, as well as setting 'ground rules' to ensure that all contributions to both live and asynchronous discussions are treated with equal respect. Some modules also include a reflective workbook, which students can download at the beginning of the module. This follows the sequence of lessons, with prompts given at various points to record any reflections on areas such as how theories and learning relate to personal experience, learners' own perspectives on themes studied and if/how values may be challenged or reinforced. The aim of this is to encourage ongoing, active reflection in a safe space. The workbook is not assessed and does not have to be handed in, however they are encouraged to share any reflections with which they are comfortable in subsequent collaborative forums.

Active collaboration/peer learning

Meyers (2008) emphasises the value of promoting learner engagement and collaborative participation in both live sessions and asynchronous discussion forums. He particularly encourages activities that enable students to think about their experiences, beliefs and biases and how these relate to the academic concepts taught. Hiller (2018) further cites the importance of allowing diverse voices to be heard and multiple perspectives considered. This has been actively integrated into modules using the online platform 'Padlet', which allows questions or discussion points to be set for learners to then respond to, creating a virtual 'notice board' where all responses can be seen and both learners and staff can in turn comment on each other's posts. Contributions can be kept anonymous, which reinforces the earlier principle of enabling a sense of safety. One particularly successful use of Padlet has involved learners being presented with a 'moral dilemma' scenario prior to their first live seminar. They were asked before attending to post their thoughts on how they would respond to this in terms of how their personal, professional and organisational values may influence their decision. In the live session they could then review and comment on other participants' answers and link these to topics covered in the seminar. Shortly before the next live session the same scenario was presented again, this time asking for responses based on topics of additional lessons they had completed since. Again, responses were reviewed and discussed in the live seminar to prompt consideration of any transformation in perspective, based on either new learning or first-hand experiences in the interim.

Conclusion

At the time of writing it is too early to gauge how effective these activities may be in promoting behavioural transformation. Future research could take a more longitudinal and holistic approach to assessment of transformation, involving staff at different stages of their careers, practice tutor assessors, line managers, and so on. However, there are encouraging signs from seminar discussions, comments in reflective assignments and one-to-one tutorials, in which students have actively referred to some of the transformative models taught and shared examples of how they have recognised evidence of these in their own experiences. Others have shared positive reflective examples of how being more mindful of the concept of transformation has led to the development of their worldview, sense of ethics or values and reinforced their own confidence and self-worth as practitioners. Based on themes from the more recent literature review presented at the start of this chapter and my own subsequent experiences outlined earlier, the dimensions of the proposed transformative framework have been amended and organised using the acronym 'SCOPE', outlined in Table 13.1.

While both learners and staff were positive about the concept of a transformative framework, a theme arising in research was the short timescale of the PQiP programme and the intense pressure on learners to achieve the instrumental aims of qualification. Although it is possible to embed transformative activities into the existing curriculum without adding to these pressures, Wilson et al (2007) highlight how true measures of transformative success need to include evidence of longer-term behavioural impact. A related issue raised by several participants in the staff focus group was that although with hindsight they were able to reflect on and identify transformative experiences over their own academic, professional and personal lives, they did not recognise at the time how or why these were occurring. Sweet (2022: 603) acknowledges that in relation to perspective transformation 'new meaning is not easily recognisable', emphasising the importance of educators using 'guided' critical reflection to enable learners to identify evidence of ongoing transformation in their own lives.

Reflective prompts

- What benefits of a transformative approach do you feel could most complement the 'instrumental' aims of professional qualification?
- How might the academic component of training contribute to transformation? Which parts (content and methods) could be most effective?
- How might learners know if they have experienced transformation?
- Who/what might best support learners to achieve or maintain transformation in the longer term (that is, in the workplace)?

Table 13.1: Transformative outcomes (SCOPE)

SCOPE dimension	Intended outcomes for qualifying probation officers
Self-awareness	• ncreased awareness of own strengths and limitations, positionality, potential biases, impact of prior experience on practice. • Emotional literacy in promoting personal and moral rehabilitation. • Professional curiosity.
Critical consciousness	• Critical reflection on socio-political context of work. • Recognising potential impact of political context in terms of anti-discriminatory practice. • Commitment to avoiding marginalisation and promoting social and judicial rehabilitation.
Organisational values	• Commitment to and maintenance of core organisational values of probation. • Awareness of current practice frameworks and values underpinning these. • Sensitivity to fluid nature of organisational culture and influences on practice.
Professional identity and resilience	• Confidence in 'transition' to role of qualified probation officer. • Awareness of own personal, professional and organisational values and maintaining resilience/legitimacy when there may be dissonance between these. • Confidence in professional judgement. • Commitment to ongoing professional development.
Ethical humility	• Awareness of ethical implications of practice decisions. • Recognition of complexity/fallibility and avoiding moral disengagement.

References

Bonk, C.J. and Graham, C.R. (2012) *The Handbook of Blended Learning: Global Perspectives*, Wiley

Bowen, P. (2021) Delivering a smarter approach: Probation professionalisation, Centre for Justice Innovation. Available from: https://justiceinnovation.org/sites/default/files/media/document/2021/cji_probation_2020.pdf

Boyd, R.D. (1991) *Personal Transformations in Small Groups: A Jungian Perspective* (1st edn), Routledge.

Buchanan, J. and Senior, P. (2003) Delivering the diploma in probation studies in North Wales and Dyfed Powys: On-line learning explored, *British Journal of Community Justice*, 2(2): 41–57. Available from: https://mmuperu.co.uk/bjcj/articles/delivering-the-diploma-in-probation-studies-in-north-wales-and-dyfed-powys-on-line-learning-explored/

Burrell, A. (2022) The reflective practitioner in transition: Probation work during reintegration of probation services in England and Wales, *Probation Journal*, 69(4): 434–451. https://doi.org/10.1177/02645505221117537

Burrell, A. and Petrillo, M. (2022) Delivering the four forms of rehabilitation: Training and developing probation practitioners, in L. Burke, N. Carr, E. Cluley, S. Collett and F. McNeill (eds) *Reimagining Probation Practice: Re-forming Rehabilitation in an Age of Penal Excess*, Routledge, pp 174–188.

Carr, N. (2020) Recruitment, training and professional development of probation staff, *Academic Insights 2020*, 2. Available from: https://www.justiceinspectorates.gov.uk/hmiprobation/wp-content/uploads/sites/5/2020/02/Academic-Insights-Carr-Final.pdf

Clark, R. (2016) How education transforms: Evidence from the experience of Prisoners' Education Trust on how education supports prisoner journeys, *Prison Service Journal*, 225: 3–8. Available from: https://www.crimeandjustice.org.uk/sites/crimeandjustice.org.uk/files/PSJper cent20225per cent20May percent 202016.pdf

Cooper, S. (2021) A failed social experiment: Damaged professional identity post 'Transforming Rehabilitation', *British Journal of Community Justice (BJCJ)*, 17(2): 46–66. Available from: https://mmuperu.co.uk/bjcj/articles/a-failed-social-experiment-damaged-professional-identity-post-transforming-rehabilitation/

Cranton, P. (2016) *Understanding and Promoting Transformative Learning: A Guide to Theory and Practice*, Stylus

Daloz, L. (1986) *Effective Teaching and Mentoring: Realizing the Transformational Power of Adult Learning Experiences*, Jossey-Bass.

Deering, J. and Feilzer, M.Y. (2017) Questions of legitimacy in probation practice after transforming rehabilitation, *The Howard Journal of Crime and Justice*, 56(2): 158–17. https://doi.org/10.1111/hojo.12200

Dirkx, J.M. (1998) Transformative learning theory in the practice of adult education: An overview, *PAACE Journal of Lifelong Learning*, 7: 1–14.

Forbes, D. (2010) Probation in transition: A study of the experiences of newly qualified probation officers, *Journal of Social Work Practice*, 24(1): 75–88. https://doi.org/10.1080/02650530903532781

Fowler, A., Martin, L., Watson, A. and Brown, T. (2023) Professional qualification in probation and COVID-19, in C. Kay and S. Case, *Crime, Justice and COVID-19*, Bristol University Press, pp 190–216

Freire, P. (1970) *Pedagogy of the Oppressed*, Seabury Press.

Grabove, V. (1997) The many facets of transformative learning theory and practice, *New Directions for Adult and Continuing Education*, 74: 89–96. https://doi.org/10.1002/ace.7410

Gregory, M. (2007) Probation training: Evidence from newly qualified officers, *Social Work Education*, 26(1): 53–68. doi: https://doi.org/10.1080/02615470601036575

Hiller, S. (2018) Flipping the chalk and talk with law student on and offline: The advantages of transformative pedagogy utilising technology, in K. Lindgren, F. Kunc and M. Coper (eds) *The Future of Australian Legal Education*, Thomson Reuters, pp 429–439.

HMPPS (HM Prison and Probation Service) (2022) Statutory guidance: Core probation roles and qualification requirements. Available from: https://www.google.com/url?q=https://assets.publishing.service.gov.uk/media/624323a1d3bf7f32ac2b93da/Statutory_Guidance_-_Core_probation_roles_and_qualification_requirements.docx&sa=D&source=docs&ust=1723461749338312&usg=AOvVaw1SC0i-_sjhzCiDTvlZKZz

Keysell, B. (2022) *Transformative Pedagogy of Trainee Probation Officers: A Framework for Evaluation of Outcomes and Methods*, unpublished MREs Dissertation.

Lancaster, E. (2003) Probation values: Where are we now? *British Journal of Criminal Justice*, 2(2): 25–40.

Mayo, P. (1993) When does it work: Freire's pedagogy in context, *Studies in the Education of Adults*, 25(1): 11–30.

McNeill, F. (2012) Four forms of 'offender' rehabilitation: Towards an interdisciplinary perspective, *Legal and Criminological Psychology*, 17(1): 18–36. doi: https://doi.org/10.1111/j.2044-8333.2011.02039.x

Meyers, S. (2008) Using transformative pedagogy when teaching online, *College Teaching*, 56(4): 219–224. https://doi.org/10.3200/CTCH.56.4.219-224

Mezirow, J. (1991) *Transformative Dimensions of Adult Learning*, Jossey-Bass.

Mezirow, J. (1997) Transformative learning: Theory to practice, *New Directions for Adult and Continuing Education*, 1997(74): 5–12. https://doi.org/10.1002/ace.7401

Mullineux, J.C., Taylor, B.J. and Giles, M.L. (2019) Probation officers' judgements: A study using personal construct theory, *Journal of Social Work*, 19(1): 41–59. https://doi.org/10.1177/1468017318757384

Nerstrom, N. (2014) *An Emerging Model for Transformative Learning*, Kansas State University Libraries

Parmar, D. and Nudd, D. (2021) Post-unification priorities for probation: Former practitioners' perspectives, *Probation Quarterly*, 21: 50–53. Available from: https://static1.squarespace.com/static/5ec3ce97a1716758c54691b7/t/6131db2af03e804a40a9055b/1630657358890/PQ21.pdf

Phillips, J., Ainslie, S. and Westaby, C. (2022) Lifting the lid on Pandora's box: Putting professional curiosity into practice, *Criminology and Criminal Justice*, 24(2): 321–338, https://doi.org/10.1177/17488958221163

Reamer, F.G. (2023) Ethical humility in probation, *HMIP Academic Insights* 2023/03. Available from: https://www.justiceinspectorates.gov.uk/hmiprobation/wp-content/uploads/sites/5/2023/03/Ethical-humility-in-probation.pdf

Skinner, C. and Goldhill, R. (2013) Changes in probation training in England and Wales: The Probation Qualification Framework (PQF) three years on, *European Journal of Probation*, 5(3): 41–55. https://doi.org/10.1177/206622031300500304

Sweet, S.F. (2022) Using guided critical reflection to discover deepened and transformative learning in leadership education, *Journal of Research on Leadership Education*, 18(4): 600–621. https://doi.org/10.1177/19427751221118951

Tangen, J. and Briah, R.K. (2018) The revolving door of reform: Professionalism and the future of probation services in England and Wales, *Probation Journal*, 65(2): 135–151. https://doi.org/10.1177/0264550518768398

Treadwell, J. (2006) Some personal reflections on probation training, *The Howard Journal of Crime and Justice*, 45(1): 1–13. https://doi.org/10.1111/j.1468-2311.2006.00400.x

Tsimane, T.A. and Downing, C. (2020) Transformative learning in nursing education: A concept analysis, *International Journal of Nursing Science*s, 7(1): 91–98. https://doi.org/10.1016/j.ijnss.2019.12.006

UNESCO (United Nations Educational, Scientific and Cultural Organisation) (2017) *Transformative Pedagogy for Peace-building: A Guide for Teachers*, International Institute for Capacity Building in Africa. Available from: https://unesdoc.unesco.org/ark:/48223/pf0000261349

Vipler, B., Knehans, A., Rausa, D., Haidel, P. and McCall-Hosenfeld, J. (2021) Transformative learning in graduate medical education: A scoping review, *Journal of Graduate Medical Education*, 13(6): 801–814. https://doi.org/10.4300/JGME-D-21-00065.1

Wilson, B.G., Switzer, S.H. and Parrish, P. (2007) Transformative learning experiences: How do we get students deeply engaged for lasting change? In M. Simonson (ed) *Proceedings of Selected Research and Development Presentations*, Association for Educational Communications and Technology, pp 1–12.

14

De-mystifying the mirror: a framework for the assessment of reflective practice

Julie Eden-Barnard

This chapter draws on the author's diverse experiences of engaging in and assessing reflective practice. From being a trainee probation officer being asked to reflect on practice and responding in a way that felt uncomfortable and surface level; to being a practice tutor assessor asking candidates to reflect on their practice in a way that felt robotic and did not quite capture the essence of what they needed to do; and finally being in the position of marking academic reflective writing and feeling like some accounts lacked authenticity and were the product of a learner going through the motions. Despite those experiences, the author holds a strong belief that reflective practice is fundamental to good probation practice and that assessment should be an important component of supporting the development of reflective practitioners. These experiences became the motivation to undertake a small-scale piece of action research as part of a Post Graduate Certificate in Higher Education qualification. The project sought to critically appraise the assessment of reflective practice within the academic team that the author was working in at the time, to understand how the assessment strategy could be improved and provide a more meaningful experience for learners. The findings highlighted areas which could benefit reflective assessment more generally, thus leading to a framework being devised.

This chapter aims to share learning taken from this project. It will begin with a brief exploration of literature, which will demonstrate that the challenges outlined earlier are not unique to the author, and are instead consistent with complexities that have previously been identified. It will also explore the contextual landscape of probation practice to argue that it is more important than ever before in terms of the learner experience to address these complexities. There will be a brief overview of the methodology used in this project before the Reflective Practice Assessment Framework is presented. The framework introduces key principles to consider when designing reflective practice assessments based on the research findings. These principles include curriculum design, the design of the assessment strategy and consideration of how reflective practice is modelled.

Reflective practice and probation practice

Reflective practice is integral to probation officers' professional identity (see Worrall and Mawby, 2013; Coley, 2016), and commentators have consistently raised concerns about the impact of neoliberalism and managerialism on the reflective practice culture within probation (Gregory, 2007; Eadie et al, 2012; Tangen and Briah, 2018; Burrell, 2022). Consequently, academics and practitioners alike have sought to highlight barriers to, and assert the importance of, supporting practitioners to be reflective (Goldhill, 2010; Ainslie et al, 2022). Reflection is seen as a tool for practitioners to explore their own values and emotional literacy to develop self-awareness (Coley, 2016). As highlighted in the previous section of the compendium this is particularly important in the context of personal bias, notions of fairness and commitment to anti-discriminatory practice. Practitioners also use reflection to assimilate theoretical knowledge and practical experience (Dempsey et al, 2001) and to assess their skills and knowledge, supporting them to identify areas for professional development (Coley, 2016). This, in turn, can lead practitioners to try new ways of working and increase confidence in their judgement and decision-making (Eadie et al, 2012). Reflective capacity is therefore seen as an element of practice that requires ongoing commitment and development and can be transformative for practitioners. Consequently, supporting the development of reflective practice forms part of the core curriculum of the Professional Qualification in Probation (PQiP).

Goldhill (2010) and Ainslie (2020) have both written about their experiences of reflective practice teaching in their roles as academics on the PQiP and the author shares the sentiments of importance and responsibility that are expressed in these articles. It was this sense of responsibility that led to the design of my research project that focused on assessment of reflective practice:

> Although I believe that supporting the development of reflective practice is important, I found that I often did not enjoy assessing reflective assignments. I started to explore why I felt like this and came to a few conclusions. I sometimes questioned the authenticity of the information that I was being presented with and therefore wondered whether genuine reflection had taken place. Similarly, Hobbs (2007) explores how she resorted to 'strategic deception' in her reflective assessments when she felt that her genuine accounts were not what her assessor wanted to see. In turn, this made me wonder whether the learner understood what was expected of them and whether these assessment tasks were supportive of development, or whether they were just seen as 'tick box' exercises. This is a concern that is echoed by Rich and Parker, who highlight that poor assessment can have a negative impact on the learner, and discourage the development of reflective practice (Rich and Parker, 1995, as cited in Bulman and Schutz, 2013). I therefore saw the research project as an opportunity to develop my understanding of the assessment of reflective practice and use this new knowledge to consider how our assessment strategy could be improved and developed.

Challenges with reflective practice assessment

Bulman and Schutz (2013) raise several key issues in assessing reflective practice. The first key point is around defining reflection.

In the context of probation, for example, there is no agreed definition of what reflective practice is. Although Kolb's (2014) model of Experiential Learning is often used, there are numerous models and definitions that learners can draw on, which can lead to variations in interpretation of what constitutes good reflection. This can be problematic as it does not support learners to understand what is required of them in assessment (Bulman and Schutz, 2013). Following on from this theme, it could be argued that variations in interpretation can also lead to inconsistencies between assessors.

The second issue highlighted by Bulman and Schutz (2013) is ensuring clarity around whether it is the process of reflection that is being assessed, the outcome of the reflection or both. Again, it could be argued that a lack of clarity here can confuse both learners and assessors alike. Burton (2000) highlights that if it is written reflection that is being assessed, then learners with good academic writing skills are at an advantage, and there is a danger that learners will write what they think the assessor wants to hear. For Hannigan (2001), a variety of assessment strategies must be used to encourage learners to engage in a meaningful process. Therefore, Bulman and Schutz (2013) argue that both the process and the outcome should be assessed as they are both equally as important.

Another point of consideration is whether assessment methods differentiate between learners at the beginning and the end of their programme of study (Bulman and Schutz, 2013). For some learners, the commencement of the PQiP will be their first encounter with reflective practice, and as they progress through their studies their reflective skills should develop and become more sophisticated. An assessor's expectations of those early reflections may be different from those at the end of the programme. It may be useful therefore to introduce levels of reflection (Bulman and Schutz, 2013) which would be consistent with a constructivist approach to learning. Bulman and Schutz (2013) outline that consideration should be given to an array of assessment methods (verbal and written – both summative and formative), that allow graduated development and provide different ways of demonstrating their abilities to reflect. Each method has strengths and limitations, which is why it is beneficial to use a variety of these. For example, a reflective essay may be confusing for people who have only just started to write academically, because the 'rules' around reflective essays would differ from the 'rules' of a conventional academic essay (Bulman and Schutz, 2013).

The five key areas identified by Bulman and Schutz (2013) resonated with the author's experience of assessment of reflective practice. To explore the perspectives and practices of the whole team, a questionnaire was developed based on them.

Methodology

After ethical approval was obtained from the appropriate institution, staff members from a single team (n=9) participated in the project by completing the questionnaire. Once the data had been obtained, a thematic analysis was used to explore the data using Braun and Clarke's (2006) six-phase guide. This guide enabled the researcher to explore the data holistically and systematically, following a grounded theory methodology (Noble and Mitchell, 2016). As part of this initial process, the surveys were read through and preliminary themes were identified. Themes were then revisited and revised, and in the final stage, descriptive labels were attached to data in the surveys to categorise or code the data. An overarching theme emerged related to improving consistency and eliminating ambiguity, and two distinct, but interrelated sub-themes around teaching and learning practice and principles, and relational and environmental factors. From these themes, a framework for the assessment of reflective practice has been developed. This chapter will now present this framework, drawing on the findings from this research project and the secondary literature to justify this proposal. The mirror is often used as a metaphor for reflective practice (Gibbons, 2019) and as highlighted through the exploration of previous research and literature, navigating the assessment of reflective practice can be challenging. The framework aims to support the practitioner (and learner) to navigate these complexities and therefore de-mystify the mirror.

Reflective Practice Assessment Framework

Curriculum design

Summative assessment is usually the end point of a learning journey, the point at which the learner 'officially' demonstrates that they have achieved learning outcomes. It would be difficult to explore the destination without also exploring the pathway to the destination, and in this context, the pathway is the approach to teaching and learning. Therefore, a framework for reflective practice assessment must consider curriculum design.

Participants in this project felt that it was important to ensure that reflective practice is embedded in all areas of the curriculum, with active teaching input that provides opportunities to make theory-to-practice links, so that learners are supported to develop a reflective 'habit' and 'practice' reflection. In alignment with constructivist principles of learning, some participants also expressed that teaching should become more complex or scaffolded as the learner progresses through their studies (Petty, 2018). Bourner (2003) differentiates between simply reviewing what has happened and interrogating an experience by asking searching questions, highlighting that the former does not constitute reflective thinking. To support learners in developing the necessary skills, Bourner (2003) encourages an approach to teaching reflective practice that parallels the teaching of critical thinking skills. Goodman's (1984) levels of reflection provide a good framework for scaffolding. This can be aligned with Bloom's taxonomy of thinking skills (Petty, 2018), and relevant higher education level descriptors (QAA, 2014) (see Table 14.1).

Furthermore, participants in Coley's (2016) study expressed a strong preference for peer reflection in the workplace, therefore it is important to consider the implications for this in a teaching and learning context. Martin and Fowler (2018) outline that the nature of the PQiP means that learners are often studying in isolation and highlight the impact that this has on learners' opportunity and ability to engage with other learners to test out their understanding and construct meaning. Gibbons (2019) advocates using a Problem-Based Learning (PBL) approach in professional programmes; PBL is a learner-centred approach where students learn by working together to address real-world problems. Originally developed for medical education, it is an approach grounded in the work of Schön (1983) and Kolb (2014). PBL supports the development of skills that are fundamental to reflective practice, and provides

Table 14.1: Aligning levels of reflection, thinking skills and higher education levels

Higher education level	Level 4	Level 5 and 6	Level 6, 7 and 8
Bloom's taxonomy	Knowledge and comprehension	Application and analysis	Synthesis and evaluation
Goodman's levels	Level 1: Reflection is based on technicality or competency and is therefore largely descriptive.	Level 2: Reflection explores the relationship between theory and practice. There is a rationale for practice decisions that draws on underpinning principles or theory, and there is an assessment of the implications and consequences of actions.	Level 3: Building on Level 2, this level of reflection also explores practice in a socio-political context. Considering themes of social justice, such as inequality, power and discrimination.

regular opportunity for formative assessment, primarily in the form of peer review (Gibbons, 2019). There are some distinct challenges in embedding a PBL approach in a distance learning programme that is largely delivered online and asynchronously (see Treadwell, 2006; Martin and Fowler, 2018), but taking inspiration from Meenaghan et al (2023) this is perhaps an area of teaching and learning practice where the use of Extended Reality (XR) technology could be utilised.

Similarly, Dempsey et al (2001) outline an approach to teaching reflective skills that brings together simulations of real practice with relevant theories and supports learners to become conscious of the personal lens through which they view both. They anticipated that the outcome of providing a learning environment that supported learners through a cycle of action, reflection and inquiry would encourage learners to be conscious, proactive and responsive in their practice.

Assessment strategy

There are several key areas of consideration concerning the assessment strategy itself, so these will be explored in turn.

The importance of definition

There are numerous definitions and models of reflection, different ways in which practitioners use and value reflection, and as demonstrated by participants in this study (see Table 14.2) there are a wide range of attributes that can be associated with 'good' reflective practice. This diversity may be useful in some respects, but in terms of teaching and learning this can also present challenges and uncertainties, particularly around assessment (Bulman and Schutz, 2013). It is therefore important to address these to minimise misunderstanding and confusion. Participants expressed that it was important to ensure that the parameters of reflective practice assessment were clearly defined and communicated to learners, for example: 'Emphasis that the "marks" are awarded for reflection and considering how you can improve' (Participant C).

This was important in terms of learners understanding limitations to confidentiality, for example, and being clear that

Table 14.2: What are the attributes of a 'good' reflective practitioner?

Skills	Knowledge	Behaviours
• Empathy	• Knowledge and understanding of reflective models	• Open to exploration of self
• Patience		• Reflexivity
• Emotional intelligence		• Open to self-development
• Emotional literacy	• Integrate theory and practice	• Growth mindset
• Self-critical – but balanced – able to identify good and bad	• Able to make links between theory and practice	• Critically look at practice
		• Critically consider own practice – what went well – areas for development
• Demonstrates 'practitioner wisdom'	• Understanding the meaning and interpretation of behaviour	• Demonstrate ongoing learning from experience
• Self-awareness within an organisational and social context		• Committed to lifelong learning
• Self-aware – how own feelings and behaviours impact outcomes	• Link theory to own behaviour	• Honest
	• Knowledge	• Recognise that they are on a developmental journey
• Think critically		• Open
		• Open to feedback
		• Open to learning
		• Be prepared to learn and change practice
		• Learning is ongoing

learners were not being assessed on their practice. It was felt that ambiguity around the parameters could lead to learners feeling 'unsafe' which in turn would impact on whether or not they felt they could be open and honest.

Concerning the PQiP, there is arguably a greater focus in the workplace on developing practitioner skills and behaviour, with an emphasis on developing knowledge through academic study provided by the higher education institution. Therefore, the context has implications for what is being assessed, and most significantly, what is realistic to assess. Academic assessors need to acknowledge these distinctions, particularly when they have come from practice and may have experience assessing learners in the workplace as a practice tutor assessor. Going back to that original experience of feeling like there was a lack of authenticity in reflective accounts, it might be that this was a symptom of unrealistic expectations of what a learner could demonstrate.

Linking back to the previous discussion around the importance of scaffolding learning and constructive alignment, the work of Bourner (2003) is also useful to draw on when considering definition. This highlights that one of the most significant challenges in assessing reflective learning is that often learning outcomes are based on subjective, rather than objective, knowledge. He argues this can be addressed by shifting the focus of assessment from reflective learning to reflective thinking, as this enables assessors to separate the content of the reflection (subjective) from the process of the reflection (objective). Once this shift has occurred, the principles that are followed when assessing critical thinking can be applied; has the learner simply reviewed what has happened, or have they interrogated the experience by asking searching questions? For Bourner (2003) it is this process of interrogation that separates reflective thinking from unreflective thinking.

A final point of consideration concerning definition is whether it is the process or the outcome of reflection (or both) that is being assessed. This will be explored further in the next section, but it is important to mention here that a lack of clarity around this can lead to confusion for learners and a lack of continuity from assessors.

Initial, formative and summative assessment

For many probation learners, the concept of reflection is new and this can present a challenge with meeting learning outcomes relating to reflection at Level 5 and above, where there are expectations that they can demonstrate abilities beyond knowledge and comprehension (QAA, 2014). To support the development of this learning reflective practice must not be just assessed summatively. For those learners who are new to reflective practice, initial assessment provides the opportunity to consider what they already know about reflection and what they might already do that is reflective in other areas of their life. This supports learners in making sense of this new concept (Petty, 2018). One participant in this research identified that for those who have experience of being reflective practitioners, initial assessment can also provide the learner with the opportunity to explore their barriers to engagement with reflection. As a brief example of how this could work in practice, learners could be set a short preparatory task to consider some questions that enable them to analyse their knowledge and experience of reflection. These responses can then be shared, for example via an online discussion forum, which enables the academic to better understand the learner's experience and pitch the learning and formative assessment appropriately.

Formative assessment allows learners to test out their learning and get feedback in a risk-free way. This might be particularly significant in building confidence in those learners who are new to reflective practice. When exploring her own experiences, Hobbs (2007) outlines that her reflective accounts were superficial and guarded because she did not feel comfortable expressing personal thoughts to a professor that she did not know. As discussed previously, participants in this project expressed concern that failing to clearly define the parameters of reflective practice assessment could lead to learners feeling unsafe, which could then impact how open and honest they are in reflective accounts. There are similarities here with Hobbs' experiences. So, formative assessment can provide the opportunity to assert these parameters and provide reassurance to learners so that they can be authentic in their writing.

Gregory (2007) highlights the impact of 'treadmill' moments, where learners did not feel that they were able to engage in deep learning and therefore not able to think critically or transfer learning. Formative assessment can provide these opportunities and so support learners to appreciate the value and importance of development, as opposed to just focusing on how to pass assessment criteria (Elkington, 2019). However, as expressed by a participant in this project, academic practitioners are not exempt from 'treadmill' moments either: 'What is realistic in the timeframe that we have? Timescales of the programme may result in "tick box" assessment and superficial engagement' (Participant B).

Nevertheless, the use of formative assessment is important considering the themes that have emerged from research with probation practitioners about the challenges that they experience with reflective practice in the workplace, particularly around protecting time and space to think (Coley, 2020; Ainslie et al, 2022). In the context of probation learners, formative assessment is not only important in terms of processing learning around reflective practice but also to their practice and academic knowledge.

Participants in this research identified both the process of reflection and the outcome of reflection should be assessed, and initial and formative assessments are key elements in supporting this differentiation and development (Petty, 2018). They suggested that for those at the beginning of their learning journey, formative assessment should be more structured, perhaps using a model of reflection and focusing more on the process of reflection. However, for those at the end of their learning journey, there were expectations that reflective accounts were more in-depth, and included critical reflection and links between theory and practice. Parallels can be drawn here with Goodman's (1984) levels of reflection, and Bourner's (2003) assertion that reflection should include an interrogation of practice. Further, it was felt that summative assessment for learners at the end of their learning journey should focus more on the outcome of the reflective process, with particular attention to the impact of learning on practice and professional development. Moon's (2004) Framework for Reflective Writing could be utilised here to support learners in developing a writing style that captures a greater depth of analysis and reflection.

Assessment methods

Earlier in this chapter, it was identified that one of the challenges around the assessment of reflective practice relates to the methods that are used, in as much as different methods have strengths and limitations. Participants in this research expressed that they felt that it is important to use a variety of assessment methods to provide learners with different ways of demonstrating their abilities, a point that is also emphasised in previous research (Bulman and Schutz, 2013). Elkington (2019) highlights that assessment is a significant factor in the exclusion of higher education students, because of the structural inequalities that are inherent in higher education practices and cultures that can inadvertently lead to unfair outcomes for learners. Therefore, using a range of methods is an action that can be taken to promote inclusion. This is an important consideration for probation learners, as many of them would not have chosen to undertake a degree if it was not a requirement of their training.

In the author's experience of the academic component of PQiP, reflective academic essays are privileged as the summative assessment method, and learning is formatively assessed in group discussions in 'live' sessions. There are challenges in creating variety because of the limitations of the delivery of the programme, however, there would be a benefit to learners from exploring a greater variety of methods. Variation of assessment methods was commented on by participants in this study; for example, a participant outlined that they thought that it would be good to 'have an assessment strategy that captured individual journeys and progressions, such as portfolios, logs, conversations, etc' (Participant A). Elkington (2019) asserts that it is possible to accommodate different motivations, preferences, learning needs and backgrounds of learners and also maintain academic standards. Effective feedback from assessors can also help alleviate some of these challenges (see Chapter 15).

Modelling the model

All of the participants in this project felt that they had some experience of being a reflective practitioner themselves. Although there was a range of experiences, with some expressing more confidence about their abilities than others, most identified that they felt that being able to be reflective in practice was positive, particularly in relation to learning and development: 'Sometimes when reflecting I would discover things that I didn't like about myself or things that sat against what I considered my value base to be. This can be difficult but is an important part of personal development and growth' (Participant G).

However, as highlighted throughout this chapter, there are challenges for probation practitioners in engaging with reflective practice (see Goldhill, 2010; Coley, 2016). Furthermore, participants in the study by Ainslie et al (2022) expressed that critical reflection is not modelled or supported by all senior leadership. For a PQiP learner then, the reality of this might be that reflective practice within the workplace is not always visible, and therefore the messages that they receive about the importance of reflective practice are inconsistent. In a teaching and learning context then it is important to consider ways of ensuring that reflective practices are visible. This could be about the lecturer sharing their practice reflections with learners, or about being honest when they are finding areas of teaching practice challenging and, therefore, they are trying new ideas. It could also include seeking feedback from learners about their experiences of teaching and learning and being explicit about when changes have taken place because of the feedback that has been given by learners. Goldhill (2010) questions whether it is fair for practitioners to expect learners to demonstrate reflective practice if they are not doing this themselves. Furthermore, Goldhill (2010) highlights the importance of self-disclosure and honesty in building trust with learners and normalising navigating moments of indecision and insecurity in practice through reflection. This sentiment was shared by a participant in this project: 'The employer and HEI [higher education institution] need to embrace that learners will make mistakes, weaknesses, bias and errors' (Participant A).

Finally, participants in this study, as well as those in Coley's (2016) research, placed value on the opportunity of learning and reflecting with peers. Building on this, Elkington (2019) advocates for creating formative assessment group tasks that encourage learners to explain their reasoning to each other as this can improve understanding of the requirements of assessment tasks and marking criteria, as it gives a more concrete sense of something that is otherwise quite abstract.

Conclusion

As an academic who has come from practice and has an awareness of the challenges and threats to reflection in the workplace (Coley, 2020; Ainslie et al, 2022), I have a strong sense of responsibility to ensure that learners are getting the best from their learning experience. In relation to reflection, this means an experience that supports learners to develop the skills that are fundamental to reflective practice. As a core component of the PQiP, reflective writing is assessed, but reflective accounts can sometimes seem to lack authenticity. This could be an indication that the complexities of reflective practice assessment (Bulman and Schutz, 2013) have not been appropriately considered. A lack of agreed definition leads to variation in interpretation of what constitutes reflective practice, which can be confusing for both learners and assessors, as can a lack of clarity around whether it is the process of reflection or the outcome of the reflection that is being assessed. Privileging particular assessment methods and failing to differentiate according to knowledge and experience will create an unfair advantage for some learners (Bulman and Schutz, 2013).

To mitigate these challenges, this chapter has proposed a framework of principles to guide the assessment of reflective practice. First, it is important for assessors to give attention to reflective practice in the curriculum design to ensure that there is constructive alignment (Biggs and Tang, 2011) and that learning is scaffolded (Goodman, 1984; Petty, 2018). Because of the constraints of the PQiP (Martin and Fowler, 2018) and challenges in the workplace (Coley, 2016) it is important to try to maximise the opportunities for group learning and peer reflection, preferably by using a PBL approach (Gibbons, 2019). For a distance learning programme that is largely asynchronous in its delivery, practice simulations using XR technology might offer a learning environment that supports reflection.

In relation to the assessment strategy itself, this must be clearly defined to improve consistency and avoid confusion. This involves careful consideration of the concepts that underpin the assessor's knowledge and beliefs about reflective practice, the purpose of the reflection and what is realistic for the learner to demonstrate within the limitations of the assessment and at their particular stage of learning. The strategy should use a range of assessment methods to promote inclusion and consider all types of assessment – initial, formative and summative – to support learners to develop confidence, avoid 'treadmill moments' (Gregory, 2007) and ensure that both the process and outcome of reflection are assessed.

Finally, teaching on the PQiP provides an opportunity for reflective practice to be modelled, and this is particularly important as learners might not experience this in the workplace (Ainslie et al, 2022). To support the development of safe and trusting relationships with learners, and to have authenticity as an assessor, these practices should be visible to learners (Goldhill, 2010). Group learning also provides valuable opportunities for peers to model reflective practice.

Reflective prompts

- How do you integrate reflective practice into your curriculum design?
- How might you provide opportunities for your team to improve consistency around the assessment of reflective practice?
- How do you balance the need for objective assessment with the subjective nature of reflective thinking?
- How do you ensure that your assessment methods are fair and equitable for all learners?
- What opportunities are there for you to model reflective practice?

References

Ainslie, S. (2020) A time to reflect? *Probation Quarterly*, 17: 9–12. https://static1.squarespace.com/static/5ec3ce97a1716758c5469 1b7/t/5f438e00b398394e2d99d1ac/1598262837547/PQ17.pdf.

Ainslie, S., Fowler, A., Phillips, J. and Westaby, C. (2022) 'A nice idea but …': Implementing a reflective supervision model in the National Probation Service in England and Wales, *Reflective Practice*, 23(5): 525–538. https://doi.org/10.1080/ 14623943.2022.2066075

Biggs, J. and Tang, C. (2011) *Teaching for Quality Learning at University*, McGraw-Hill Education.

Bourner, T. (2003) Assessing reflective learning, *Education and Training*, 45(5): 267–272. https://doi.org/10.1108/00400910310484321

Braun, V. and Clarke, V. (2006) Using thematic analysis in psychology, *Qualitative Research in Psychology*, 3: 77–101. http://dx.doi.org/10.1191/1478088706qp063oa

Bulman, C. and Schutz, S. (eds) (2013) *Reflective Practice in Nursing*, John Wiley and Sons.

Burrell, A. (2022) The reflective practitioner in transition: Probation work during reintegration of probation services in England and Wales, *Probation Journal*, 69(4): 434–451. https://doi.org/10.1177/02645505221117537

Burton, A.J. (2000) Reflection: Nursing's practice and education panacea?, *Journal of Advanced Nursing*, 31(5): 1009–1017. https://doi.org/10.1046/j.1365-2648.2000.01395.x

Coley, D. (2016) Reflective practice: The cornerstone of what we all do, Probation Institute. Available from: https://www.essex.ac.uk/-/media/documents/directories/human-resources/reflective-practice---digital-(1).pdf

Coley, D. (2020) Probation staff supervision: Valuing 'me time' within congested spaces, *Probation Journal*, 67(3): 228–245. http://doi.org/10.1177/026455050926581.

Dempsey, M., Halton, C. and Marian, M. (2001) Reflective learning in social work education: Scaffolding the process, *Social Work Education*, 20(6): 631–641. https://doi.org/10.1080/02615470120089825

Eadie, T., Wilkinson, B. and Cherry, S. (2012) Stop a minute: Making space for thinking in practice, *Probation Journal*, 60(1): 9–13. https://doi.org/10.1177/0264550512470188.

Elkington, S. (2019) Assessment: Understanding the basics, in S. Marshall (ed) *A Handbook for Teaching and Learning in Higher Education: Enhancing Academic Practice* (5th edn), Taylor & Francis, pp 116–125.

Gibbons, J. (2019) Reflection, realignment and refraction: Bernstein's evaluative rules and the summative assessment of reflective practice in a problem-based learning programme, *Teaching in Higher Education*, 24(7): 834–849. https://doi.org/10.1080/13562517.2018.1514374

Goldhill, R. (2010) Reflective practice and distance learning: Problems and potentials for probation training, *Reflective Practice*, 11(1): 57–70. https://doi.org/10.1080/14623940903500085

Goodman, J. (1984) Reflection and teacher education: A case study and theoretical analysis, *Interchanges*, 15: 9–26. https://doi.org/10.1007/BF01807939

Gregory, M. (2007) Probation training: Evidence from newly qualified officers, *Social Work Education*, 26(1): 53–68. https://doi.org/10.1080/02615470601036575.

Hannigan, B. (2001) A discussion of the strengths and weaknesses of 'reflection' in nursing practice and education, *Journal of Clinical Nursing*, 10: 278–283. https://doi.org/10.1111/j.1365-2702.2001.00459.x

Hobbs, V. (2007) Faking it or hating it: Can reflective practice be forced?, *Reflective Practice*, 8(3): 405–417. https://doi.org/10.1080/14623940701425063

Kolb, D.A. (2014) *Experiential Learning: Experiences as the Source of Learning and Development*, Pearson Education.

Martin, L. and Fowler, A. (2018) A pedagogical response to the challenges of delivering collaborative probation education in online environments, 4th International Conference on Higher Education Advances (HEAd'18) Universitat Politecnica de Valencia. Available from: http://dx.doi.org/10.4995/HEAd18.2018.8147

Meenaghan, A., McDermott, M. and Haggar, L. (2023) XR technology and risk assessment: The future of probation training? *Criminology & Criminal Justice*. https://doi.org/10.1177/17488958231200346.

Moon, J.A. (2004) *A Handbook of Reflective and Experiential Learning: Theory and Practice*, Taylor & Francis.

Noble, H. and Mitchell, G. (2016) What is grounded theory?, *Evidence-Based Nursing*, 19: 34–35. https://doi.org/10.1136/eb-2016-102306

Petty, G. (2018) *Teaching Today* (4th edn), Nelson Thomas.

QAA (Quality Assurance Agency for Higher Education) (2014) *The Frameworks for Higher Education Qualifications of UK Degree-Awarding Bodies*. Available from: https://www.qaa.ac.uk/docs/qaa/quality-code/qualifications-frameworks.pdf.

Schön, D.A. (1983) *The Reflective Practitioner: How Professionals Think in Action*, Basic Books.

Tangen, T. and Briah, R.K. (2018) The revolving door of reform: Professionalism and the future of probation services in England and Wales, *Probation Journal*, 65(2): 135–151. https://doi.org/10.1177/0264550518768398

Treadwell, J. (2006) Some personal reflections on probation training, *The Howard Journal*, 45(1): 1–13. https://doi.org/10.1111/j.1468-2311.2006.00400.x

Worrall, A. and Mawby, R.C. (2013) Probation workers responses to turbulent conditions: Constructing identity in a tainted occupation, *Australian and New Zealand Journal of Criminology*, 46(1): 101–118. https://doi.org/10.1177/0004865812469976

15

Critical reflection: key principles for Professional Qualification in Probation students and assessors providing feedback

Ceri Halfpenny

Reflective practice is integral to effective probation work (Coley, 2016) and as such, reflective practice is prominent in the learning and teaching of trainee probation officers for their Professional Qualification in Probation (PQiP) programme. Mullineux et al (2019: 54) argues that reflective practice is pivotal in developing 'professional effectiveness'. However, students often struggle to write reflectively (Johnson, 2020) and teachers can find it difficult to provide reflective practice feedback (Dekker et al, 2013). Despite this, there is limited research regarding reflective practice assignment feedback for PQiP students. Drawing on research I completed for my PGCert in Higher Education, which investigated the quality of written feedback for PQiP student's reflective practice assignments, this chapter attempts to address the gap in literature to support assessor feedback and aid PQiP students to improve their critical reflection within assessments.

From my own experiences, PQiP students recognise the benefits of reflecting on their practice with a peer or mentor but may not recognise the benefit of critical reflection within academic assessments. Therefore, the purpose of this chapter is to help PQiP students develop a good understanding of what critical reflective practice is and to help them improve their critical reflective writing. This chapter also highlights some key effective feedback principles, and considers my own research, particularly discussing my thematic analysis of reflective practice feedback, with a focus on developmental, 'close the gap' (Sadler, 1989: 138) comments. These are essentially comments which provide students with strategies to help them improve their work. This stemmed from my desire to improve my practice, answering the question 'What makes good feedback for reflective practice assignments?'. Drawing on analysis of the literature, this chapter highlights the core principles of effective reflective practice feedback for teachers. It also helps PQiP students understand and develop the skills to reflect, analyse and integrate theory and practice when writing reflective practice assignments. The chapter concludes with reflective prompts for markers and PQiP students to aid them in developing their reflective practice academic writing skills.

The importance of reflective practice in Professional Qualification in Probation training

Prior to teaching on the PQiP programme, I had a career in the Probation Service. When I was a newly qualified probation officer beginning to navigate the challenges of managing a high caseload, I appreciated the value that reflection could bring to my practice. However, during my training, as with many of the PQiP students that I now teach, I found it difficult to write reflectively (Ainslie, 2020; Johnson, 2020) and to understand what is meant by the term reflective practice, especially in an academic writing context. Reflective practice is more than just thinking about what happened in a supervision session, or even 'deep thinking' (Bassot, 2016: 1). There is not sufficient time in this chapter to fully explore the term reflective practice (see Chapter 2) but one key aspect is integrating theory and practice, a requirement of education and training by HM Prison and Probation Service (HMPPS) (Carr, 2020). This helps ensure that academic research underpins approaches to practice, ensuring effective probation work and the best outcomes for individuals under probation supervision. Probation practitioners work with a wide variety of individuals, which inevitably means that they will encounter situations, often difficult, that they have not been specifically trained for. Thompson and Thompson (2008: 14) argue that professional knowledge rarely 'gives direct practice guidance on what to do and how to do it'. Therefore, reflection enables PQiP students to improve their future practice by thinking about what they could do differently, taking into account literature and theory to underpin the work that they do.

A further benefit of reflective practice for probation practitioners is the development of professionalism (Coley, 2016), which is now part of the Probation Service agenda with the introduction of the professional register and Probation Professional Registration Standards (HMPPS, 2024). This is supported by wider research regarding the importance of reflective practice in professional development (Fergusson et al, 2019; Goh, 2019). Cardwell and Wright (2023: 41) also highlight that 'HMPPS is increasingly recognising the benefits of reflective practice in promoting staff wellbeing', which is important given concerns about PQiP students and probation practitioners leaving the service due to burnout (Phillips et al, 2020). Continued reflective practice should therefore contribute to having 'a skilled, responsive and resilient workforce' (HMPPS, 2021: 8).

Within PQiP training, the focus is on more than just reflective practice, instead the aim is to help students develop skills in critical reflection. Bassot (2016: 2) states that this includes 'paying attention to your emotional responses and being prepared to challenge your assumptions … examining our personal values and issues of power in the context of working relationships'. This is supported by Ainslie (2020: 10) who adds that it is 'vital' in enabling individuals to be effective probation practitioners, but she acknowledges that it is challenging to learn how to critically reflect. Thompson and Thompson (2008) argue that critical reflective practice can have a transformative impact (see Chapter 14). Due to this, critical reflective practice has been, and continues to be, prominent in the learning, teaching and assessment process of PQiP students (Knight and White, 2001; Petrillo, 2007; Gregory, 2010; Goldhill, 2017; Ainslie, 2020). Therefore, this chapter seeks to help PQiP students understand the term critical reflective practice, know what markers are looking for in their academic reflective assignments and to help them develop the skills to write good critical reflective assignments.

Reflective practice feedback

Cathro and O'Kane (2017: 427) state that minimal research has been undertaken exploring how assessors mark reflective practice assignments. Price et al (2010) argue that it is necessary to measure the effectiveness of feedback provided to students as it is a 'powerful tool' (Kim et al, 2019: 100) to improve practice. This led to my research exploring the principles of effective written feedback for reflective practice assignments, with the aim of improving the quality of teaching and learning for our PQiP students.

Moon (2004: 149) asserts that assessment and feedback is similar in reflective practice to other academic writing. Therefore, I initially sought to explore the principles of effective feedback. Sadler (1989) highlights three conditions for effective feedback. First, that students must understand what high quality work is. Second, they must be able to evaluate their work against high quality work. Third, they must be given strategies to improve their work, referred to as 'gap closure' comments (Sadler, 1989: 138). The importance of this developmental, forward-looking aspect of feedback is widely supported (Jessop et al, 2011; Boud and Molloy, 2013; Winstone and Nash, 2016).

Methodology

My research was undertaken at one of the higher education providers where students undertake the academic component of their PQiP studies. I undertook explorative research into the quality of feedback provided to students for a sample of reflective assessments The literature review strongly emphasised the importance of 'feed forward' and 'gap closure' comments and, therefore, this was used to determine quality feedback (Sadler, 1989: 138; Jessop et al, 2011: 15). Stratified sampling techniques (Cochran, 1977) were used to select a sample of 17 scripts, out of 97 submissions (just under 20 per cent), to ensure that there was a consistent amount of marking analysed by each of the six markers and to be in line with the external examiner sampling policy.

All data was anonymised and transcribed onto Atlas software and thematic analysis was used to analyse the data (Clarke and Braun, 2006). As Sadler (1989: 138) identifies 'strategies for gap closure' as key for effective feedback, the first focus of the analysis was to determine if any of the feedback was developmental. I used a broad encompassing criteria to determine if the feedback was a developmental comment. If the comment went beyond simply stating what was negative or positive and had some possibility of helping the student improve it was included. Comments that encouraged the inclusion of further information in the work were also included, such as: 'Your essay needed to include more critical reflection upon the knowledge, skills …' (S1).

This comment was included as it attempted to give the student advice on how to improve, and therefore it was assessed as a 'feed forward' comment (Sadler, 1989). I then systematically worked through the anonymised feedback to develop initial codes regarding the main focus of the feedback comments. Further analysis was undertaken regarding all the comments which had the code 'reflective writing'. From this analysis three broad themes were identified; reflection, integrating theory and practice and analysis. The following sections will discuss these themes further in relation to implications for PQiP students and assessors.

Learning for Professional Qualification in Probation students: writing reflectively

A common issue with reflective writing is the tendency for students to be overly descriptive (Chanock, 2000). Moon (2004) highlights the variation that can be seen within attempts to write reflectively, highlighting the subjective and unstructured nature of the learning process. Reflective writing benefits from a move away from description to a more detailed level of reflective account (Moon, 2004). In line with this, many of the feedback comments analysed were aiming to help students develop the analysis within their reflective writing. Eleven out of 35 comments in this theme were in essence asking the student to 'reflect more', rather than describing or only briefly reflecting on the situation. The assignment guidance contained questions to guide the students based on Kolb's (1984) experiential learning cycle. The cycle has four stages: (1) concrete experience, the experience being reflected on; (2) reflective observation, looking back at the experience, reflecting on your feelings, skills and knowledge; (3) abstract contextualisation, learning from your experience, drawing on the evidence and developing new insights; and (4) active experimentation, putting in place new learning.

Reflective models can provide useful structure and prompts to aid reflection. There are numerous reflective models, so students are advised to use a model that suits their learning style. Most reflective models should also prompt students to think about what else they need to learn and how they can continually improve their practice. Thirteen feedback comments encouraged the students to think about how they could improve their supervision skills in the future, highlighting that this is another key area for PQiP students to include in their reflective assignments. Some questions PQiP students can use to help inform their forward-looking reflections and areas for professional development are: What went well? What did not go so well? Are there any policies or research that I could read to help me improve my practice in the future? How has this knowledge and learning changed my practice?

Learning for Professional Qualification for Probation students: integrating theory and practice

HM Inspectorate of Probation (HMIP, 2020: 8) emphasises the importance of practitioners using 'evidenced based practice' because this should result in a reduction in reoffending. However, HMIP (2020: 5) also notes that 'there is no "one size fits all" and that practice needs to be attentive and tailored to the diversity of service users'. Reflective practice can ensure that practitioners are adapting their approach by taking account of diversity issues (both their own and that of the individual under probation supervision) and by applying their knowledge of best practice gained through research and training. It also helps ensure that practitioners are considering and challenging their own beliefs, assumptions and stereotypes and reflecting on where their personal values may impact practice.

Using a reflective model should help prompt students to write in short reflective cycles throughout their essays, in order to link theory to practice. The skill of integrating theory and practice is supported by Carr (2020: 8), who states that it is very important that probation staff 'understand the evidence base underpinning areas of practice ... this is particularly important in the area of risk assessment, where any tool should be used to assist professional judgement, rather than to replace it'. This is another key skill for PQiP students to develop in their reflective writing, to explain how research and literature underpins their approach to their practice. Smyth and Watson (2018: 68) interviewed probation students qualifying in 2016 and highlighted that 'the most valuable learning from the programme ... referred to theoretical underpinning and practical application in areas such as risk management'. Improving this aspect of integrating theory and practice should help PQiP students become more confident and effective probation officers.

Learning for Professional Qualification in Probation students: developing critical reflection

A dominant theme in the feedback comments (n=63) was the need for students to develop their critical reflection. It is likely that many students, especially those who have not studied in higher education for a long time, may struggle to understand what 'critical reflection' means (Ainslie, 2020; Johnson, 2020). A starting point for this can be to consider what went well and what did not go well. However, Bassot (2016: 130) encourages students to go further than just reflecting on positives and negatives, and emphasises the importance of reflecting on thoughts and feelings. Encouraging PQiP students to reflect on their emotions, values and bias, can help ensure that they are treating individuals under their supervision fairly, which Petrillo (2007) argues is important due to the power imbalance in the relationship. Another key part of reflective practice for PQiP students is reflecting on how their own values and attitudes impact the decisions they make regarding individuals under their supervision. Goldhill (2017: 279) states that this form of critical reflection is essential for practitioners to overcome any prejudice, enabling them to respect diversity and treat every person on probation in a fair and appropriate manner. Houston (2015) supports this approach to reflective practice, arguing that practitioners should reflectively examine themselves, in order to be aware of how they influence and respond to others.

Another benefit of critical reflective practice, particularly focusing on feelings and emotions, is to help PQiP students develop the skill of emotional intelligence, which was an outcome in the BA Hons (Petrillo, 2020: 7). As it is inevitable that probation officers will have to have difficult conversations it is important that PQiP students are able to be aware of and manage their emotions and be empathic in order to build positive working relationships with individuals on their caseload. This point is supported by Knight (2014), noting that the probation caseload is challenging and therefore developing emotional literacy is a key skill for the professional practitioner.

Critical reflection can also help PQiP students develop 'professional curiosity' (HMIP, 2022: 8) which improves the 'quality of supervision' (HMIP, 2022: 1). Bassot (2016: 132) also encourages students to use 'curiosity in professional practice ... posing questions such as "What is happening here?", "What made the person respond in that way?"'. This self-reflecting and self-questioning approach is supported by HMIP (2022: 67) as it emphasised the importance of professional curiosity, encouraging probation staff to 'take every opportunity to be curious' in their practice.

Learning for assessors: providing effective feedback for reflective assignments

This section will now focus on key principles of effective feedback for reflective practice assignments. One of the primary findings from my research was that students can struggle to understand how to write reflectively, and often wrote descriptively instead. In an attempt to help students write more reflectively, some feedback stated that students needed to 'develop their discussion' (n= 16), however, students may struggle with how to do this. Nicol (2010) argues that effective feedback should be understandable. Sometimes, students do not understand their feedback and Gibbs (2015: 1) describes these students as 'assessment illiterate', highlighting that if they knew how to, for example, 'develop their discussion', they would. Another similar phrase used was 'more depth'. These phrases alone do not seem to be very clear on strategies that students could use to 'close the gap' (Sadler, 1989: 138). This could possibly leave some students confused as to how to create 'more depth'. The concern here is that as the feedback is not effective, students could just ignore it (Gibbs, 2015). Therefore, a key principle of effective feedback is ensuring that it is useful for the student and that it signposts them where to find further support.

Often to help students write more reflectively, they are encouraged to use a reflective model to guide their writing. Three feedback comments advised the students that they would benefit from using a model of reflection. However, it is very difficult for a marker to know if a model was used or not, and therefore, it may not be very motivating for a student to read this, especially if they had used a model of reflection, albeit not very well. Fenwick (2001: 41) supports this, providing advice for feedback on reflective writing, including focusing on strengths and sensitively challenging the student. This highlights the importance of assessors reflecting on their feedback, to ensure that language used is motivating, helpful and avoids assumptions.

Hyatt (2005) reinforces the benefits of positive comments. From my own reflections, I recognise this is something that I need to do more of, especially in busy periods at work. Henderson et al (2019) assert that the quality of feedback can be impacted by volume of marking, workload pressures and tiredness, which I can relate to. A way to help ensure that the feedback is motivating is to start with a positive phrase. For example: 'Great reflection, however, you could have developed this further' (S6).

Another key area that emerged from my research was to help the students develop the skill of 'emotional reflection' (Bruno and Dell'Aversana, 2017: 250). The majority of the feedback comments in this category were written in the form of a question; prompting students to develop aspects of their reflections, such as: 'What were you anxious about?' (S6), or 'Why is this important in this context?' (S1).

These 'why' questions were mainly asking the students to explain their thought process and decision-making. Knight and White (2001: 206) state that probation officers need a thorough understanding of 'the "why" – a range of theoretical perspectives that will inform their professional development as well as their day-to-day perspectives'. Dekker et al's (2013: 5) research into the characteristics of written feedback that were perceived to stimulate students' reflective competence found that 'comments that were rated as stimulating reflection were predominantly phrased as questions and were phrased in a more positive tone'. It can be difficult to be certain how the tone of the question will come across to the student, and arguably a question beginning with 'why' may not be read as having a positive tone (see Chapter 4). None of the questions with 'why' had any specific positive praise in the comment. Ivanič et al (2000: 58) suggests questions that engage in dialogue with the student from the 'perspective of an interested reader' appear to come across in a more positive tone. Therefore, this is another area for myself and academic staff to reflect upon when writing feedback.

Another way to encourage students to develop their critical reflection is to consider their own potential bias. There were seven comments which asked the students to reflect on this. For example: 'You make some good reflection on the need to avoid unconscious bias but need to expand on what this could have looked like specifically for X and how you took it into account' (S15).

This comment provides positive praise, reiterates what the student has done well and also tells the student how to improve, which is a helpful guide in providing effective feedback. Goldhill (2017) supports this approach highlighting the importance of PQiP students reflecting on and challenging their own values to ensure anti-discriminatory practice. Again, a form of question could be beneficial here. Such as: 'could it also be an expression of the discrimination that he has experienced and a fear this will happen again?' (S6).

This is asking the student to question their own assumptions about an individual's behaviour and the possible reasons for this. Reflective practice can therefore support practitioners in adapting their practice by taking account of research and diversity issues.

Some of the markers' comments were very clear about why integrating theory and practice was important. For example:

> Overall, there needs to be more links to the academic literature and relevant policy material to develop your

critique – this was a missed opportunity to explore the evidence base that is specific to women, and as a consequence your links between theory and practice – and your understanding of how the evidence base can be applied to your practice with women is limited. You talk about developing confidence in your decision making, arming yourself with this knowledge will support you in doing that. (S13)

This tells the student how to improve and why it is important. This is a central aspect of effective feedback (Nicol and Macfarlane-Dick, 2006) which assessors should try and include in their feedback comments.

Conclusion

This chapter has highlighted some of the key benefits of critical reflective practice for PQiP students, including developing 'professional effectiveness' (Mullineux et al, 2019: 54), professionalism (Coley, 2016) and staff well-being (Cardwell and Wright, 2023). It then discussed some key areas that PQiP students should focus on to help them improve their critical reflective practice assignments. The first area was writing reflectively, rather than descriptively. The second area was integrating theory and practice. Through this integration, practitioners can consider how research is informing their approach to practice, and the ways that they may adapt this to ensure inclusivity. Reflecting on theory and practice should help PQiP students ensure that they are using 'evidenced based practice' and thereby reducing reoffending (HMIP, 2020: 8). The third area for PQiP students to focus on is developing their critical reflection. This includes reflecting on their strengths and their areas of development. Bassot (2016: 130) highlighted the importance of reflecting on thoughts and feelings. Critically reflecting on their values, biases and their own impact on supervision should help PQiP students tailor their practice to the diversity of their caseload (HMIP, 2020: 5) and enable them to overcome any prejudice, thereby treating every person on probation in a fair and appropriate manner (Goldhill, 2017: 279).

This self-questioning and self-reflection should help PQiP students 'to take every opportunity to be curious' (HMIP, 2022: 67) in their practice and enable them to become effective practitioners who consistently use professional curiosity.

This chapter also argued the importance for academics to reflect on their own feedback because feedback is a 'powerful tool' (Kim et al, 2019: 100) to improve practice. Some key areas for academics to reflect upon when providing reflective practice feedback include helping students understand what high quality work is and providing feedback that gives students strategies to improve their work (Sadler, 1989: 138). This section also highlighted the importance of academic markers being very clear about how the students can improve and encouraged academics to reflect on the feedback they provide and consider if the student can easily understand the feedback comments (Nicol, 2010). Other key principles discussed were focusing on strengths and sensitively challenging (Fenwick, 2001: 41), including positive comments (Hyatt, 2005), and stimulating reflecting by using questions (Dekker et al, 2013: 5) ideally in the form of an 'interested reader' (Ivanič et al, 2000: 58). In order to help PQiP students develop critical reflection, makers should also encourage 'emotional reflection' (Bruno and Dell'Aversana, 2017: 250) in their feedback comments.

Reflective prompts

- As a practitioner, how do my feelings, values and opinions impact on my approach to working with people on probation?
- What are the strengths and weaknesses of my practice when working with diversity needs? How could I improve my practice using the evidence base?
- As an assessor is my feedback clear, constructive and encouraging? Does it help guide future improvement?
- Is my feedback clear in explaining to the student what they need to do to improve in the future?
- Within my feedback, how can I foster emotional reflection, either in myself or in others? What questions can I use to encourage deeper reflection?

References

Ainslie, S. (2020) A time to reflect?, *Probation Quarterly*, 17: 9–12. Available from: https://tinyurl.com/485jf42c

Bassot, B. (2016) *The Reflective Practice Guide: An Interdisciplinary Approach to Critical Reflection*, Routledge.

Boud, D. and Molloy, E. (2013) Rethinking models of feedback for learning: The challenge of design, *Assessment and Evaluation in Higher Education*, 38(6): 698–712. doi: http://dx.doi.org/10.1080/02602938.2012.691462

Bruno, A. and Dell'Aversana, G. (2017) Reflective practice for psychology students: The use of reflective journal feedback in higher education, *Psychology Learning & Teaching*, 16(2): 248–260. doi: https://doi.org/10.1177/1475725716686288

Cardwell, V. and Wright, P. (2023) Coaching: A valuable tool to support wellbeing and resilience in the prison workforce, *Prison Service Journal*, 268: 38–44. Available from: https://tinyurl.com/4a752wud

Carr, N. (2020) *Recruitment, Training and Professional Development of Probation Staff*, 2020/02, HM Inspectorate of Probation. Available from: https://tinyurl.com/496eu7vp

Cathro, V. and O'Kane, P. (2017) Assessing reflection: Understanding skill development through reflective learning journals, *Education and Training*, 59(4): 427–442. doi: https://doi.org/10.1108/ET-01-2017-0008

Chanock, K. (2000) Comments on essays: Do students understand what tutors write?, *Teaching in Higher Education*, 51(1): 95–105. doi: https://doi.org/10.1080/135625100114984

Clarke, V. and Braun, V. (2006) Using thematic analysis in psychology, *Qualitative Research in Psychology*, 3(2): 77–101. doi: https://doi.org/10.1191/1478088706QP063OA

Cochran, W.G. (1977) *Sampling Techniques* (3rd edn), Wiley.

Coley, D. (2016) *Reflective Practice: The Cornerstone of What We All Do*, Probation Institute. Available from: https://tinyurl.com/2hyvua3y

Dekker, H., Schönrock-Adema, J., Snoek, J.W., van der Molen, T. and Cohen-Schotanus, J. (2013) Which characteristics of written feedback are perceived as stimulating students' reflective competence: An exploratory study, *BMC Medical Education*, 13(94): 1–7. doi: https://doi.org/10.1186/1472-6920-13-94

Fenwick, T.J. (2001) Responding to journals in a learning process, *New Directions for Adult & Continuing Education*, 90: 37–47.

Fergusson, L., van der Laan, L. and Baker, S. (2019) Reflective practice and work-based research: A description of micro- and macro-reflective cycles, *Reflective Practice*, 20(2): 289–303. doi: https://doi.org/1080/14623943.2019.1591945

Gibbs, G. (2015) *53 Powerful Ideas All Teachers Should Know About*, Idea Number 28, Staff and Educational Development Association, pp 1–3. Available from: https://tinyurl.com/efj8jvd4

Goh, A. (2019) Rethinking reflective practice in professional lifelong learning using learning metaphors, *Studies in Continuing Education*, 41(1): 1–16. doi: https://doi.org/10.1080/0158037X.2018.1474867

Goldhill, R. (2017) Videoing supervision: Messages for probation practice, *Journal of Social Work Practice*, 31(3): 279–292. doi: https://doi.org/10.1080/02650533.2016.1253005

Gregory, M. (2010) Reflection and resistance: Probation practice and the ethic of care, *British Journal of Social Work*, 40(7): 2274–2290. doi: https://doi.org/10.1093/bjsw/bcq028

Henderson, M., Ryan, R. and Philips, M. (2019) The challenges of feedback in higher education, *Assessment & Evaluation in Higher Education*, 44(8): 1237–1252. doi: https://doi.org/10.1080/02602938.2019.1599815

HMIP (HM Inspectorate of Probation) (2020) *Effective Practice Guide: Case Supervision – Adult*, HM Inspectorate of Probation. Available from: https://tinyurl.com/42cppbdu

HMIP (2022) *Practitioner: Professional Curiosity Insights Guide*, HM Inspectorate of Probation. Available from: https://tinyurl.com/25zm9wvn

HMPPS (HM Prison and Probation Service) (2021) *The Target Operating Model for Probation Services in England and Wales: Probation Reform Programme*, HM Prison and Probation Service. Available from: https://tinyurl.com/y24w9t3w

HMPPS (2024) *Probation Professional Register Policy Framework*. Available from: https://assets.publishing.service.gov.uk/media/66fa78c0a31f45a9c765ee6e/2024_09_30_Prof_Reg-Probation_Professional_Register_policy_framework.pdf

Houston, S. (2015) *Reflective Practice: A Model for Supervision and Practice in Social Work*, Northern Ireland Social Care Council.

Hyatt, D. (2005) 'Yes, a very good point!': A critical genre analysis of a corpus of feedback commentaries on Master of Education assignments, *Teaching in Higher Education*, 10(3): 339–353. doi: http://dx.doi.org/10.1080/13562510500122222

Ivanič, R., Clark, R. and Rimmershaw, R. (2000) What am I supposed to make of this? The messages conveyed to students by tutors' written comments, in M. Lea and B. Stierer (eds) *Student Writing in Higher Education: New Contexts*, Open University Press, pp 47–66.

Jessop, T., El-Hakim, Y. and Gibbs, G. (2011) The TESTA project: Research inspiring change, *Educational Developments*, 12(4): 2–16. doi: https://tinyurl.com/2p9pema2

Johnson, I. (2020) '#39 The best way to surf the reflective wave?', *Take 5*, 30 January. Available from: https://tinyurl.com/hzxcz4ms

Kim, S., Raza, M. and Seidman, E. (2019) Improving 21st-century teaching skills: The key to effective 21st-century learners. *Research in Comparative & International Education*, 41(1): 99–117. doi: https://doi.org/10.1177/1745499919829214

Knight, C. (2014) *Emotional Literacy in Criminal Justice: Professional Practice with Offenders*, Palgrave Macmillan.

Knight, C. and White, K. (2001) The integration of theory and practice within the diploma in probation studies: How is it achieved?, *Probation Journal*, 48(3): 203–210. doi: https://doi.org/10.1177/026455050104800306

Kolb, D. (1984) *Experiential Learning: Experience as the Source of Learning and Development*, Prentice-Hall.

Moon, J.A. (2004) *A Handbook of Reflective and Experiential Learning: Theory and Practice*, RoutledgeFalmer.

Mullineux, J.C., Taylor, B.J. and Giles, M.L. (2019) Probation officers' judgements: A study using personal construct theory, *Journal of Social Work*, 19(1): 41–59. doi: https://doi.org/10.1177/1468017318757384

Nicol, D. (2010) From monologue to dialogue: Improving written feedback processes in mass higher education, *Assessment & Evaluation in Higher Education*, 35(5): 501–517. doi: https://doi.org/10.1080/02602931003786559

Nicol, D.J. and Macfarlane-Dick, D. (2006) Formative assessment and self-regulated learning: A model and seven principles of good feedback practice, *Studies in Higher Education*, 31(2): 199–218. doi: https://doi.org/10.1080/03075070600572090

Petrillo, M. (2007) Power struggle: Gender issues for female probation officers in the supervision of high risk offenders, *Probation Journal*, 54(4): 394–406. doi https://doi.org/10.1177/0264550507083538

Petrillo, M. (2020) *BA Community Justice Student Handbook: Course Supplement 2020 (Release 3)*, University of Portsmouth.

Phillips, J., Westaby, C. and Fowler, A. (2020) *Recruitment, Training and Professional Development of Probation Staff*, 2020/03, HM Inspectorate of Probation. Available from: https://tinyurl.com/4ndvafaf

Price, M., Handley, K., Millar, J. and O'Donovan, B. (2010) Feedback: All that effort, but what is the effect?, *Assessment & Evaluation in Higher Education*, 35(3): 277–289. doi: https://doi.org/10.1080/02602930903541007

Sadler, D.R. (1989) Formative assessment and the design of instructional systems, *Instructional Science*, 18(2): 119–144. doi: https://www.jstor.org/stable/23369143

Smyth, G. and Watson, A. (2018) Training for a transformed service: The experience of learners in 2016, *Probation Journal*, 65(1): 61–76. doi: https://doi.org/10.1177/0264550517748361.

Thompson, S. and Thompson, N. (2008) *The Critically Reflective Practitioner*, Palgrave Macmillan.

Winstone, N.E. and Nash, R.A. (2016) *The Developing Engagement with Feedback Toolkit*, Higher Education Academy. Available from: https://tinyurl.com/ycx3zu72

16

Navigating trauma in higher education: reflections on applying trauma-informed approaches to teaching criminology and Professional Qualification in Probation (PQiP) students

Megan Thomas

Trauma-informed approaches are recognised as a key overarching strategy for building supportive relationships and providing positive outcomes for organisations that work with a wide range of people. This chapter asserts that trauma-informed approaches (Covington, 2007) in higher education (HE) enhance student outcomes and experiences. It provides an overview of trauma-informed practice, introduces its application to teaching in HE, and reflects on my experience delivering a trauma-informed module. The final section draws together the arguments from the chapter. It proposes a model for trauma-informed practice in HE that will aid academics and professionals in developing their approaches within teaching and professional training.

Positionality statement

I am a white British, cis-gendered woman in my mid-40s currently working as a Senior Teaching Fellow with over two decades of experience in HE, teaching criminology and the Professional Qualification in Probation (PQiP) across various learning environments. My understanding of trauma initially developed within the context of the criminal justice system (CJS) and has evolved to inform my approach to education. Additionally, I have undergone training with One Small Thing on Becoming Trauma Informed, which has enhanced my appreciation of trauma-informed methodologies and their application to education.

Definitions of trauma-informed approaches

Trauma is a pervasive force with broad and multifaceted impacts (Fallot and Harris, 2009). Exposure to trauma elevates the risk of lifelong difficulties affecting physical health, mental health, substance abuse, relationships, academic attainment and involvement in the CJS, among other aspects (Tobin, 2016; Ford et al, 2019; Treisman, 2021). Adverse Childhood Experiences (Felitti et al, 1998) recognise that childhood trauma – examples include neglect, abuse and household dysfunction – negatively influences adult health and well-being, prompting interventions and support within education and the CJS (Hardcastle et al, 2018; Ford et al, 2019).

The Substance Abuse and Mental Health Services Administration defines individual trauma as resulting 'from an event, series of events, or set of circumstances that is experienced by an individual as physically or emotionally harmful or life-threatening and that has lasting adverse effects on the individual's functioning and mental, physical, social, emotional or spiritual well-being' (SAMHSA, 2014: 7). This comprehensive definition highlights the event, the individual's reaction and its ongoing impact on their life. Covington (2007) outlines that the response to an incident is central to its long-term effects on the individual and those around them. It is recognised that individuals may experience the same event and respond differently. Furthermore, Treisman (2021) broadens the definition to encompass community trauma (for example, war, natural disasters) and intergenerational trauma (for example, racism, poverty), thereby demonstrating its increasing scope and the growing number of affected individuals.

Exposure to trauma has been shown to impact brain development (Tobin, 2016) and the ability to learn (Sadin, 2022). The direct impact on academic performance is related to language acquisition, memory formation, cognitive processing speed, and the regulation of emotions (Sadin, 2022). These areas can impair learning and educational attainment (Harrison et al, 2023) which has led to the call for trauma-informed approaches to reframe the question of 'What is wrong with you?' to 'What has happened to you?' (Treisman, 2021) to provide supportive and inclusive environments.

Vicarious trauma, defined as the impact of engaging with individuals who have undergone traumatic experiences, whether through listening to or reading their accounts (Treisman, 2021), is a significant consideration in criminology and PQiP HE qualifications. These courses incorporate materials that discuss real-life crimes and victim experiences, potentially causing vicarious traumatisation and re-traumatisation for students (Carello and Butler, 2015). Nikischer (2019) outlines that vicarious trauma can impact individuals working directly with trauma survivors in five key areas: trust, safety, control, esteem and intimacy. Given that the course content draws on real-world experiences and case studies, it is plausible that students exposed to traumatic material may experience similar effects. The application of trauma-informed approaches in HE should aim to 'do no harm' (Carello and Butler, 2014) and actively resist re-traumatisation (Harrison et al, 2023: 183).

Fallot and Harris (2009) define a trauma-informed service as one that integrates awareness of trauma and routes to healing into all aspects of delivery, aiming to prevent re-traumatisation for clients and staff. Trauma-specific services, by contrast, focus on directly addressing trauma and facilitating recovery. In this context, HE settings aim to be trauma-informed rather than trauma-specific. Treisman (2021) likens developing a trauma-informed approach to a river, where stages can overlap and the pace of change varies. The four stages – trauma-sensitive, trauma-aware, trauma-informed, and trauma-responsive – represent an ongoing journey rather than a final destination.

A trauma-informed approach is built on the five core values (Fallot and Harris, 2009: 3) demonstrated in Figure 16.1.

Figure 16.1: The five core values of a trauma-informed approach

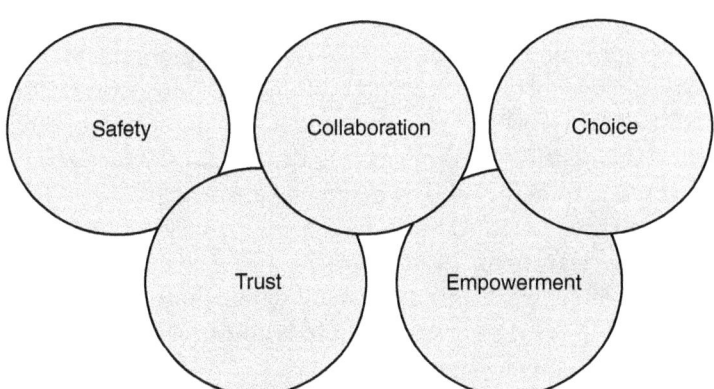

A programme or organisation is trauma-informed when it consistently embodies these values in all interactions, environments, relationships and activities. Furthermore, this ethos must be apparent in the experiences of both staff and students. Some American settings also include cultural, historical and gender issues as a sixth value (Bitanihirwe and Imad, 2023).

Mental health and higher education

While the rising prevalence of mental health issues among university students is a global concern (Macaskill, 2013) this chapter specifically examines UK data (Lewis and Bolton, 2023). Official figures for UK home students in 2021/2022 indicate a significant increase in mental health issues, with 5.5 per cent having a diagnosed mental health condition, marking a three-and-a-half-fold rise from the rates recorded in 2014/2015 (Lewis and Bolton, 2023). However, self-report studies conducted by Student Minds (2023) and Cibyl (2022) reveal more nuanced perspectives, with 57 per cent of students acknowledging current mental health issues, and 81 per cent experiencing challenges according to Cibyl's (2022) research, up from 60 per cent in the previous year.

Contributing factors to mental health challenges for students include moving away from home, workload pressures, financial strains and transitional phases (Lwis and Bolton, 2023). Certain demographics, such as disadvantaged, international, mature and neurodiverse students, are at higher risk of mental health conditions and suicide (Lewis and Bolton, 2023). The changing demographic of the student population, with more students from disadvantaged backgrounds now attending university (IPPR, 2017), and the COVID-19 pandemic (Chen and Lucock, 2022) have been identified as exacerbating these factors. Mental health can impact student attendance and engagement (Oldfield et al, 2018) and their potential for re-traumatisation or vicarious trauma within the classroom. PQiP learners, being mature, part-time students, often work in emotionally demanding environments (Lee, 2017) while pursuing their studies, rendering them susceptible to mental health challenges.

While universities do provide support for student mental health (Lewis and Bolton, 2023), this chapter argues that implementing trauma-informed approaches can enhance this support. This chapter aligns with Carello and Butler's (2014: 157) assertion that in moving towards a trauma-informed approach the initial step is 'First, do no harm'.

Individuals who have experienced trauma and adversity in their early life may be more inclined to pursue careers in caring professions (Treisman, 2021; Bryce et al, 2023b). This includes roles in the Probation Service or charities supporting people involved in the CJS. Trauma-informed approaches have been developed and implemented in several areas of the CJS, for example, the Probation Service (Petrillo and Bradley, 2022) and Police Service (Gillespe-Smith et al, 2020). This chapter reflects on the Gender and Crime module, which discusses gender-responsive and trauma-informed approaches, especially for women in the CJS (Covington, 2007). While delivering this content, I identified key themes of a trauma-informed approach and concluded that my teaching should be 'informed and consistent' with the curriculum (Carello and Butler, 2015: 264).

Trauma-informed teaching

The application of trauma-informed practice in schools and educational settings has been widely discussed (Brummer, 2020; Brunzell and Norrish, 2021; Jacobson, 2021). The extensive evidence base outlines strategies for 'creating supportive learning environments' (Brunzell and Norrish, 2021: 26) where teachers ensure that pupils feel 'safe, secure, welcomed and accepted' (Brunzell and Norrish, 2021: 30) within classrooms. Trauma-informed classrooms ensure all areas of practice recognise how trauma and stress affect students, their behaviour and their ability to learn. However, trauma-informed approaches in HE have yet to be fully embraced and implemented. The initial focus has been on social work education, where students train to work in situations exposing them to stories of trauma and adversity (Hitchcock et al, 2021; Sanders, 2021). The COVID-19 pandemic of 2020 led to a renewed interest in the concept of trauma-informed approaches in HE, largely due to the transition to online teaching and the growing recognition of the collective experiences of trauma (Carello and Thompson, 2021).

Within HE, trauma-informed approaches refer to practices that consciously create inclusive and supportive learning environments (Parrotta et al, 2021; Bitanihirwe and Imad, 2023). Comparisons can be drawn to disability-informed organisations that strive to ensure their services are accessible to all (Carello and Butler, 2015), recognising that the problem is the environment we ask people to function in rather than the disability. The same can be said of those who have experienced trauma. Students who are presented with materials in a trauma-informed environment will develop increased empathy, self-reflection and personal growth which are all relevant skills for potential future careers (Parrotta et al, 2021). Andragogy or adult learning theory (ALT) (Bryce et al, 2023a) specifically refers to teaching approaches with adults who have chosen to study and have agency in their learning. Consequently, strategies for this cohort must acknowledge the potential impact of personal trauma, systemic oppression and previous educational trauma, which may hinder learning if not effectively addressed (Daniels, 2021). A central element of a trauma-informed approach is to 'remove possible barriers to learning, not to remove traumatic, sensitive or difficult material from the curriculum' (Carello and Butler, 2015: 265). To address this, Miller (2001) urges formal discussion of trauma and its impact within the curriculum, as this will aid student understanding and reduce potential re-traumatisation.

The discussion will now turn to three key areas concerning the implementation of trauma-informed approaches in HE: the use of trigger warnings, the application of a growth mindset, and the adoption of a restorative justice approach.

Trigger warnings

The term 'trigger warning' originated with female bloggers, initially used to caution readers about explicit online discussions of sexual assault (Campbell and Manning, 2018). Repurposed for educational settings they are defined as 'explicit statements alerting learners that discussed content may contain distressing material' (Bryce et al, 2023a: 2883). Trigger warnings in classrooms aim to prevent re-traumatisation or vicarious trauma, sparking widespread debate, especially in the United States, with critics contending they have shifted from aiding trauma survivors to becoming a 'silver bullet to address all social ills in the classroom' (Dickman-Burnett and Geaman, 2019: 36). Bryce et al's (2023a) literature review suggests trigger warnings positively impact trauma-informed or inclusive organisations but may harm students if used in isolation without broader support.

Acknowledging that students in criminology or PQiP courses will engage with potentially traumatic topics, some methods can mitigate the impact. Stringer (2016: 65) reflects on incorporating 'content forecasting', a term she deems 'benign and accessible' compared to trigger warnings, into her 'Critical Victimology' course, emphasising their role in supporting trauma survivors and preventing disruptions. Cunningham (2004) suggests that integrating trigger warnings and understanding vicarious trauma into the curriculum can offer a theoretical framework to assist students in managing their reactions to the material.

The application of a growth mindset

A growth mindset is 'the belief that human capacities are not fixed but can be developed over time' (Dweck and Yeager, 2019: 481). This is in opposition to a fixed mindset, the belief that intelligence and attributes cannot be changed (Yeager et al, 2022). Extensive research has explored the application of growth mindset approaches in education, revealing a positive impact on students' learning approaches, even amid ongoing challenges (Dweck and Yeager, 2019). In HE, linking a growth mindset with trauma-informed approaches is clear, as promoting belief in human capacity flexibility aligns with providing empathetic support for diverse student needs, including trauma survivors.

McKinsey and Desmarais (2023: 579) discuss the application of a growth mindset to the education of criminal legal professionals in America by identifying that mindset impacts how people 'confront bias, face challenges and perceive others'. An example of a growth mindset teaching exercise is 'saying-is-believing' (McKinsey and Desmarais, 2023) which encourages students to learn about the brain's malleability and apply it to themselves, making the message feel more relevant and easier to recall. Applying this exercise to criminology and PQiP teaching, students could reflect on case studies or people they have worked with to identify positive changes in attitude and behaviour, in doing so recognising the potential for both themselves and others to change.

Despite its positive impact, it is crucial to acknowledge the potential limitations of the growth mindset concept. Although mindset theory suggests that endorsing a growth mindset can predict achievement by influencing self-regulatory processes after failure (Dweck and Leggett, 1988), its application in trauma-informed teaching may face challenges. Trauma-affected students may exhibit difficulties in engaging with growth mindset strategies, as their cognitive responses to feedback and challenges can be influenced by the lasting effects of trauma. For example, PQiP students, who are consistently involved in 'trauma work' (Lee, 2017) through supporting people on probation, face unique difficulties relating to the combination of academic study and work with marginalised people. Addressing these challenges is crucial for implementing growth mindset principles in trauma-informed education.

A restorative justice approach

Restorative justice is a 'criminal justice process in which offenders, victims and other persons with a stake in an offence or conflict are enabled to participate in responding to that offence' (Marder et al, 2022: 529).

These principles have been applied to education within schools (Brummer, 2020) with an emphasis on developing a strong sense of community. Equally, restorative justice approaches have been implemented within some HE institutions, for example, Maynooth University in Ireland (Marder et al, 2022). The similarity to trauma-informed teaching is a shared commitment to compassionate and understanding educational environments that prioritise the needs of students. A central tool of this approach is circle time, where the educator and students sit in a circle, and everyone is encouraged to respond to a question. Circle processes in HE teaching promote active listening, respect and deep reflection on diverse experiences. They foster connection, and support, and prevent the dominance of louder voices in conversations (Marder and Wexler, 2021). Circle time can be utilised within a trauma-informed classroom to develop collaboration, trust and safety.

Reflections on applying a trauma-informed approach

These reflections centre on the delivery of Gender and Crime, an optional module for campus-based final-year undergraduates, delivered face-to-face in interactive two-hour sessions. Framed by the five values of a trauma-informed approach, the discussion explores the author's experiences of module delivery through a trauma-informed lens. While specific to a campus-based academic setting, the identified key learning points have broader relevance in HE or professional training.

The module examines gendered experiences in the CJS, focusing on gender-specific and trauma-informed approaches. Developing the content prompted me to embody 'practising what I teach' (Carello and Butler, 2015) and explore trauma-informed approaches in HE. During the first two years of their course, the cohort faced disruptions from the pandemic and online learning, along with a lack of community-building activities. This highlighted the need for a teaching style that fosters community, safety and trust. The module was delivered through lectures and seminars using a collaborative, learner-centred approach.

Empowerment

Empowerment is the process of providing people with information so that they can develop their agency, self-esteem and ability to make informed decisions. Within the Virtual Learning Environment, I defined my approach as trauma-informed, but I felt apprehensive about stating this verbally during the first teaching session. It was a significant statement, and it is plausible that I perceived myself as an individual making the assertion rather than as a representative of a trauma-informed organisation. My hesitation may also stem from the possibility of a student challenging the assertion. I now recognise that this is part of an ongoing process 'that needs constant attention, re-evaluation and deliberate effort' (Treisman, 2021: 30). Moreover, this self-critical stance stems from a lack of practical understanding regarding the implementation of trauma-informed practices. Carello and Butler (2015) discuss the importance of being kind to ourselves as instructors who are aiming to present in a trauma-informed way. It will not always be possible to achieve this fully but we can move from asking ourselves what went wrong to what happened to prevent that session from being trauma-informed (Carello and Butler, 2015)? Furthermore, providing students with a clear overview of what trauma is, how it affects people and how to recognise vicarious trauma can give them the knowledge to identify and address it themselves.

Safety and collaboration

Safety refers to the physical and emotional feelings of both students and educators. Collaboration promotes a sense of shared ownership in the pursuit of shared objectives.

To foster a sense of safety and community within the group, I employed the restorative justice circle time approach (Marder and Wexler, 2021). Initially, the students exhibited a certain degree of hesitancy, possibly influenced by the need to rearrange the furniture and the novelty of the activity. The first circle used a two-word check-in to ascertain their emotional state, the first student to speak said they were 'tired and hungry' (the session was at 1pm) and several other students in the group repeated the same words. We laughed about it and engaged in a discussion about the timing of the session and the collective mood, yet it left me initially doubting the success of the circle. At that moment, I failed to fully recognise the group's sincerity. I had anticipated that our discussions would evoke more profound emotions, but as we were not familiar with each other as a group, this did not occur. As the module progressed, I used this approach to open each session, with mixed results. Building a sense of safety takes time (Treisman, 2021) yet this method facilitated active involvement from all participants. Its consistent implementation established it as a core activity, thereby enhancing feelings of safety and collaboration.

Choice

Choice encourages recognition of autonomy and the individual's ability to make decisions about their own life. The Virtual Learning Environment provided students with an overview of each taught session. This included a trigger warning so students could make an informed choice about how the content might affect them. After one session, a student informed me that it was beneficial for them to be aware that the subsequent session would address the topic of stalking. They had first-hand experience of stalking and felt that knowing the focus of the session would enable them to mentally prepare. However, they also wished to attend to hear what was said and to contribute their thoughts and experiences. This relates to Bryce et al's (2023a) discussions of trigger warnings as the student used them not to avoid the session but to enable preparation and participation. In response to the disclosure, I provided 'supportive acknowledgement as a teacher' (Miller, 2001: 168), discussed the potential impact of the session and checked that they were receiving formal support.

The Virtual Learning Environment did not explicitly discuss the trigger warnings. To develop this approach, it would be beneficial to outline the content and purpose of the trigger warnings for the students. Additionally, discussions on how to recognise and address vicarious trauma should be included as a central part of the curriculum (Cunningham, 2004; Bryce et al, 2023a).

Trust

Trust can be defined as providing a safe and consistent environment where students can feel confident in approaches within the classroom. I have taught the module previously and due to time constraints, I re-used case studies within seminar activities. A conversation with a student helped me recognise that I was not fully aware of the potential impact of the content of the case studies. This lack of awareness could be attributed to desensitisation or compassion fatigue (Nikischer, 2019). During a group task, I observed a student who appeared to be experiencing some degree of distress. Upon speaking with them, it became evident that they grasped the exercise but found the subject matter challenging. I assessed the impact of the materials and stressed the importance of acknowledging any discomfort. With their consent, I raised this issue in the group discussion, identifying the possibility of re-traumatisation and vicarious trauma. This is an example of the safety and trust (Carello and Butler, 2015) built within the group as the student was open and shared their feelings. Graziano (2001) identified instances where students shared personal experiences of trauma in class. They found that such experiences could influence the direction of the discussion and the learning outcomes. However, they also emphasised the importance of ensuring that students feel safe and supported. Carello and Butler (2015) highlight that it is important to discuss and normalise the unsettling feelings that can arise when learning about trauma. The preparation of materials from a trauma-informed perspective would have facilitated a more focused consideration of the content and how it was shared with students, with the use of trigger warnings and references to vicarious trauma being employed at an early stage of the module.

Conclusion

The application of trauma-informed approaches within HE holds the potential for significant benefits to students, particularly as mental health issues become more prevalent. This chapter has critically explored the evolving field of trauma-informed education, examining its application in the CJS, schools and HE.

The literature and reflections provided highlight the following key components for achieving positive outcomes in teaching and learning:

- Introduction of trauma from the outset of the module.
- Outline vicarious trauma at the outset of the module.
- Utilise a growth mindset perspective to deliver the content.
- Address the five values of trauma-informed approaches for both students and educators.
- Deliver as part of a fully trauma-informed organisation.

This is summarised in Figure 16.2.

Treisman (2021) states that a trauma-informed organisation recognises and responds to trauma in all its work. To be fully trauma-informed it takes time to introduce the approach,

Figure 16.2: The five components required to apply a trauma-informed approach and achieve positive outcomes in teaching and learning

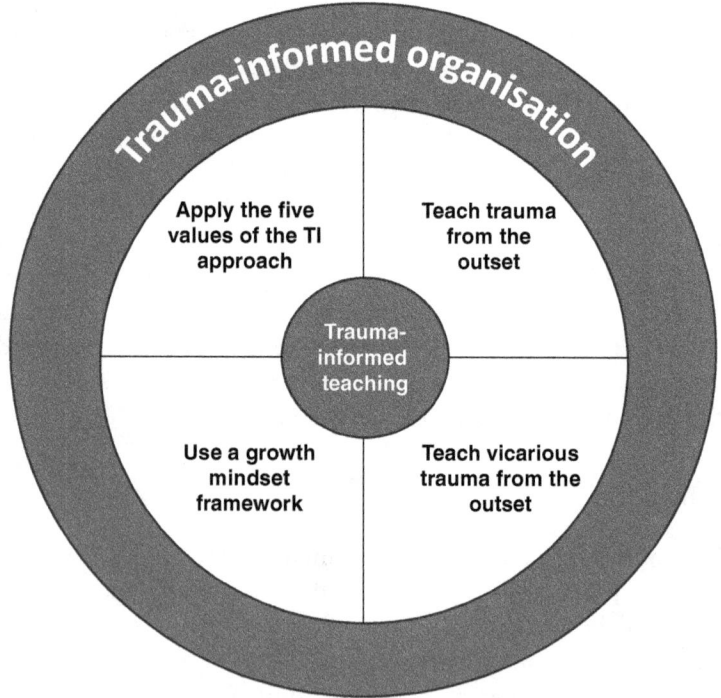

educate everyone and fully embed it (Fallot and Harris, 2009). Implementing this approach in HE is anticipated to result in improved outcomes for both students and staff, attributed to enhanced support mechanisms. Even implementing only the first four steps of the aforementioned model in a developing organisation would likely yield positive outcomes. However, further research is required to ascertain the efficacy of the model and to gain insight into the experiences of students and educators.

In summary, the application of trauma-informed teaching within HE accentuates its transformative potential. The relationship between theory and practice, exemplified in the Gender and Crime module, demonstrates the impact a trauma-informed perspective can have on both students and educators. As we recognise the increasing number of people in society with experiences of trauma and corresponding mental health issues the salience of trauma-informed teaching within HE becomes apparent. It transcends being merely a *teaching* strategy; rather, it emerges as a guiding principle steering us towards more empathetic, supportive and inclusive learning environments. The reflections presented in this chapter highlight the importance of applying trauma-informed approaches, not solely as a theoretical construct but as an experiential paradigm fostering the five trauma-informed values. For educators and professionals alike, the implications are unequivocal – the integration of trauma-informed principles is not just advantageous; it is imperative. This chapter extends an invitation to contemplate the far-reaching ramifications of trauma-informed teaching within your own educational or professional sphere.

Reflective prompts

- Consider the role of trauma in the educational experiences of students and educators. Reflect on how understanding trauma can enhance empathy, communication and support in the learning environment, drawing from personal experiences.
- Reflect on the impact of vicarious trauma in the CJS, schools or HE. Explore ways to incorporate awareness of vicarious trauma into your setting and identify strategies to recognise and address it for both students and staff.

- Reflect on the practical application of the five values of a trauma-informed approach in teaching and learning scenarios. Provide specific examples where these principles could lead to positive outcomes or potential challenges in their adoption.

References

Bitanihirwe, B. and Imad, M. (2023) Gauging trauma-informed pedagogy in higher education: A UK case study, *Frontiers in Education*, 8: 1–2. doi: https://doi.org/10.3389/feduc.2023.1256996.

Brummer, J. (2020) *Building a Trauma-informed Restorative School: Skills and Approaches for Improving Culture and Behavior*, Jessica Kingsley Publishers.

Brunzell, T. and Norrish, J. (2021) *Creating Trauma-Informed, Strengths-Based Classrooms: Teacher Strategies for Nurturing Students' Healing, Growth, and Learning*, Jessica Kingsley Publishers.

Bryce, I., Horwood, N. and Gildersleeve, J. (2023a) Pulling the trigger: A systematic literature review of trigger warnings as a strategy for reducing traumatization in higher education, *Trauma, Violence, & Abuse*, 24(4): 2882–2894. doi: https://doi.org/10.1177/15248380221118968

Bryce, I., Pye, D. and Du Preez, J. (2023b) A systematic literature review of the career choice of helping professionals who have experienced cumulative harm as a result of adverse childhood experiences, *Trauma, Violence, & Abuse*, 24(1): 72–85. doi: https://doi.org/10.1177/15248380211016016

Campbell, B. and Manning, J. (2018) *The Rise of Victimhood Culture: Microaggressions, Safe Spaces, and the New Culture Wars*, Palgrave Macmillan.

Carello, J. and Butler, L.D. (2014) Potentially perilous pedagogies: Teaching trauma is not the same as trauma-informed teaching, *Journal of Trauma & Dissociation*, 15(2): 153–168. doi: https://doi.org/10.1080/15299732.2014.867571

Carello, J. and Butler, L.D. (2015) Practicing what we teach: Trauma-informed educational practice, *Journal of Teaching in Social Work*, 35(3): 262–278. doi: https://doi.org/10.1080/08841233.2015.1030059

Carello, J. and Thompson, P. (eds) (2021) *Lessons from the Pandemic: Trauma-Informed Approaches to College, Crisis, Change*, Palgrave Macmillan.

Chen, T. and Lucock, M. (2022) The mental health of university students during the COVID-19 pandemic: An online survey in the UK, *PLoS ONE*, 17(1): e0262562. https://doi.org/10.1371/journal.pone.0262562.

Cibyl (2022) *Student Mental Health Study 2022*, 7 October. Cibyl. Available from: https://tinyurl.com/384r7nf2

Covington, S.S. (2007) The relational theory of women's psychological development: Implications for the criminal justice system, in R. Zaplin, *Female Offenders: Critical Perspectives and Effective Interventions* (2nd edn), Jones & Bartlett Publishers, pp 135–164.

Cunningham, M. (2004) Teaching social workers about trauma: Reducing the risks of vicarious traumatization in the classroom, *Journal of Social Work Education*, 40(2): 305–317.

Daniels, E. (2021) *Building a Trauma-Responsive Educational Practice: Lessons from a Corrections Classroom*, Routledge.

Dickman-Burnett, V.L. and Geaman, M. (2019) Untangling the trigger-warning debate: Curating a complete toolkit for compassionate praxis in the classroom, *Journal of Thought*, 53(3/4): 35–52.

Dweck, C.S. and Leggett, E.L. (1988) A social-cognitive approach to motivation and personality, *Psychological Review*, 95(2): 256–273.

Dweck, C.S. and Yeager, D.S. (2019) Mindsets: A view from two eras, *Perspectives on Psychological Science*, 14(3): 481–496. doi: https://doi.org/10.1177/1745691618804166

Fallot, R.D. and Harris, M. (2009) Creating Cultures of Trauma-Informed Care (CCTIC): A self-assessment and planning protocol, Community Connections. Available from: https://tinyurl.com/mryv85un

Felitti, V.J., Anda, R.F., Nordenberg, D., Edwards, V., Ross, M.P., Marks, J.M., et al (1998) Relationship of childhood abuse and household dysfunction to many of the leading causes of death in adults: The Adverse Childhood Experiences (ACE) study, *American Journal of Preventive Medicine*, 14(4): 245–258. doi: https://doi.org/10.1016/S0749-3797(98)00017-8

Ford, K., Barton, E., Newbury, A., Hughes, K., Bezeczky, Z., Roderick, J., et al (2019) *Understanding the Prevalence of Adverse Childhood Experiences (ACEs) in a Male Offender Population in Wales: The Prisoner ACE Survey*, Public Health Wales NHS Trust & Bangor University. Available from: https://tinyurl.com/ypsmp862

Gillespie-Smith, K., Brodie, Z., Collins, K., Deacon, K. and Goodall, K. (2020) *Moving Towards Trauma-Informed Policing: An Exploration of Police Officers Attitudes and Perceptions Towards Adverse Childhood Experiences*, The Scottish Institute for Policing Research. Available from: https://tinyurl.com/3pthajak

Graziano, R. (2001) Teaching trauma: A true story, *Journal of Teaching in Social Work*, 21(3–4): 177–185. doi: https://doi.org/10.1300/J067v21n03_13

Hardcastle, K., Bellis, M.A., Ford, K., Hughes, K., Garner, J. and Rodriguez, G.R. (2018) Measuring the relationships between adverse childhood experiences and educational and employment success in England and Wales: Findings from a retrospective study, *Public Health*, 165: 106–116. doi: https://doi.org/10.1016/j.puhe.2018.09.014

Harrison, N., Burke, J. and Clarke, I. (2023) Risky teaching: Developing a trauma-informed pedagogy for higher education, *Teaching in Higher Education*, 28(1): 180–194. doi: https://doi.org/10.1080/13562517.2020.1786046

Hitchcock, L.I., Creswell Báez, J., Sage, M., Marquart, M., Lewis, K. and Smyth, N.J. (2021) Social work educators' opportunities during COVID-19: A roadmap for trauma-informed teaching during crisis, *Journal of Social Work Education*, 57(sup1): 82–98. doi: https://doi.org/10.1080/10437797.2021.1935369

IPPR (2017) Not by degrees: Improving student mental health in the UK's universities. Available from: https://www.ippr.org/research/publications/not-by-degrees

Jacobson, M.R. (2021) An exploratory analysis of the necessity and utility of trauma-informed practices in education, *Preventing School Failure*, 65(2): 124–134. doi: https://doi.org/10.1080/1045988X.2020.1848776

Lee, R. (2017) The impact of engaging with clients' trauma stories: Personal and organizational strategies to manage probation practitioners' risk of developing vicarious traumatization, *Probation Journal*, 64(4): 372–387. doi: https://doi.org/10.1177/0264550517728783

Lewis, J. and Bolton, P. (2023) *Student Mental Health in England: Statistics, Policy, and Guidance*, Research Briefing 8593, House of Commons Library, pp 1–43. Available from: https://tinyurl.com/2u75t635

Macaskill, A. (2013) The mental health of university students in the United Kingdom, *British Journal of Guidance & Counselling*, 41(4): 426–441. doi: https://doi.org/10.1080/03069885.2012.743110

Marder, I.D. and Wexler, D.B. (2021) Mainstreaming restorative justice and therapeutic jurisprudence through higher education, *University of Baltimore Law Review*, 50(3): 399–424.

Marder, I.D., Vaugh, T., Keny, C., Dempsy, S., Savage, E., Weiner, R., et al (2022) Enabling student participation in course review and redesign: Piloting restorative practices and design thinking in an undergraduate criminology programme, *Journal of Criminal Justice Education*, 33(4): 526–547. doi: https://doi.org/10.1080/10511253.2021.2010781

McKinsey, E. and Desmarais, S.L. (2023) Impact of growth mindset-enhanced trauma education on criminal legal professionals' attitudes and perceptions, *Criminal Justice and Behavior*, 50(4): 578–599. doi: https://doi.org/10.1177/00938548221143529

Miller, M. (2001) Creating a safe frame for learning: Teaching about trauma and trauma treatment, *Journal of Teaching in Social Work*, 21(3–4): 159–176. doi: https://doi.org/10.1300/J067v21n03_12

Nikischer, A. (2019) Vicarious trauma inside the academe: Understanding the impact of teaching, researching and writing violence, *Higher Education*, 77(5): 905–916. doi: https://doi.org/10.1007/s10734-018-0308-4.

Oldfield, J., Rodwell, J., Curry, L. and Marks, G. (2018) Psychological and demographic predictors of undergraduate non-attendance at university lectures and seminars, *Journal of Further and Higher Education*, 42(4): 509–523. doi: https://doi.org/10.1080/0309877X.2017.1301404

Parrotta, K., Bergquist, A.C. and Hans, K.R. (2021) Student perspectives on trauma-informed education practices in criminal justice and forensic science, *Journal of Criminal Justice Education*, 32(3): 323–343. doi: https://doi.org/10.1080/10511253.2021.1958885

Petrillo, M. and Bradley, A. (2022) Working with trauma in adult probation, *Research & Analysis Bulletin* 2022/02, HM Inspectorate of Probation. Available from: https://tinyurl.com/4tft9bky

Sadin, M. (2022) *Trauma-Informed Teaching and IEPS: Strategies for Building Student Resilience*, Association for Supervision & Curriculum Development

SAMHSA (Substance Abuse and Mental Health Services Administration) (2014) *SAMHSA's Concept of Trauma and Guidance for a Trauma-Informed Approach*, HHS Publication No. (SMA) 14-4884, U.S. Department of Health and Human Services. Available from: https://tinyurl.com/ex3c7p7c

Sanders, J.E. (2021) Teaching note: Trauma-informed teaching in social work education, *Journal of Social Work Education*, 57(1): 197–204, doi: https://doi.org/10.1080/10437797.2019.1661923

Stringer, R. (2016) Reflection from the field: Trigger warnings in university teaching, *Women's Studies Journal*, 30(2): 62–66.

Student Minds (2023) Student Minds: Research briefing – February '23, Student Minds. Available from: https://tinyurl.com/ypm7d62v

Tobin, M. (2016) *Childhood Trauma: Developmental Pathways and Implications for the Classroom*, Australian Council for Educational Research.

Treisman, K. (2021) *A Treasure Box for Creating Trauma-Informed Organizations: A Ready-To-Use Resource for Trauma, Adversity, and Culturally Informed, Infused and Responsive Systems*, Jessica Kingsley Publishers.

Yeager, D.S., Carroll, J.M., Buontempo, J., Cimpian, A., Woody, S., Crosnoe, R., et al (2022) Teacher mindsets help explain where a growth-mindset intervention does and doesn't work, *Psychological Science*, 33(1): 18–32. doi: https://doi.org/10.1177/09567976211028984

17

Extended Reality: a new dimension for reflective learning

Laura Haggar, Michelle McDermott and Amy Meenaghan

Rapid growth and interest in Extended Reality (XR) technology – an umbrella term that incorporates Virtual Reality (VR), Augmented Reality and Mixed Reality – is fostering an ever-growing appetite for its use to replace or enhance existing education and training. Yet, in the criminal justice domain, the evidence for effective application is in the fledgling stages compared to, for example, military and medical applications (van Gelder et al, 2019). Recent developments suggest that XR technology holds potential for rehabilitative interventions (Ticknor, 2019), professional training and pedagogical opportunities within the field (Smith, 2021). Drawing upon our own research with probation practitioners, this chapter explores the potential for utilising XR to promote reflective practice within criminal justice work.

Training opportunities for probation practitioners have increasingly moved to remote, online formats (HMPPS, 2022). While these platforms have strengths in terms of resources and access to training, there are potential limitations when applied to some of the deeper learning and feedback mechanisms required within the complexity of the role. For example, developing practitioners' professional curiosity is a consistent area of development seen within safeguarding and serious further offence analysis (HMIP, 2023a). Furthermore, the role of home visits within risk assessment practice is a regular feature of Inspectorate reports (HMIP, 2023b), with opportunities for staff members, particularly those who are early in their careers, to embark on active home visit training limited post-pandemic (Meenaghan et al, 2023). Therefore, we sought to explore whether the use of XR could be beneficial for this learning and development of these skills.

The focus on practitioner risk decision-making and the development of professional curiosity within the research led naturally to considerations of reflection and how this could be enabled within the training environment. The proof of concept study used two conditions: (1) 360 video; (2) VR. We noted that differences could be seen within the different tools, and opportunities for developing reflection are explored within this chapter.

The benefits and limitations of Extended Reality in experiential learning

Simulated environments, including those that use a variety of XR tools, have been demonstrated to be effective in facilitating the development of intuitive, implicit and functional knowledge (Swaak et al, 1998). XR has the ability to recreate life-like environments, with recent advances in technology providing multi-sensory experiences enabling users to see, hear, touch and even smell their virtual world (Petit et al, 2022). When such real-life simulations are provided in learning spaces, they offer the opportunity to practice new skills and make mistakes in a risk-free environment. From a pedagogical position, this realism can tap into emotion (Smith, 2021), which is of particular importance in the criminal justice field, where decisions have a human impact. Unlike real life, simulations can enable repetition of the experience with the same conditions, promoting the development of higher-order thinking skills and allowing learners to test their knowledge and understanding. XR technology can assist in closing the feedback loop, offering both immediate and delayed feedback, enabling deeper engagement in reflection of practice, and supporting the reinforcement of learning and skill development (University of Glasgow, 2023). Further, Witmer and Singer (1998) indicated an improvement in transfer of knowledge and skill to the real world, as demonstrated by the recent application of VR in criminal justice where it has been used to improve the predictive validity of risk assessment instruments through the depiction of real-life scenarios (Cornet and van Gelder, 2020).

Despite these benefits, XR is not without limitations. Cost is an obvious issue, particularly in relation to VR headsets, which can limit accessibility (Hamad and Jia, 2022). There is the risk of motion sickness or eye strain (Chang et al, 2020) in some participants. Furthermore, with a desire to embrace technology in training and education, there is a concern that they are simply seen as novel, without clear pedagogical alignment (Kluge et al, 2022).

The use of XR technology can be seen to hold real potential within the criminal justice domain, however, for probation professional training it requires empirical testing and development to ensure that this meets the needs of practitioners, in a way that can mitigate the risks outlined.

The role of observation and reflection in probation officer training

In setting their priorities for learning and development, the Probation Service Learning Strategy (HMPPS, 2022: 8) highlights the need for learner-centred training that takes place 'in a safe learning environment where you can be open, share mistakes and grow'. Further, it acknowledges the importance of 'using technology to develop engaging, interactive learning for all' (2022: 10). This latter point reflected the growing need of the Probation Service to engage with technological advances, not only in professional development but in case management following the COVID-19 pandemic, which undoubtedly accelerated the adoption of remote learning for probation officer qualification (Fowler et al, 2023) and the onset of remote supervision through the Exceptional Delivery Model (see Chapter 9 for further details).

Probation practitioners have a complex role that requires ongoing assessment of risk, as well as promoting desistance of individuals under their supervision. A core feature of the academic component of the Professional Qualification in Probation is the application of theoretical knowledge to case management. This is fundamental in the development of practitioner skills that align with the core aims of the Probation Service to Assess, Protect and Change (HMPPS, 2021). Skills acquisition takes place within the vocational learning in the role, supported by practice tutor assessors (PTAs) and line managers. Reflection on practice provides a critical thread between these aspects of case supervision in both trainees and qualified probation practitioners. Indeed, reflective practice is important at all stages of a practitioner's career, with the Probation Professional Register firmly placing it as a 'fundamental part of ongoing professional development, enhancing practice' (HMPPS, 2024: 10).

Through the guidance of PTAs and line managers, the practice of trainee officers is observed and discussed (Skills for Justice Awards, 2016), with a view to reflecting both in and on action (Schön, 1983). The value of practice observations as a means of developing critical reflection can be seen across a range of professions that require emotional literacy and high-stakes decision-making (for example, social work, healthcare, police and probation). They can build confidence in both the practitioner and the assessor/line manager, and the overall profession that the student is ready to practice (Westaby et al, 2021; Pye, 2024). Observations can be used for both the assessment *of* learning, for example, what officers do in real time, and the assessment *for* learning, identifying what they do well and what they need to develop (Andolsek and Simpson, 2017). Further, both the validity and credibility of this as an assessment method is significantly increased when it incorporates an explicit reflective component (Ruch, 2015). However, there are potential challenges for practitioners in engaging in reflection, more broadly, and within the context of observations. For instance, high workloads restrict the time required for reflective conversations (Ainslie et al, 2022), and reflecting on high-stake interactions can often be confronting, requiring practitioners to challenge their thinking and behaviours (Westaby et al, 2021). A lack of managerial support in prioritising reflective practice creates barriers to open reflective conversations, further, when reflection is used as a means of assessment it can lead to reflections being superficial or taking a 'paint by numbers' approach (Boud, 2010: 28).

When considering observations of practice, problems can arise from a practical perspective in relation to accessibility (for example, service user consent is required), and whether the session available for observation meets the learning requirements. There can be issues with congruence between the observer and the participant, particularly given the observer uses their experienced lens to assess an inexperienced practitioner (Edmonds, 2017). Further is the existence of cognitive bias in reflective practice, where the practitioner's recollection of events may be clouded or interpreted inaccurately, or the practitioner possesses biases that impact how they think (Mahon and McNeil, 2020). For example, in their study of Canadian social workers involving engagement pre and post a simulated online session, Occhiuto et al (2024) found divergence between what participants said they did in the simulation and what was observed. In understanding the misalignment between reflections during the post simulation interviews and observation of practice the researchers identified three themes: (1) understanding of the client and the session in the moment can be understood differently post engagement; (2) reflections of behaviours can be tied up with who we want to be, not necessarily who we are in the moment; (3) reflections are linked to perceptions of self (Occhiuto et al, 2024: 2649).

Facilitated simulations, with the opportunity for immediate feedback, however, can offer standardisation, maximising objectivity of the assessor (Ruch, 2015) and mitigate learners' eagerness to please (Occhiuto et al, 2024). They can provide a safe learning environment for practitioner growth while enabling the ability to change the script and build complexities to test different competencies (Mayne and Green, 2020). When these simulations are recorded another dimension of learning is offered, supporting the development of critical reflection (Occhiuto et al, 2024). Therefore, this chapter will explore the use of XR technology as a tool to support this critical reflection on practice, through analysis of a proof of concept study exploring XR and risk decision-making.

Extended Reality technology to support practitioner risk assessment: a proof of concept

Rationale for the study

Technology has the potential to enhance a variety of criminal justice and rehabilitation practices. In developing a small-scale research study, we sought to provide a proof of concept in relation to using 360 images and VR technology to enhance probation practitioner risk assessment decision-making, within the context of a home visit environment. This chapter explores the utility of this technology as a means of developing reflective practice in a way which can address some of the potential limitations identified within practice observations.

As well as beginning to uncover the effectiveness of these two forms of technology as a tool for risk assessment, as researchers we were keen to elicit information about the user experience both from a practical perspective (that is, the navigation of the simulation and use of the technology), and a personal perspective (that is, any perceived barriers to the use of the technology, or any ways in which the technology exceeded prior learning experiences). Through this feedback, we were able to consider the implications for these technologies within blended learning, as well as the opportunities for the promotion of reflective practice.

Authenticity and utility was important to us as researchers, and so rather than just designing a VR simulation that 'transports' learners to a scene or event, we were keen to initiate discussions among training providers, academic researchers, criminal justice experts and learning designers to ensure that any tools incorporated into educational and training efforts were 'fit for purpose' and could inform the development of future training packages.

Methodology

The proof of concept research was designed to align with current risk assessment training provision for early career probation officers. A fictional case study was prepared outlining offending history, current offence details and pertinent background details relevant to making risk assessment judgements. A small bedsit (unused student accommodation) was secured for the creation of the initial home visit scenario, and was dressed to reflect the information in the case notes. Ten risk factors and protective factors were incorporated into the scene. Some of these were deliberately ambiguous to encourage professional curiosity and enable discourse surrounding their indication of a potential risk or protective influence on the person on probation. An Insta360 camera was used to capture 360 images, and these were edited and stitched together into a virtual tour using Adobe PremierPro and 3D Vista software. Embed codes, hyperlinks and QR codes were created to allow the tour to be accessed and shared using a mobile device or laptop.

A VR version of the same tour was created using the Unity Pro Engine (v2021.3.45f1), and was a direct replica of the 360 tour. Dimensions and positions of objects were mapped using the Unity Builder to reflect the physical appearance of the bedsit, and the same risk and protective factors were incorporated into the scene using pre-existing assets available through Unity, or through modelling scanned items using Blender (an online 3D modelling software tool). The VR home visit was built to be accessed using an Oculus Quest 2 Head Mounted Display.

Following institutional and organisational ethical approval, early career and trainee probation officers (n=23) were recruited to one of two conditions via advertisements in probation offices and probation staff newsletters.

Condition 1 (360 video) could be accessed remotely at a time and place convenient to the participant. The link to the 360 was embedded into a survey tool that provided the client details, case notes, instructions for completing the home visit and questions designed to elicit details of their risk assessment decision-making, and any recommendations for actions for the client to be completed post-home visit. The 360 condition allowed participants to move around the property by clicking on 'hotspots', but they could not move independently or interact with items in the scene. Participants had the opportunity to reflect on their experience of using the virtual tool after completion of the task.

Condition 2 (VR) required that participants complete the risk assessment task in person at a probation office, in the presence of the researchers. The procedure was as for the 360 condition, instead they used a VR headset and could explore and interact with the virtual property in their own time. In this condition, we were able to observe participants' interaction with the simulation.

Summary of findings

The findings of the research demonstrated that there were no statistically significant differences between conditions in relation to the number of risk and protective factors that were identified by the participants, thus both tools held promise in terms of their utility for future training (see Meenaghan et al, 2023).

Early career and trainee officers embarking on training during the Exceptional Delivery Model implemented during the pandemic were likely to have limited opportunities to observe colleagues on home visits. Thus the opportunity to 'practice' a home visit and consider the implications for risk assessment before embarking on a 'real-world' visit was considered to be of great value. When asked about their experiences of the proof of concept tool, one participant reflected that it was 'Really good. Liked being able to be tested about Home Visits in a safe environment, especially due to there being nothing surrounding this currently' (PPT010, 360 condition). Another stated: 'Really useful way of experiencing a home visit for the first time, especially if you don't have the opportunity to observe someone' (PPT011, VR condition).

Overall, feedback suggested that the opportunities for observation of colleagues' practice was considered to be the most valuable method for developing learning (n=15). This consideration of practice opportunities for those who were very early in their careers provided an interesting perspective when considering live observations of practice. With this in mind, there is potential to utilise these tools as a means of creating safe spaces for individuals to build confidence and discuss their experiences within the simulated environment. While based on a small sample, the results provide a foundation for the ongoing replication and development of research projects to empirically test a range of immersive and non-immersive tools that can be incorporated into existing and future training programmes.

Condition 1: 360 images

While comparisons between the 360 condition and VR condition did not indicate significant differences in risk assessment decision-making, participants in the 360 condition were more likely to comment on the unkempt presentation of the flat. The use of real world photography compared to computer generated images is a realism factor to be explored with future simulations. The potential for the 360 videos enhancing learner experience can be seen with this participant response:

> I think it's incredibly useful and more useful than training I have completed myself to do with risk management, so many of the training events I have done involve case studies, but case study after case study doesn't feel real, and people don't find themselves getting a lot out of them, whereas the 360 view interactive way of doing it is far more inviting to trainees. (PPT008, 360 condition)

The responses of this participant suggest that 360 simulations may have the potential to bridge a gap between training and practice, in a more effective way than current case study approaches. Additionally, this may support more effective reflection 'in-action' with subsequent practice experience. Furthermore, the extent of practitioner motivation to engage in different forms of training is highlighted. As part of the proof of concept we were keen to avoid using technology as a novelty, rather than a meaningful tool, thus these responses provide insight into the potential utility of these in practice.

When considering the opportunities for the enhancement of reflective practice, the participant feedback suggests that technology may provide some important benefits for prompting reflective discussion, as can be seen here:

> I think this was a useful exercise and the location/scenario used was realistic based on my previous experiences. I find it useful to have to think about why something concerns me rather than just repeating what I have learnt, and this could be a useful tool to complement existing learning. (PPT002, 360 condition)

As this was a proof of concept, we reflect that there could be some further opportunities to integrate reflection and feedback mechanisms into the training experience within this condition. For example, while the accessibility of the 360 video tool was viewed as positive, the use of this in isolation could be seen to limit the reflective learning opportunities. Therefore, it is considered that this tool could be used in conjunction with peer discussion and PTA facilitation to enhance the '[v]alue of engaging in reflective processes ... as a collective activity with multiple perspectives' (Occhiuto et al, 2024: 2655). In this way potential bias and links to theory could be explored, as well as addressing the potential disconnect between training and practice as described in the experiences of case study-based training. It also provides an opportunity for immediate feedback (Ruch, 2015). Furthermore, within the training packages themselves, prompts and links to literature provide scope for immediate feedback mechanisms.

Condition 2: Virtual Reality simulation

The in-person nature of the VR condition itself led to some interesting insights regarding how technology can enhance learning and reflective discussion. As noted, there was not a significant difference in the number of risk or protective factors identified in the two conditions, but there was a bias towards greater identification using VR. Participant responses indicated the more interactive nature of the task may have impacted this observation: '[V]ery useful, my training has been case study and teams discussion. To see something in real life helps to learn from experience which suits my learning style. Practice based training is interesting, I liked it and think it is better than talking about' (PPT003, VR condition). Similarly, the use of VR provided an additional layer of authenticity to the training experience, in a way that more traditional methods had been unable to capture, based upon this participant's feedback:

> I think it should be used in every training. I have had HV training where a health and safety person lectured at us about using our solo/safety personal measures. I walked into a make shift room with a 'SPO' pretending to be an offender which is extreme. This is much more realistic, can have time to walk around. think can be helpful to use in all scenarios eg breach, even collecting someone from reception – something

can make you change your decision about then using a duty room etc. (PPT004, VR condition)

The opportunity for an authentic experience to reflect upon can be seen here, and may help to address some of the lack of congruence between the participant and observer in these types of role play observational exercises.

An interesting finding in the feedback related to the ways that VR has the potential to prepare early career practitioners emotionally for a home visit scenario and the idea that there is an opportunity, through the use of technology, to provide a safe test simulation:

Like the idea about being able to simulate home visit without first one being the real thing; would be stressed on first home visit. VR creates an opportunity to experience. Bit subjective; not for everyone ie. felt a little queasy, may need adapting. Can create secure situation where people can take attention to the details. Will help be prepared for real scenarios; might help to enable officers used to looking for risks. Would like to do it as a learner and particularly useful early on. (PPT005, VR condition)

However, this notion of having a 'secure situation' to support risk decision-making is one that shows promise moving forward, with the potential to address some of the issues in practitioner-based observations that are highlighted within the literature.

This participant feedback also demonstrates that such a simulation may not be suitable for all, and there are practical and resource implications to using such tools in a training environment. Furthermore, there may be individual differences such as neurodiversity (Dahlstrom-Hakki et al, 2024), disability, accessibility (Stendal and Bernabe, 2024) and expectations of digital literacy (Lin et al, 2024). Therefore, variation of tools, within a broader training package, should be considered to assist in meeting individual needs. In terms of reflecting on risk assessment and the actions that should be undertaken following a home visit, the VR condition did lead to a higher number of referrals suggested by participants post-visit, aligning with the increased identification of risk factors by these participants. As this participant highlights, the simulation enabled future-focused thinking: 'It's realistic. Able to look at the next steps. More realistic than a case study' (PPT012, VR condition).

This suggests that this experience assisted in the recollection of events, and may minimise the effects of cognitive bias, with more alignment with the understanding in the moment of the experience. It is also worth noting that within both conditions there was an absence of the person on probation in the home visit environment. This was due to realism within the proof of concept and is something for further exploration. However, this may have also impacted the complexity of the recollections of the experience within these conditions. That said, more developed VR and 360 video simulations can include sensory experiences such as background noises, and for the VR conditions, interactions with others that can heighten the realism and emotional response of the experience being reflected upon.

Researcher observations and reflections

While the purpose of the proof of concept study was to test the impact of different simulation environments on participants' decision-making it became apparent that the use of immersive learning provided a tool for enabling critical reflection. This was particularly clear in the VR condition, where as researchers we were able to experience the event with participants while enabling them to 'talk aloud' about what they were seeing, feeling and thinking at the time. The simulations were not recorded in the process of this research, however, there are opportunities within the technology to record the observations and practitioner 'journey' around the space and analyse participant focus around the simulation. The ability to go back and 'review' actions and behaviours of practice within a simulated environment can support practitioners' development by countering concerns of 'wanting to please' their assessors, or adopting superficial levels of reflection as identified in the literature. This also enables 'real-time' reflection in-action, that may support more authentic engagement with the reflective process, particularly in relation to responses to stimuli within the environment and potential biases in terms of perceived risks within the environment.

Conclusion

The findings of this research demonstrated that both 360 images and VR simulations have potential utility as training tools to aid risk-assessment decision-making for probation practitioners. The similarity in identification of risk and protective factors, and the capacity of both modalities to promote professional curiosity in the process of undertaking risk judgements, provides encouraging support for the potential for the use of both types of technologies, but in a way that considers the needs and barriers for the individual learner. The potential for such tools to be utilised within broader packages to enhance reflection and experiential learning can be seen from the findings of the proof of concept.

There are some limitations to the use of VR in training in terms of cost and practical limitations to the wide-scale use of such technology. In addition to the costs associated with the development of simulations, it is not practical to assume that all training providers will have access to the required equipment, the required space and the required time to ensure a consistent approach across all trainees on a national scale. 360 video, by contrast, can easily be shared using web-links, and can be accessed using the learner's personal or work devices at a time and place to suit them.

On a similar note, we became acutely aware of the potential for VR technology to be an inclusivity 'double-edged sword'. The potential for enabling access to hard-to-reach, dangerous and impossible-to-replicate scenarios using VR is well documented (Cornet and van Gelder, 2020). What has been less documented is the potential to exclude some individuals from the training experience. Specifically those with medical or personal reasons that prohibit the wearing of a Head Mounted Display and those who experience motion sickness. Additionally, we noted the discomfort that some individuals displayed when using a headset in the presence of others. The immersive nature of the experience means that the user is essentially removed from the room while still being physically present. As such, we were all concerned about ways to address any power imbalances and inequalities that might exist in a training environment that may exacerbate any such feelings.

Nonetheless, the process of planning and undertaking this research gave us great hope for the future of the use of technological advancement in criminal justice education. Key to this chapter, we felt that the most beneficial outcome of the user experience was the identification of, and opportunity to discuss, personal and individual perceptions (and perhaps misconceptions) related to objects in the virtual environments. As such, the effective use of appropriate technology can enable a reflexive approach to learning, supporting the development of professional curiosity.

This ability to elicit critical reflection on an authentic experience provides an exciting opportunity for the development of future training of probation practitioners. While this chapter focuses upon a proof of concept research study, it has highlighted the possibilities for training packages to utilise feedback and reflection mechanisms alongside the tools that were developed. Future research must take a holistic approach to design, testing and implementation, and ideally will be supported by shared learning and ongoing collaboration between educators, learning designers, professional experts and software developers. In this way, training packages (rather than training tools) can be developed that address not only the specific needs of current practice, but also are responsive to the needs of individual learners in a collaborative training context.

While XR, and VR in particular, has the potential to open up spaces that are either hard to replicate or inaccessible to certain individuals, this must be weighed against the real possibility that technology will likely create its own barriers for those with specific learning preferences and requirements.

Reflective prompts

- What have your experiences of practice observation been, and how do these align with the strengths and limitations identified within the literature review of this chapter?
- Have you had experience of using technology to enhance learning? How might these experiences enable you to reflect on your practice?

- How might you be able to add reflective prompts to existing training opportunities?
- What opportunities might there be for recording practice to enhance the discourse and reflection around decision-making?
- How might you develop professional curiosity in relation to home visits? What barriers might be present and how might you overcome these?

References

Ainslie, S., Fowler, A., Phillips, J. and Westaby, C. (2022) 'A nice idea but ...': Implementing a reflective supervision model in the National Probation Service in England and Wales, *Reflective Practice*, 23(5): 525–538. doi: https://doi.org/10.1080/14623943.2022.2066075

Andolsek, K.M. and Simpson, D. (2017) Direct observation reassessed, *Journal of Graduate Medical Education*, 9(4): 531–532. doi: https://doi.org/10.4300/JGME-D-17-00328.1

Chang, E., Kim, H.T. and Yoo, B. (2020) Virtual reality sickness: A review of causes and measurements, *International Journal of Human–Computer Interaction*, 36(17): 1658–1682. doi: https://doi.org/10.1080/10447318.2020.1778351

Cornet, L.J.M. and van Gelder, J.L. (2020) Virtual reality: A use case for criminal justice practice, *Psychology, Crime and Law*, 26(7): 631–647. doi: https://doi.org/10.1080/1068316X.2019.1708357

Boud, D. (2010) Relocating reflection in the context of practice, in H. Bradbury, N. Frost and S. Kilminster (eds) *Beyond Reflective Practice*, Routledge, pp 25–36.

Dahlstrom-Hakki, I., Alstad, Z., Asbell-Clarke, J. and Edwards, T. (2024) The impact of visual and auditory distractions on the performance of neurodiverse students in virtual reality (VR) environments, *Virtual Reality*, 28(1). doi: https://doi.org/10.1007/s10055-023-00933-6

Edmonds, C. (2017) The practice educator lens: Bringing student practice into focus using the direct observation, *The Journal of Practice Teaching and Learning*, 14(3): 46–63. doi: https://doi.org/10.1921/jpts.v14i3.1014

Fowler, A., Martin, L., Watson, A. and Brown, T. (2023) Professional qualification in probation and COVID-19, in C. Kay and S. Case (eds) *Crime, Justice and COVID-19*, Bristol University Press, pp 190–216.

Hamad, A. and Jia, B. (2022) How virtual reality technology has changed our lives: An overview of the current and potential applications and limitations, *International Journal of Environmental Research and Public Health*, 19(18). doi: https://doi.org/10.3390/ijerph191811278

HMIP (HM Inspectorate of Probation) (2023a) HM Inspectorate of Probation annual report 2023: Serious further offences. Available from: https://www.justiceinspectorates.gov.uk/hmiprobation/wp-content/uploads/sites/5/20F23/06/120623-FINAL-SFO-Annual-report-2023-v1.3.pdf

HMIP (2023b) A thematic inspection of work undertaken, and progress made, by the Probation Service to reduce the incidence of domestic abuse and protect victims. Available from: https://www.justiceinspectorates.gov.uk/hmiprobation/wp-content/uploads/sites/5/2023/07/Domestic-Abuse-Thematic-inspection-report-v1.3.pdf

HMPPS (HM Prison and Probation Service) (2021) The target operating model for probation services in England and Wales. Available from: https://assets.publishing.service.gov.uk/government/uploads/system/uploads/attachment_data/file/1061047/MOJ7350_HMPPS_Probation_Reform_Programme_TOM_Accessible_English_LR.pdf

HMPPS (2022) The learning strategy for the probation service (2022–2024). Available from: https://welcome-hub.hmppsintranet.org.uk/wp-content/uploads/2022/11/Probation-Learning-Strategy-2022-2024-V1.pdf

HMPPS (2024) Probation professional register policy framework. Available from: https://assets.publishing.service.gov.uk/media/66fa78c0a31f45a9c765ee6e/2024_09_30_Prof_Reg-Probation_Professional_Register_policy_framework.pdf

Kluge, M.G., Maltby, S., Keynes, A., Nalivaiko, E., Evans, D.J.R. and Walker, F.R. (2022) Current state and general perceptions of the use of Extended Reality (XR) technology at the University of Newcastle: Interviews and surveys from staff and students, *Sage Open*, 12(2). doi: https://doi.org/10.1177/21582440221093348

Lin, X.P., Li, B.B., Yao, Z.N., Yang, Z. and Zhang, M. (2024) The impact of virtual reality on student engagement in the classroom: A critical review of the literature, *Frontiers in Psychology*, 15. doi: 10.3389/fpsyg.2024.1360574

Mahon, P. and McNeil, M. (2020) Through the looking glass: The rabbit hole of reflective practice, *The British Journal of Nursing*, 29(13). Available from: https://www.britishjournalofnursing.com/content/professional/through-the-looking-glass-the-rabbit-hole-of-reflective-practice

Mayne, R. and Green, H. (2020) Virtual reality for teaching and learning in crime scene investigation, *Science and Justice*, 60(5): 466–472. doi: 10.1016/j.scijus.2020.07.006.

Meenaghan, A., McDermott, M. and Haggar, L. (2023) XR technology and risk assessment: The future of probation training?, *Criminology & Criminal Justice*. doi: https://doi.org/10.1177/17488958231200346

Occhiuto, K., Tarshis, S., Todd, S. and Gheorghe, R. (2024) Reflecting on reflection in clinical social work: Unsettling a key social work strategy, *The British Journal of Social Work*, 54(6): 2642–2660. doi: https://doi.org/10.1093/bjsw/bcae052

Petit, O., Velasco, C., Wang, Q.J. and Spence, C. (2022) Consumer consciousness in multisensory Extended Reality, *Frontiers in Psychology*, 13. doi: https://doi.org/10.3389/fpsyg.2022.851753

Pye, J. (2024) Direct observations of practice in social work education: The role of professional autonomy in policy enactment, *Social Work Education*, 1–17. doi: https://doi.org/10.1080/02615479.2024.2400205

Ruch, G. (2015) Evidence scope regarding the use of practice observation methods as part of the assessment of social work practice, *Research in Practice*. Available from: https://www.researchinpractice.org.uk/media/bkobv1uz/rip_evidence_scope_regarding_the_use_of_practice_observation_methods_as_part_of_the_assessment_of_social_work_practice_2015.pdf

Schön, D. (1983) *The Reflective Practitioner: How Professionals Think in Action*, Temple Smith.

Skills for Justice Awards (2016) *Qualification Handbook Level 5 Diploma in Probation Practice*. Available from: https://sfjawards.com/wp-content/uploads/2020/03/Qualification-Handbook-L5-Diploma-in-Probation-Practice-2016-v1.pdf

Smith, H.P. (2021) The role of virtual reality in criminal justice pedagogy: An examination of mental illness occurring in corrections, *Journal of Criminal Justice Education*, 32(2): 252–271. doi: https://doi.org/10.1080/10511253.2021.1901948

Stendal, K. and Bernabe, R.D.L.C. (2024) Extended Reality: New opportunity for people with disability? Practical and ethical considerations, *Journal of Medical Internet Research*, 26. doi: https://doi.org/10.2196/41670

Swaak, J., Joolingen, W. and Ton de Jong, T. (1998) Supporting simulation-based learning: The effects of model progression and assignments on definitional and intuitive knowledge, *Learning and Instruction*, 8(3): 235–252. doi: https://doi.org/10.1016/S0959-4752(98)00018-8

Ticknor, B. (2019) Virtual reality and correctional rehabilitation: A game changer, *Criminal Justice and Behavior*, 46(9): 1319–1336. doi: https://doi.org/10.1177/0093854819842588

University of Glasgow (2023) *XRED: Preparing for Immersive Education*. Available from: https://www.gla.ac.uk/media/Media_1030423_smxx.pdf

van Gelder, J.-L., de Vries, R.E., Demetriou, A., van Sintemaartensdijk, I. and Donker, T. (2019) The virtual reality scenario method: Moving from imagination to immersion in criminal decision-making research, *Journal of Research in Crime and Delinquency*, 56(3): 451–480. doi: https://doi.org/10.1177/0022427818819696

Westaby, C., Phillips, P., Fowler, A. and Ainslie, S. (2021) An evaluation of the implementation of reflective practice supervision standards in the national probation service, Sheffield Hallam University. Available from: https://shura.shu.ac.uk/28842/1/SEEDS2%20RPSS%20Report%20Final.pdf

Witmer, B.G. and Singer, M.J. (1998) Measuring presence in virtual environments: A presence questionnaire, *Presence: Teleoperators and Virtual Environments*, 7: 225–240. doi: http://dx.doi.org/10.1162/105474698565686

Conclusion

Laura Haggar, Michelle McDermott and Jennifer Grant

This edited collection has brought together the academic and practical knowledge of the contributors to provide a range of insights and reflective prompts to aid the process of reflection, and explore the challenges and potential of this, within probation practice. The chapters demonstrate open and honest reflections of practice experiences, drawing on the evidence base to provide opportunities to consider the implications for future practice, and developments within the field. The reflective prompts provided within each chapter of this collection are designed to support personal reflection on the issues and key learning from each of the chapters. Whether early or later in their career, the reader is invited to pause, reflect and revisit these prompts as they continue their professional journeys, particularly at times when reflection may seem difficult, and the barriers to reflection are felt. To draw together the learning from the compendium, we encourage you to engage with the final reflective prompts identified to support the practical application that each part of this collection provides.

Part I highlighted how reflection is not simply a tool that we learn in training, but rather is something that is fundamental to our professional and personal development as probation practitioners. Through continued active engagement with the reflective process, we are able to become habitual reflectors, enabling us to navigate our everyday experiences and challenges. In considering the core themes of this section the reader may benefit from giving thought to; how they are able to develop reflection holistically, as part of a group and as part of their everyday lives, as well as evaluating the context of the sources of information which they base their reflections on. Having read this section you might ask yourself: how will I continue to develop the way I engage in reflection?

While many of the chapters in Part II reflect on a range of barriers impacting the time and space that practitioners have to reflect, a core message throughout this collection is that through ongoing engagement with this process we are able to approach the challenges that we face in a way that explores our own reflexivity and positionality. Here we can consider organisational challenges, and how we respond to these within a variety of roles that we may have within our careers. How do the organisational frameworks through which we operate increase or decrease the opportunities for reflection, and how might we seek to overcome these challenges? This section also focused on working in partnership with other agencies, as well as opportunities for collective creative reflection. How might other agencies and organisations provide further opportunity to overcome the barriers to reflection you have just identified?

In exploring diversity, Part III invited us to unpick the personal challenges that we experience in the role. The reflections within this section provide us with an opportunity to analyse our values and positionality to take a reflexive approach to our critical reflection. In exploring our positionality and diversity, we can develop empathy for the people on probation, our colleagues both in and out of the service, and ourselves. Through this approach we are able to promote the safety of one another in the workplace, and explore the issues that increase emotional labour and burnout for individuals. Taking into account your own positionality, how will you take your own reflections from this section into your everyday interactions with your colleagues and the people you supervise?

Finally, in Part IV, the role of reflective practice within training and development was considered. Here we explored the development of reflection as a tool for probation practitioners early in their careers, as well as ongoing professional development. This section explores the roles of higher education providers and assessors within the workplace to be responsive to the needs of the workforce. If you work with trainee probation officers, how can you continue to enhance your approach to teaching, assessment and feedback? If you support the professional development of probation staff, how can you use trauma-informed approaches and technology to further develop your approach to training?

This compendium has demonstrated that practitioners at every stage of their career can benefit from considering the learning and opportunities for ongoing professional development. The academic literature demonstrates that there is an appetite to develop the evidence base in relation to probation practice and reflection and this edited collection demonstrates the multifaceted nature of reflection within the nuances of the role, and the individuals who work both with and for the service. While acknowledging the significant pressures faced by the Probation Service, such as limited resources, time constraints and bureaucratic demands, there is also recognition of the need to create space for reflection. At the heart of this is a desire to provide safety and opportunity for people on probation and through engagement with the chapters contained within this collection, there is an opportunity to reflect upon how this can be achieved within an ever-changing, and challenging, environment.

Index

References to figures appear in *italic* type; those in **bold** type refer to tables.

A

active collaboration/peer learning 240–241
active reflection 231, 236, 240
Adair-Stantiall, A. 15, 17, 18, 21
Adverse Childhood Experiences 283
affordances 20–21, 22
age and supervisory relationship 196, 197
Ainslie, S. 3, 35, 37, 38, 47, 55, 57, 63, 67, 84, 85, 87, 88, 90, 249, 250, 258, 260, 261, 262, 267, 268, 272, 304
Andrews, D.A. 51, 159
Annison, J. 35, 194
Ansbro, M. 47, 55, 101
anti-discriminatory practice, reflecting on 38, 275
Anti-Racist Charter 168–169
applied theatre and creative practice 135–136, 138–141
  practical application 141–143
  supporting staff well-being and reflection 143–146, *144*, *147*
Argyris, C. 32
Armani, J. 183
Ashforth, B.E. 15, 20
assessment of reflective practice, framework for 248–265
assessment strategy 254–258, 261–262
  assessment methods 259
  formative assessment 254, 257–258, 260–261
  importance of definition 255–256, **255**
  initial assessment 257
  summative assessment 258
authenticity of reflective writing 248, 250, 256, 261
challenges 250–252
curriculum design 252–254, **254**
methodology 252
modelling the model 259–261
reflective practice and probation practice 249–250
using a variety of methods 251–252
attachment theory 47
authenticity of reflective writing 248, 250, 256, 261

B

Baines, S. 175, 182, 183
Bambling, M. 49–50
Barr, U. 211, 221
barriers to engagement
  gender dynamic in therapeutic relationship and 195–200, 201–202
  for probation service users 181–182
  with reflective practice 55–56, 84, 137, 304
  in leadership 87–93
Bassot, B. 267, 268, 272, 273, 276
Bateson, Gregory 13, 22
BearFace Theatre (BFT) 135–136
  applied theatre and creative practice 138–141
  practical application 141–143
  supporting staff well-being and reflection 143–146, *144*, *147*
  Working with Trauma Silver Quality Mark 140
Bendall, review into case of Damien 38, 99, 100, 110
Bennett-Levy, J. 63, 64, 65, 68, 70, 74

Index

bias
  dismantling 166
  linguistic. *see* linguistic profiling
  racial 166, 167
  senior probation officers 89–91, 93
Black and ethnic minority
  groups in criminal justice
    system 174–191
  barriers to engagement with
    probation services 181–182
  Black men's experience
    of probation and
    co-creation 178–181
  co-creation in practice 182–185
  disproportionate challenges faced
    by 157–158, 161
  distrust of law enforcement
    agencies 176, 180
  over-representation 174–175, 176
  racial disparity in system 175–177
Black and ethnic minority probation
  staff 160, 167, 168–169
  see also racially minoritised female
    staff, reflections in
    COVID-19 pandemic
Black Lives Matter 157–158, 161
'Blackness' and deviance 175, 176–177
Borrelli, B. 45, 55
boundaries between work and
  home, blurring of 69, 201, 203
Bourgon, G. 53
Bourner, T. 253, 256, 258
Boyd, R. D. 233
Boyd, R.D. 232
'bridging questions' 70–71
Bulman, C. 250, 251, 252, 255, 259, 261
bureaucracies and reflective
  practice 34
Burke, L. 35, 106, 108
Burman, M. 138, 141
burnout 49, 69, 93, 134, 137, 202, 268
Burrell, A. 63, 65, 66, 81, 84, 89, 230, 231, 232, 233, 235, 236, 249
Burt, C.H. 102
Butler, L.D. 284, 286, 287, 290, 291, 292

C

Cardwell, V. 268, 276
Carello, J. 284, 286, 287, 290, 291, 293
Carr, N. 134, 160, 161, 180, 213, 235, 267, 272
change, reflective practice in times
  of 29–43, 134–135
  author reflections 39–40
  a challenging and demanding
    process 33–34
  defining reflective practice 30–31
  enabling 34–39
  importance of reflective
    practice 31–34, 38–39
  reflection as active practice 32
Charman, S. 110, 161
child protection practice 99, 100–101, 106
  good safeguarding practice 107–109
  legal responsibility for 106–107
  work experience in 110
Children Act 1989 106
Children Act 2004 106
circle time 290, 291–292
Citizenship supervision
  programme 51–52, 56
closed-mindedness 16
co-creation of criminal justice
  provision 180–181
  barriers to engagement 181–182
  critique 185
  in practice 182–185
'code-switching' 165–166, 167
cognition, new understanding
  of 19–22
  embedded and extended
    cognition 21–22
  embodied cognition 21
  enactive cognition 19–21
Coley, D. 1, 2, 3, 33–34, 35, 36, 38, 67, 68, 82, 87, 93, 125, 126, 134, 249, 253, 258, 260, 261, 266, 268, 276
Collett, C. 106, 108
Commission on Racial
  Inequalities 157–158
Community Policy
  Framework 83, 85
continuous professional
  development 2–3, 70, 85, 88, 89, 136
  limited opportunities for 236
  SPO-led reflective supervision to
    support 82–83, 84, 93
Cooney, M. 102

COVID-19 pandemic 287
  remote working in 29, 37–38
  Exceptional Delivery
    Model 159–162, 165, 168
  and linguistic profiling 158,
    164–167
  see also racially minoritised
    female staff, reflections in
    COVID-19 pandemic
Cramer, H. 193, 196, 211
Cranton, P. 235, 238, 239
Crawley, E.M. 219
Create Reflect Unite Women
  (CRUW) 144–145, 148
creative arts and third sector,
  reflective practice and learning
  from 134–153
  applied theatre and creative
    practice 138–141
  exercises 139–140
  collaboration and
    co-production 142
  critical reflection in probation
    practice 136–138
  practical application 140–143
  supporting staff well-being and
    reflection 143–146, *144*, *147*
Crewe, B. 200, 204
critical consciousness 230–231, **243**
Critical Race Theory 166
critical reflection 2, 266–281
  creating safe spaces for 240
  effective feedback for reflective
    assignments 273–276, 277
  benefits of positive
    comments 274
  focusing on strengths 274
  integrating theory and
    practice 275–276
  'why' questions 274–275
  Extended Reality technology
    to support 305–313
  importance in PQiP
    training 267–269
  learning for PQiP
    developing critical
      reflection 272–273, 276–277
    integrating theory and
      practice 271–272
    writing reflectively 270–271
  methodology 269–270
  observation of practice in
    developing 304–305, 308

in probation practice 136
reflective practice feedback 269
cultural competency 177, 184
Culture Health and Wellbeing
  Alliance (CHWA) 137
curriculum design 252–254, **254**

D

Daloz, L. 232, 238
De Jaegher, Hanne 16, 17
Declarative-Procedural-Reflective
  (DPR) model 64–66, 68
  example 72–74
  integrating PPs in 68, 71–72
deep acting 92, 202
Dekker, H. 266, 275, 277
desistance 141, 177, 183
  and family relationships for
    offenders 117–118
  LGBTQIA+ community
    and 215–216, 217, 221
  role of identity changes in 18–19
  therapeutic relationship and 120–
    121, 217–218
Dirkx, J.M. 230, 233
distance learning *see* online learning
diversity, reflecting on approaches to
  issues of 214–215
domestic abuse 100–101
  Labour government policy on 110
  punishment for 102–103
Dominey, J. 99, 119, 142, 159,
  168, 194
Dowden, C. 51
DPR (Declarative-Procedural-
  Reflective) model *see*
  Declarative-Procedural-
  Reflective (DPR) model

E

Ekemezie, C. 165
Elkington, S. 258, 259, 260
embedded cognition 21–22
embodied cognition 21
emotional intelligence 134, 273
emotional labour 69, 201, 202, 203
  a barrier to effectiveness of
    casework supervision 91–93,
    93–94
  and emotional well-being 91,
    92, 93
  in remote working 168
emotional literacy 67–68, 249, 273

emotional reflection 272–273, 274, 277
empowerment 291
enactive cognition 19–21
Equality Act 2010 159
'ethical' cognition 19
ethical humility 230, 234–237, **243**
ethnic minorities in criminal justice system *see* Black and ethnic minority groups in criminal justice system
ethnic minority probation staff *see* Black and ethnic minority probation staff
Eurich, T. 66
evidenced based practice 271–272
Exceptional Delivery Model (EDM) 159–162, 165, 168
experiential learning, benefits and limitations of Extended Reality in 302–303
experiential learning cycle 251, 270–271
extended cognition 22
Extended Reality (XR) technology 254, 261, 301–318
  benefits and limitation in experiential learning 302–303
  inclusivity 313–314
  role of observation and reflection in probation officer training 303–305, 308
  to support practitioner risk assessment 305–313
    360 video 306–307, 308–310, 313
    methodology 306–307
    rationale for study 305–306
    researcher observations and reflections 312–313
    summary of findings 307–308
    Virtual Reality simulation 302–303, 306, 307, 310–312, 313

F

Fallot, R.D. 283, 284, 295
families of prisoners
  maintaining connections 116–117
  and supporting desistance efforts 117–118
  visitor centre staff supporting 122–127

feedback on reflective assignments 269, 273–276, 277
  benefits of positive comments 274
  focusing on strengths 274
  integrating theory and practice 275–276
  'why' questions 274–275
Felix, B. 219–220
female probation practitioners, reflections on working with male offenders 192–209
  male power and therapeutic alliance 195–197
  misogyny 200
  opportunities for positive experiences 203–204
  'paradoxical feminisation' of Probation Service 194–195
  romanticisation 200
  spaces for reflective practice 199–200, 202, 204
  threats and intimidation 197–200
  vulnerability 197, 201–203
  see also racially minoritised female staff, reflections in COVID-19 pandemic
feminisation of Probation Service 194–195
fidelity framework 45–49, 55–56
  step 1: staff reflective practice 45–46
  steps 2–3: implementation 46–48
  steps 4–6: impact/outcomes 48–49
Finlay-Jones, A. 68
formative assessment 254, 257–258, 260–261
'4e' cognition 19–22
Fowler, A. 67, 236, 253, 254, 261, 303
Freire, P. 141, 230
Fuchs, T. 17

G

Gender and Crime module, reflections on delivery of 290–293, 295
gender of probation staff 160, 192, 194
Gibbons, J. 252, 253, 254, 261
Gibbs, G. 46, 55, 273, 274
Goffman, E. 218–219
Goldhill, R. 33, 37, 63, 65, 82, 134, 137, 231, 234, 249, 250, 260, 262, 268, 272, 275, 276

Gomes, R. 219–220
'good' reflective practitioner attributes 255, **255**
group-based reflective practice 45–46, 57
growth mindset 288–289, 294

H

Haarhoff, B. 64, 71
Haggar, L. 161
Harris, M. 283, 284, 295
Hart, Kyle 36–37
The Heart of the Dance: A Diversity Strategy 214
hegemonic masculinity 193, 195–196
Hessick, C.B. 102
Hiller, S. 237, 238, 239, 240, 241
HM Inspectorate of Probation (HMIP) 3, 29, 31, 36, 37, 38, 81, 84, 85, 86, 91, 94, 99, 100, 106, 107, 108, 109, 158, 159, 161, 162, 167, 168, 218, 271, 273, 276, 277, 301
HM Prison and Probation Service (HMPPS) 3, 83, 93, 94, 116, 120, 160, 194, 195, 196, 212, 234, 267, 268, 301, 303, 304
Hobbs, V. 257
home visit training 301–302
  Extended Reality technology to support 305–313
homophobia 219, 220
hybrid working 167, 168

I

'I Need' 144
identity
  changes and role in desistance 18–19
  getting stuck in 15–16
  resilience and professional 230, 232–233, 234, 237, **243**
  transformation 232–233
Indeed 109
individuation 233
initial assessment 257
intersubjectivity 16–17, 23
intimidation and threats 197–200
introspection 66

J

Jack the Ripper 102
Jones, L. 16, 19
journaling 72

K

Kelly, George 16
Keysell, B. 236
Kirkwood, S. 192, 204
Knight, C. 67, 68, 134, 212, 268, 273, 274
knowledge, critiques of prevalent forms of 12–19
  getting stuck 15–16
  getting together 16–17
  inhabiting a position 18–19
  people as systems 14–15
  variables as abstractions 12–13
  web of relations 13–14
Kolb, D. 251, 253, 270
Koski, S.E. 16, 17
Kyselo, M. 16, 21, 22

L

Laing, R.D. 22
Laroche, J. 20, 21
lesbians 210–226
  of colour 212–213
  current intervention practices and how they relate to 215–218, 221
  desistance 215–216, 217, 221
  Risk, Need, Responsivity approach 216–218
  depictions in prison and crime dramas 213
  disclosures of sexuality 215, 219–220, 221–222
  diversity issues 214–215
  experiences in prison 213
  lack of research on criminal justice system and 211
  over-represented in criminal justice system 210, 211–213, 221
  reflections on being lesbian probation practitioners 218–220, 221
LGBTQIA+ community
  bullying and victimisation at school 212
  life trajectories 215–216
  resilience in 217
  Risk, Need, Responsivity approach 216–217
linguistic profiling 158
  and remote working 158, 164–167
Lutze, F.E. 216, 217

M

Makarios, M. 53
male offenders, female probation practitioners working with *see* female probation practitioners, reflections on working with male offenders
male power 195–197, 200–202
masculinity, hegemonic 193, 195–196
McCann, Joseph 44–45
McDermott, M. 161
McNeill, F. 118, 231
Meenaghan, A. 254, 302, 308
mental health
  and higher education 285–286
  intersections of race, victimisation and 163, 166
  issues and imprisonment 116
  trauma and impact on 283
Meyers, S. 237, 238, 239, 240
Mezirow, J. 231–232, 233, 238
Millings, M. 40
Milne, D. 45, 49, 55
mindfulness practices 69
Ministry of Justice (MoJ) 83, 85, 89, 93, 101, 102, 105, 110, 116, 119, 135, 174, 192, 212
misogyny 195, 200, 204
Moon, J.A. 258, 269, 270
Mor Barak, M.E. 49, 51, 54
Mullineux, J.C. 232, 266, 276
Multi Agency Public Protections Arrangements 105–106
multi-agency working and third sector partners 118–120, 121
music intervention 183
'My Direction' programme 183

N

Nahouli, Z. 160, 196, 200
Nash, M. 100, 101
National Criminal Justice Arts Alliance (NCJAA) 135
National Offender Management Service 118, 119, 214
Needs, A. 15, 16, 17, 18, 19, 21
neurodiversity training 123
Nikischer, A. 284, 293
Nudd, D. 233
Nyamwiza, N. 176

O

OASys Initial Sentence Plan 31–32
observation and reflection in probation officer training 303–305, 308
Occhiuto, K. 305, 310
Offender Management in Custody Model, HMPPS 120
Offender Personality Difficulties (OPD) pathway strategy 44
  attachment theory as core model 47
  reflective practice 44–45, 45–46, 48–49, 54, 55–56
online learning 31, 214, 239
  challenges and limitations 37, 239, 254, 301–302
  in COVID-19 pandemic 236–237, 239
  and Extended Reality technology 254, 261
  and use of Padlet 241
organisational values 230, 234, 240, 241, **243**
Osborne, S.P. 181

P

Padlet 241
Parmar, D. 233
'Pathways to Resettlement' 117–118
Pearson, D. 52
peer learning 240–241
people as systems 14–15
performance management and supervision 82–83, 87–88, 91–92
'permission' to take time for reflection 145
personal construct theory 23
Personal Practices (PP) model 68–69, 69–70, 76
  integration in DPR model 68, 71–72
  reflective practice 71
'personal self' 65–66, 68, 69, 70, 72, 73
personality difficulties, reflective practice and impact on clients with 44–62
  learning from literature on clinical supervision 49–53
  outcomes for staff 49

training in effective supervision 51–53
recommendations moving forward 56–58
reflection and implications 53–56
impact of wider organisational support 55–56
impact of workloads 54–55
staff reflective practice 45–49
perspective transformation 231–232
Petrillo, M. 3, 137, 182, 194, 195, 196, 198, 200, 201, 202, 204, 230, 231, 232, 233, 235, 268, 272, 273, 286
Phillips, J. 36, 69, 91, 135, 136, 137, 157, 159, 202, 203, 233, 268
police culture 220
Pope, L. 177, 181
position, inhabiting a 18–19
positionality, exploring 177, 320
PP model *see* Personal Practices (PP) model
'practitioner self' 65–66, 68, 69, 70, 72, 74
prison
 behaviour towards female prison officers 200
 dramas 213
 experiences of lesbians in 213
 'jail gays' 213
 racism 179
Prison Reform Trust 175, 178
prison, relational role in 116–133
 establishing a rehabilitative culture 121–122
 family relationships and desistance 117–118
 multi-agency working and third sector partners 118–120, 121
 therapeutic relationship 120–122
 visitor centre staff 122–127
  bureaucratic support 122–124
  functional support 124–125
  stress-reducing support 126–127
Probation Professional Registration Standards 268
Probation Service Learning Strategy 303
Problem- Based Learning (PBL) 253–254
procedural justice 179

professional curiosity 38, 105, 233, 273, 301
'professional effectiveness' 266, 276
professional identity and resilience 230, 232–233, 234, 237, **243**
Professional Qualification in Probation (PQiP)
 experiences of online teaching in pandemic 236–237, 239
 importance of reflective practice 267–269
 learners susceptible to mental health challenges 286
 learning for students
  developing critical reflection 272–273, 276–277
  integrating theory and practice 271–272
  writing reflectively 270–271
 providing effective feedback for student reflective assignments 273–276
 role of observation and reflection in 303–305, 308
 teaching and modelling reflective practice 260, 262
 typical entrant to training programme 194
 see also assessment of reflective practice, framework for; SCOPE revised framework of transformative outcomes for PQiP; trauma-informed approaches to teaching criminology and PQiP students
professionalism 39, 234, 268
'Pulse Train' exercise 139

R

Race Equality in Probation report 158, 161–162, 167–168
racial disparities
 in criminal justice system 175–177
 for minority probation staff 167–168
racially minoritised female staff, reflections in COVID-19 pandemic 157–173
 Exceptional Delivery Model 159–162, 165, 168

linguistic profiling and remote
  working 158, 164–167
ongoing racial disparities 167–168
supervising a racially prejudiced
  individual 162–164
racism
  Anti-Racist Charter 168–169
  barriers to reporting instances
    of 164
  in prison 179
Radcliffe, K. 48, 54
Rasheed, S.P. 66
Reamer, F.G. 234, 235
reflection-in-action 63, 136
reflective models 271–272, 274
reflective practice 1–3
  barriers to engagement with
    55–56, 84, 137, 304
  in leadership 87–93
  a challenging and demanding
    process 33–34
  defining 30–31, 251
  enabling 34–39
  group-based 45–46, 57
  importance of 31–34, 38–39
  in PQiP training 267–269
  probation and 67–69, 249–250
  'safe' spaces 137, 138, 214, 240
  self-awareness and 66–67
  technical expertise prioritised
    over 34
reflective practice and impact on
  outcomes for clients with
  personality difficulties 44–62
  learning from literature on clinical
    supervision 49–53
  outcomes for staff 49
  training in effective
    supervision 51–53
  recommendations moving
    forward 56–58
  reflection and implications 53–56
  impact of wider organisational
    support 55–56
  impact of workloads 54–55
  staff reflective practice 45–49
Reflective Practice Supervision
  Standards (RPSS) 46, 47, 81,
  84, 85, 88–89, 93, 94
reflective processes in criminal
  justice contexts, psychological
  perspectives on 11–28
  challenges to 11–12

critiques of prevalent forms of
  knowledge 12–19
  getting stuck 15–16
  getting together 16–17
  inhabiting a position 18–19
  people as systems 14–15
  variables as abstractions 12–13
  web of relations 13–14
new understanding of
  cognition 19–22
  embedded and extended
    cognition 21–22
  embodied cognition 21
  enactive cognition 19–21
Rehabilitating Probation project 85
rehabilitation, forms of 231
remote working
  in COVID-19 pandemic 29, 37–38
  Exceptional Delivery
    Model 159–162, 165, 168
  linguistic profiling and 158, 164–167
resilience and professional
  identity 230, 232–233, 234,
  237, **243**
restorative justice approach 289–290
  circle time 290, 291–292
retention of staff 91, 160–161
  reflective supervision to
    address 83, 93
Rice, P. 158, 165
Rietveld, E. 20
risk assessment and
  management 88–89, 91–92
  and difficulties with co-creation 182
  Extended Reality technology to
    support 305–313
Risk, Need, Responsivity (RNR)
  model 216–218
Robinson, G. 85
Robson, R. 211
Roig-Palmer, K. 216, 217
romanticisation of therapeutic
  relationship 200
Russell, A. 135, 136, 141, 142–143
Russell, Justin 29, 168
Rutter, N. 211, 217, 221

S

Sadler, D.R. 267, 269, 270, 274, 277
'safe' spaces
  for reflective practice 137, 138,
    214, 240
  of supervision 83, 87, 93

safeguarding 99–115
  assumptions leading to limited action on 102–103
  cases 104–106
  core task of public protection 100–101
  expectation of new staff for involvement in 100, 109–110
  failings in Bendall review 99, 100, 110
  action plan in response to 110–111
  good practice 107–110
  legal responsibilities 106–107
  multi-agency collaboration 107
safety
  and collaboration 291–292
  and 'safe allocation' of cases 163, 168
  threats to personal 198–200
Scarman Report 180
Schön, D.A. 2, 23, 24, 30, 31, 32, 33, 34, 38, 39, 63, 136, 253, 254, 304
Schutz, S. 250, 251, 252, 255, 259, 261
SCOPE revised framework of transformative outcomes for PQiP 229–247
  challenges 235, 242
  critical consciousness 230–231, **243**
  ethical humility 230, 234–237, **243**
  framework **243**
  gauging effectiveness 241–242
  literature review 230–233
  organisational values 230, 234, 240, 241, **243**
  professional identity and resilience 230, 232–233, 234, 237, **243**
  research findings and reflections 237–241
    active collaboration/peer learning 240–241
    safe spaces for critical reflection 240
    teaching activities and methods 238–239
    teaching transformative content 239–240
  self-awareness 230, 231–232, 233, **243**
SEEDS (Skills for Effective Engagement Development and Supervision) 36, 81, 83

SEEDS2 (Skills for Effective Engagement Development and Supervision 2) 84, 88
self-awareness 249
  and reflective practice 66–67
  SCOPE revised framework 230, 231–232, **243**
self-disclosure 203
  of sexuality 219–220
self-reflection 63–78
  Declarative-Procedural Reflective (DPR) model 64–66
  examples 72–74
  integration of 69–72
  and probation 67–69
senior probation officers (SPOs) fostering reflective practice 81–98
  management oversight 85–93
  dual role barrier to 87–89, 94
  emotional labour barrier to 90–93, 93–94
  SPO bias barrier to 89–91, 93
  reflective practice in supervision 83–84
  senior leadership 85
  supervision 81–82, 82–83, 93–94
Sentencing Council 102
Serious Further Offence reviews 36, 38, 85, 99, 108
Shaw, J. 44, 48, 54
Sherbersky, H. 139, 140
Shingler, J. 17, 177, 181
Skills for Effective Engagement Development and Supervision (SEEDS) 36, 81, 83
Skills for Effective Engagement Development and Supervision 2 (SEEDS2) 84, 88
skills for probation work 31–33, 38, 255, **255**
  in early probation service 108
Smyth, G. 272
Snowdon, D.A. 50
social bond theory 118
social capital, development of 215, 216
staff shortages 161, 163
Stevanovic, M. 16, 17
Strategic Training in Community Supervision (STICS) 53
strengths-based approach 182

Substance Abuse and Mental Health Services Administration (SAMHSA) 283
summative assessment 258
supervision
  and personal safety 199–200
  remote 159, 168, 303
  'safe' spaces of 83, 87, 93
  see also senior probation officers (SPOs) fostering reflective practice
supervision, learning from literature on clinical
  impact on client outcome 49–53
  outcomes for staff 49
  recommendations for supervision 57
  training in effective supervision 51–53
systems, people as 14–15

T

theory and practice, integrating 271–272, 275–276
therapeutic alliance 120–122
  challenges in building 159–160
  male power and 195–197
  personal disclosures within 203
  romanticisation of 200
  supervising a racially prejudiced individual during pandemic 162–164
  see also female probation practitioners, reflections on working with male offenders
threats and intimidation 197–200
360 video 306–307, 308–310, 313
Thwaites, R. 64, 71
time constraints 84, 137, 304
Transforming Rehabilitation (TR) 30, 33, 84, 134, 233, 240
trauma-informed approaches to teaching criminology and PQiP students 282–300
  core values 284–285, *285*
  in criminal justice system 283, 286, 290
  definitions 283–285
  impact of trauma on educational attainment 284
  key components for positive outcomes 294–295, *294*
  mental health and higher education 285–286
  positionality statement 282–283
  reflections on application in higher education 290–293
    choice 292
    empowerment 291
    safety and collaboration 291–292
    trust 293
  in schools 286–287, 290
  trauma-informed teaching in higher education 284, 286–290, 295
    growth mindset 288–289
    restorative justice approach 289–290
    trigger warnings 288
trauma-informed practice 137–138, 146, 148
trauma and creative arts 140–141
Treisman, K. 134, 137, 138, 140, 141, 146, 283, 284, 291, 292, 298
trigger warnings 288, 292
trust 176, 180, 203, 293
Tuddenham, R. 82, 89

V

values, organisational 230, 234, 240, 241, **243**
Van der Kolk, B. 140
variables as abstractions 12–13
vicarious trauma 284, 288, 293, 294
victim blaming 200–201
victimisation in probation work 163, 166
violence
  changing attitudes to crimes of 101–102
  normalizing 199–200
  by women 211
  against women and children 100
  see also domestic abuse
Virtual Reality simulation 302–303, 306, 307, 310–312, 313
visitor centre staff in prisons 122–127
  bureaucratic support 122–124
  functional support 124–125
  stress-reducing support 126–127
Vold, K. 22
vulnerability 197, 201–203

W

Wainwright, J. 160, 161, 166
Watson, A. 272

web of relations 13–14
Webster, N. 1, 45, 48, 54, 67, 93
well-being
  creative spaces supporting reflection and staff 143–146, *144, 147*
  emotional labour and emotional 91, 92, 93
  organisational change and impact on 134–135
  reflective practice promoting staff 1, 5, 48–49, 268
Westaby, C. 48, 55, 68, 69, 81, 83, 84, 86, 87, 88, 89, 91, 92, 93, 94, 199, 304
'What I want to see' *147*

whole systems approach 46, 83–84, 93–94, 180, 183
  support of senior leadership for 85, 89, 93
Wilson, K 212
Woodall, J. 117, 122, 126, 127
work/home boundaries, blurring of 69, 201, 203
workload
  impact on engagement with reflective practice 54–55, 84, 134–135, 137, 304
  of a newly qualified probation officer 162
  of SPOs 86, 88
Wright, P. 268, 276

www.ingramcontent.com/pod-product-compliance
Lightning Source LLC
Chambersburg PA
CBHW051525020426
42333CB00016B/1784